Instructor's Manual and Test Bank

Your Guide to College Success

Strategies for Achieving Your Goals

Fifth Edition

Prepared by

Cynthia Jenkins
The University of Texas at Dallas

Alice Lanning
University of Oklahoma

Kathy Maalouf
Tidewater Community College

THOMSON

WADSWORTH

Australia   Brazil   Canada   Mexico   Singapore   Spain   United Kingdom   United States

Instructor's Manual and Test Bank
Your Guide to College Success: Strategies for Achieving Your Goals, Fifth Edition

Director, College Success: Annie Todd
Editorial Assistant: Dan DeBonis
Senior Technology Project Manager: Stephanie Gregoire
Content Project Manager: Sarah Sherman

Print Buyer: Betsy Donaghey
Cover Designer: Dutton and Sherman Design
Printer: West Group
Cover photo: © Kevin Radford/Superstock

Thomson Higher Education
25 Thomson Place
Boston, MA 02210-1202
USA

For more information about our products, contact us at:
Thomson Learning Academic Resource Center
1-800-423-0563
For permission to use material from this text or product, submit a request online at **http://www.thomsonrights.com**
Any additional questions about permissions can be submitted by e-mail to **thomsonrights@thomson.com**

ISBN-10: 1-4130-3261-3
ISBN-13: 978-1-4130-3261-1

Table of Contents

WHAT THIS MANUAL HAS TO OFFER

Welcome to the Instructor's Manual/Test Bank for Santrock and Halonen's *Your Guide to College Success*, Fifth Edition. You will find that this manual provides an extremely comprehensive guide to the purpose, process, and practice of teaching a college success course. Acknowledging that some of you are completely new to this rare and wonderful experience, and many of you are seasoned experts, the manual offers instructions, insights, and ideas that are potentially useful to all.

For those who are embarking on this adventure for the first time, you can get a feel for the uniqueness of the opportunity you have in the section titled ***About the Course*** and ***Your Role in the Classroom***. ***Designing Your Course*** will guide you through the basics of how to establish you college success format using journals and pop culture to engage students. The section on ***The Syllabus*** will both ensure that you incorporate all of the necessary elements, as well as provide input as to using it to make a bold first impression. ***Heading Off the Challenges*** addresses several of the more common issues that arise when teaching college success with several suggestions for overcoming them. ***Creative Applications of the Text Features*** provides a look at each of the elements contained in *Your Guide to College Success* and presents new and varied ways to use them with your students.

The ideas just explode in the ***Chapter Features*** section, where each chapter from the text is represented and topics, activities, and demonstrations are explicitly presented in the areas of *introductory exercises, ice breakers, exercises for discussion or reflection, exercises for major chapter themes, campus connections and resources, collaborative learning suggestions with evaluation ideas, alternative teaching strategies, using the Learning Portfolio, chapter quiz suggestions,* and *summary project ideas for the chapter.*

If all of this seems overwhelming, don't worry, as the ***Lesson Planning Grids*** clearly illustrate how various elements of each chapter relate to one another. They are very useful for getting an overall picture of what the chapter deals with and the many options for exploring the material. If at any time during your college success tenure you would like to link up with other experienced instructors around the country, you will find names and e-mail addresses of individuals of varying expertise who will welcome your inquiries, and be more than happy to share advice, ideas, and information.

I now invite you all to explore this manual. For those of you who are setting out into unfamiliar territory, it will serve as your map and compass, guiding you to your destination that is a successful college success course, making clear the path to take while showing you the way to adventure. For those of you who have traveled this way before, I encourage you to perceive your journey in a different light. Blaze a new trail to the same end, enjoying the experience anew.

— *Cynthia Jenkins, Ph.D.*

The college success course is different from every other type of college course. It is totally unique in that it is designed for the sole benefit of the students who take it. In order to earn credit for taking discipline-based courses such as psychology or college algebra, students are required to demonstrate an understanding of a long established set of information, standard across most institutions of higher learning. It is not a requirement that students enjoy the class, or the subject matter; it doesn't particularly matter if they like the instructor, or make friends along the way. The goal of all college courses is to present the necessary information and evaluate students' performance on the material. Not so for college success.

When the primary objective of the course is to provide students the motivation, skills, and confidence to successfully navigate the challenges, demands, and opportunities of the college experience, there is a shift in focus from espousing a required set of information to listening to the students. Their input is vital to the efficacy of the course. If their interest is not sparked, if their motivational fire is not lit, if their needs are not met, the course itself becomes a moot point.

Imagine the possibilities of such a course! Students who recognize that their needs and wants come first, and actually make up the core of the content are much more likely to respond with interest, excitement, and be motivated to participate. The material often covered in college success courses is tremendously varied, including everything from how to make a budget, to test-taking tips, and even the ups and downs of romantic relationships. With the great mix of topics, you, as the instructor, have almost unlimited options for addressing the information. It is a course that enables you to employ numerous different strategies for teaching, doing so in accordance with your own personal style. College success is a class that's flexible, dynamic, and useful to every student in your class.

Each college and university typically outlines its own specific goals for college success, yet they are most likely based on the following:

- Achieving academic success
- Discovering an appropriate major field of study
- Establishing healthy interpersonal relationships
- Gaining a better understanding of self, and building self-esteem
- Developing a personal health and wellness life plan
- Understanding the nature of higher education and their particular school's mission.

These six focal areas (as reported by the National Resource Center for The First Year Experience and Students in Transition at the University of South Carolina) hold tremendous potential for a course rich in content, and rife with variety. This, combined with the uniqueness of its purpose, makes the college success course a learning – and teaching – opportunity not to be missed!

YOUR ROLE IN THE CLASSROOM _____

Teaching a course in college success covers such a wide range of topics so the roles of the instructor may be varied. The main role is that of a teacher, assuring that students learn the important skills to succeed in their classes and college. You will also be their informal advisor, possibly assisting them in developing their academic and career plans, in addition to advising them about their rights and responsibilities as students. The course allows the opportunity for you and your students to get to know each other; therefore, many students will come to you when they don't know where else to go. You will play the role of a liaison or mediator by helping them with any issues relating to other staff members at the institution. At times, you may have to be the student's advocate when issues arise that may challenge their ability to navigate a situation successfully. You may also find yourself serving as a mentor to your students, encouraging, supporting, and guiding them through their journey towards success.

The roles that you take on when teaching your course are entirely up to you. You need to determine which ones you feel comfortable in, and those that work with your goals for the course. Remember, the unique nature of the college success class provides you with a number of different opportunities to expand your teaching experience, and the manner in which you choose to relate to your students can enhance that experience in a very rewarding way!

DESIGNING YOUR COURSE _____

Designing a course in college success skills can be very exciting. If your school already has the course outline developed for you, then your focus will be on the instructional format. If you are starting from scratch, there are a few variables to take into consideration, such as your goals and objectives for the course, the overall experience you want the students to have, student involvement and evaluation, and class format.

What Are My Goals For the Course?

Keeping those of your institution in mind, establish your *own* personal set of goals for your college success students. Think about what you want the students to get out of the course and how it will benefit them. Ten core competencies that are usually recurring goals in college success courses include:
- Knowledge of college procedures and resources, such as the catalog, handbook, schedule book, and student services
- Knowledge of the rights and responsibilities of students
- Career development and exploration
- Academic and transfer planning
- Time management skills
- Knowledge of learning styles
- Study and reading strategies
- Note-taking and listening skills
- Test-taking strategies

What Kind of Experience Do I Want My Students to Have?

This is not an entirely separate question from the first, but it does relate more to the *atmosphere* of your class. Consider how formal or relaxed you want the classroom atmosphere to be. Ultimately, this will be defined by your own teaching style, depending on how structured you are. The "feel" of your class can vary anywhere along the continuum from highly serious to extremely relaxed, and it will certainly be related to your particular goals. Whatever atmosphere you hope to create, it is important to communicate the importance of the class, as well as command a respect for it and for yourself.

What Kind of Involvement and Evaluation Do I Want My Students to Have?

Guidelines on how to evaluate students may already be developed by your institution; however, most institutions provide you with academic freedom, allowing you to decide how to evaluate students. The aspects of student learning you perceive as important will determine how you involve and evaluate students. Some important aspects of student evaluation and involvement, especially in a course in college success, include attendance, participation, journals and other writing assignments, campus events, and group activities. Formal tests and quizzes may be part of student evaluation or you may choose to involve students more by testing their knowledge through in-class game shows, oral presentations, or student-created tests.

An important factor in considering what your students will do to earn their grade is how much time you have for the course. The requirements should be appropriate for the number of credit hours offered; thus, you are much more limited if you teach a one-hour course.

Journals

A great writing assignment for students in college success courses is the weekly writing in a journal. This enables students to explore their thoughts and feelings regarding all of their new and challenging circumstances in a way that's relaxed and comfortable. Journal writing usually leads to open and honest sharing of true feeling. Although it is important to collect journals and provide some feedback and a grade, the focus should be on the time, effort, and thought students put into their work, rather than grading the more formal elements of grammar, spelling, punctuation, and content structure. If you would like to work with students on the latter, by all means incorporate more structured papers into your course.

Blogs

Blogging is the new online journaling activity that is highly popular with college students. Some students will have their own blog – a place online where they record various thoughts, experiences, and updates as to what they are doing. Others will simply post to other people's blogs, in which selected "members" are invited to write things, respond to what others have written, ask questions looking for feedback, etc.

If you would like to have your students write, but have experience resistance from journaling assignments, or you would simply like to incorporate this technological new trend into your class, consider setting up a class blog. You can set up a blog specifically for your class at www.blogger.com . It is free and has simple directions to follow for creating your blogspot. Once you receive your students' email addresses, you will need to "invite" them to be a part of the blog. Once your students have joined, you can then post your questions, and they will respond by commenting.

This is a great way to prompt your students to think about and discuss issues relevant to their adjustment to college, and because all members can see everyone else's comments, the students can both respond to one another and see that they are not alone in their new experiences. Of course, if you want students to write on more sensitive subject matter, continue using the pencil and paper journal format that remains confidential.

Other ideas for using the blog include enabling students to post in order to get feedback from their classmates (and you), and if you have an older peer leader who is part of your FYE class, consider having them develop and post the blog questions. This is a great opportunity for them to take charge of an element of the class – reviewing student responses, replying to their comments, and keeping track of participation. Of course, you should plan to work together to determine what questions will be posted, how to deal with any questionable responses, and what comments satisfy the requirements for a grade if you choose to include your blog in the course requirements.

If you like the idea of having students respond to weekly question prompts through a class blog, it can work well as part of their participation grade, or it can have a stand alone grade. Plan to post a certain number of questions across the semester (once a week, every other week) and decide on the minimum number you expect students to respond to (10 out of 12 posted, 8 out of 16, all of them), then allot a certain number of points per blog response. If you don't require them to respond to all the blogs you post, this is a nice way to give a little bit of extra credit. If you make this a formal part of the course requirements, consider specifying some guidelines for students, such as:

Appropriate – While you should feel comfortable expressing your true thoughts and feelings through this medium, please recognize that you are communicating with university staff as well as a diverse group of classmates. Please refrain from using profanity or expressions that might be offensive. Express your views appropriately for a class assignment.

Relevant – The prompts posted by your instructor have a purpose related to the course content. Your responses should reflect your thoughts, ideas, experiences, etc. related to that topic. You are welcome to expand and add your own prompt for classmates on other issues, but in order to receive credit for your response, it must address the issue(s) put forth by the instructor.

Substantial – In order to receive credit for your response, you must contribute a distinct thought, or share a unique experience or example to illustrate your point. It is not acceptable to simply say "I agree with X on this point." Read through other people's posts and consider their responses when giving your input. Make a contribution that other's can gain from – either through a new perspective, interesting story highlighting the issue, or a useful strategy.

Incorporating Pop Culture

The uniqueness of the college success course enables you to use a number of approaches to connect with and engage your students in learning. One very salient and dynamic method is through the use of pop culture. When you can bring some of the students' world into the class (such as the blog), it allows them an opportunity to identify and become more interested in the topics at hand. They are also more likely to feel *you* are someone they can relate to.

Pop culture is everywhere. Some great resources to use in the classroom include popular magazines such as *Cosmopolitan, Rolling Stone, People,* and *Entertainment Weekly*. Magazines often profile popular figures and celebrities that students admire and possibly seek to emulate. Students pay attention to and can associate with someone who is their role model. Popular television shows such as *Gray's Anatomy,* MTV's *Real World,* the *OC, CSI*, and *Entertainment Tonight* are also a great resource for pop culture. Movies also offer some great opportunities for learning through discussion of the lessons presented. Best-selling books such as *Tuesdays with Morrie, Who Moved My Cheese?,* and *Fish!*, can be assigned as group projects on related topics.

With a database of over a million references that include the latest articles in numerous journals, magazines, and *Info Trac* offer a good opportunity for a pop-culture based research project. Enabling students to become familiar with online research tools, and investigate a topic relating to their generation, InfoTrac can be used to have students present their own findings on the impact of pop-culture trends.

There are unlimited possibilities for incorporating pop culture. Different resources can be utilized as tools for exploring significant issues relating to goals, physical and mental health, career exploration, communication, motivation, and relationships. To help inspire you, examples of using pop culture in the college success course are presented throughout the manual. Have fun with this opportunity, and feel free to let your students guide you. They may discover on their own just how hip College Success can be!

The websites Facebook and MySpace have exploded in their popularity among college students, and many faculty and staff have pages as well. There are many lessons than can stem from this new means of cyber communication and self-presentation. Consider creating your own Facebook page (you don't have to include all of the personal information if you don't wish to) and create some in-class activities and discussions on the topic of connecting this way, as well as what students are telling the world (yes, the world!) about themselves through their own pages. Like anything, these sites have both positive and negative aspects to participation and the issues are growing by the day. Bringing this into your class will help you understand your students better, and prompt them to sit up and take more notice of you and the lessons that you are teaching.

The primary thing to keep in mind when considering incorporating pop culture in your course is that everything has potential to demonstrate some of the fundamental topics we try to teach our students. Keep your eyes and ears open to what and who your students talk about, the things that excite them, and what they like to do in their spare time. When we use their culture and world perspective, they will be all the more willing to participate more fully and consider the issues at a deeper level that speaks to them with greater meaning.

Class Format

As things begin to fall in place: your goals, class atmosphere, kind and number of assignments, you can begin to envision what you will do in class each week. This does not mean that you have to, or even should, specifically plan out every day ahead of time. In fact, flexibility and spontaneity may be your format! This is an area in which you also have lots of options and may involve students as much as you desire.

Even though lecturing is the most common method of teaching in college, it is not the most recommended format for teaching college success. You may want to limit the amount of lecturing; however, some certain topics are addressed most effectively by a formal presentation. Having guest speakers visit your class to present their areas of expertise is a great way to create variety and cover vital information relevant to the students' needs. One way to address important issues and cover the appropriate material without monopolizing class time with lectures is to have your students present the information. This serves a number of different functions, including their learning about the topics, working with others, and gaining experience with public speaking. Media sources such as film and videos are also alternatives to help teach college success. Many college classrooms are now wired for internet connection, and many students have laptops (some with wireless capability). For some activities or online exploration, you might invite all students who have laptops to bring them to class then have those without computers look on with those who do. This works well for teaching students to navigate your institution's website, and offers the possibility of some in-class research time.

After being presented with the material, students should engage in class discussions and in-class activities to enhance their learning and experience. You may want to begin or end each class with an open question and answer session in which both you and your students address each other's issues. You may want to discuss the film or video and how it relates to the topic at hand. Students seem to learn so much more when they are able to discuss the topics together, and it makes the class more fun. Another engaging activity is for you and your students to get out of the classroom. You may want to take tours of various campus facilities such as the library, computer center, or career services center.

THE SYLLABUS _____

After you design the course, you want to develop the course syllabus. The syllabus is essentially the contract between you and your students – they are expected to understand the requirements and abide by the policies contained within, as are you. The more explicit your syllabus, the more confident you can be that your students are fully aware of the expectations you have for their time, their performance, and their behavior in class. The information that you should include in your syllabus is:

- The course name, number, and credit hours earned.
- Required text and other reading and study materials.

- Your name, position at the institution, office number, hours, phone number, e-mail.
- Course objectives (purpose of course).
- Assignments (number and nature).
- Grading policy.
- Outline of topics.
- Schedule of class, including important dates (assignment due dates, exams, drop date)
- Your policies regarding:
  - -Attendance
  - -Tardiness
  - -Late work
  - -Format of work (typed, double spaced, etc.)
  - -Use of Internet sources for research
  - -Make-up exams
  - -Cheating/plagiarism
  - -Food and drink
  - -Cell phones and pagers
  - -Talking and doing other homework in class

You can, of course, include anything you want in your syllabus, but if you address all of the above, you can feel quite confident that you are providing your students with what they need to function successfully in the course. Remember, the syllabus is the first impression students get of your course, so be sure to make a good one!

Below is an example of a general syllabus for College Success Skills. Please feel free to use it as a guideline when developing your own.

SDV 100- College Success Skills

Instructor: Kathy Maalouf, MS Ed.
Office: A115 Counseling Center
Phone: 822-7211
Email: kmaalouf@tcc.edu

Course Description:

Assists students in transition to college. Provides overviews of college policies, procedures, and curricular offerings. Encourages contacts with other students and staff. Assists students toward college success through information regarding effective study habits, career and academic planning, and other college resources available to students.

Course Objectives:

The transition from high school to college and the transition that returning students make to college are complex experiences for which few students are totally prepared. This course is designed to assist students in adjusting to college and the various expectations and responsibilities of college life. There are ten core competencies:

1. College Resources
2. College Academic and Student Services and Procedures
3. Rights and Responsibilities of Students
4. Career Development and Planning
5. Academic Planning
6. Time Management
7. Learning Styles
8. Study and Reading Strategies
9. Note-taking and Listening Skills
10. Test-taking and Test Anxiety

Required Texts:

Your Guide to College Success, 4th edition—Santrock and Halonen
College Catalog, Student Handbook, and *Schedule Book*

Attendance:

Fullest growth and learning are obtained through consistent attendance. Attendance is required and points will be taken off for absences. One can receive up to 20 points for perfect attendance. If a student is bordering between two grades, lack of attendance may cause the lower of two grades. There will be no makeup work for absences, **so please come to class and be on time!!**

Assignments:

Attendance and Participation	20 points
Information Search	10 points
Academic Plan	10 points
Career Report	10 points
Knowledge is Power	10 points
Group Work	20 points
Final Exam	20 points

Grading Scale:

90 – 100	A
80 – 89	B
70 – 79	C
60 – 69	D
0 – 59	F

Support Services:

I am here to help you succeed in this course and in your college experience. Please feel free to stop by my office in the counseling center if you ever have any questions or need to talk about anything. Let me know if you have any concerns about assignments or issues relating to your college experience. Tutoring is available on the 2nd floor of the library on the VB Campus. A variety of services are available for students with disabilities. Please set up an appointment with either Gary Medlin or Vickie Rogers, our disability counselors located in the Counseling Center on the VB Campus.

Academic Dishonesty:

Academic dishonesty or cheating will not be tolerated in this course. Academic dishonesty can take a variety of forms—plagiarism, copying off another student's work, obtaining copies of exams prior to exam date, or submitting someone else's work under your name. If reasonable evidence exists that indicates you have cheated, you will receive a failing grade for this course. So please be honest and do your own work.

Class Cancellation Policy:

If I am to be away for a conference or other scheduled activity, I will notify you in advance and provide you with an assignment for the chapter to be covered for the class meeting. If I am ill, a notice will be posted on the classroom door the day of my illness. The notice will also list the assignment for which you are responsible. These make up assignments will be due the following class meeting.

If severe weather conditions occur, a notice will be provided by the TCC Information Center (757-822-1122) in addition to local radio and television stations.

Important Dates:

January 18-   Last day to add or change a course
January 21-   Last day to drop for tuition refund
March 7-12-   Spring Break
March 18-   Last day to withdraw without academic penalty

COURSE OUTLINE

January 13   Welcome—Review Syllabus
                    Commit to College Success—Chapter 1
January 20   Rights and Responsibilities of Students—Student Handbook
January 27   College Procedures and Resources—College Catalog
                    Explore Your Campus, Courses, and Computer—Chapter 4
                    INFO SEARCH IS DUE
February 3   Academic and Transfer Planning
February 10   Explore Careers—Chapter 13

	ACADEMIC PLANNING FORM IS DUE
February 17	Diversify Your Learning Styles—Chapter 2
February 24	Be a Great Time Manager—Chapter 3
March 3	Be a Great Money Manager—Chapter 5
March 10	**SPRING BREAK**
March 17	Take It In: Notes and Reading—Chapter 6
	CAREER REPORT IS DUE
March 24	Enhance Your Study Skills—Chapter 7
March 31	Succeed on Tests—Chapter 8
April 7	Expand Your Thinking—Chapter 9
April 14	Refine Your Expression—Chapter 10
April 21	Communicate and Build Relationships—Chapter 11
April 28	Take Charge of Your Physical/Mental Health—Chapter 12
	KNOWLDEGE IS POWER IS DUE
May 5	Counselor for A Day
	TAKE HOME FINAL EXAM IS DUE

Acknowledgement of Understanding:

I, _____, have read the syllabus for SDV 100 College Success Skills and have a clear understanding of the class policies, grading procedures, assignments, due dates, etc. I understand it is my responsibility as the student to read and be aware of all the information contained in the syllabus. In some cases, the instructor will amend the syllabus and I will be responsible for following the revised syllabus. I am aware of the requirements and expectations for my participation in this course. Should I have any questions or need any clarification about assignments, I will contact Ms. Kathy Maalouf immediately or at the next class meeting depending on the urgency of the matter.

Signed _____

Date _____

HEADING OFF THE CHALLENGES _____

As wonderful an opportunity as it is to teach college success, it is not without its challenges. If you have past experience with this course, you are probably well aware of the particular difficulties it may present. You have also probably experienced a new set of challenges with each new class you've encountered. For those of you who are new to this realm of instruction, it will help you to be aware of a few of the more common occurrences that will make you think and work a little bit harder to develop a truly beneficial experience for your students. As you read the following, keep in mind that each and every class has its own unique circumstances, and when you think you've figured it all out, you are likely to encounter something intriguing, yet again.

The "Attitude" (with and without a required course)

Some students perceive a course in college success as a waste of time and money. If you've experienced the "attitude", you'll know exactly what I'm referring to, and if not, you most likely will at some point. Many students right out of high school may have graduated at the top of their class and may have been in honors courses. They feel like they already know it all and do not realize the difference between high school and college success. Other students may be returning adults that have been in the work force for many years and feel that they have been successful at work and will be successful at school without the need for a course to teach them college success. All in all, some students will have an attitude when they come in to class. It is up to you to show them the benefits of the course and motivate them to learn. Your enthusiasm is the most important element in this course and it will rub off on them.

Suggestion: Promote the Course

One of the best things that you can do for your college success course, required or not, is promote it in a fun and interesting light. Dispel rumors about it simply being a "study skills" course by delineating the wide variety of topics it deals with. There are numerous ways to do this, and I encourage you to involve past students, student teachers, your orientation team members – any students on campus who want to get involved.

You may want to make a specific presentation about the nature and benefits of the course incorporated into orientation or potential student information packets and tours. The sooner students become aware of the course and its benefits, the more likely they'll be prepared to take it, and it will prevent the surprise of being told they must take it at registration.

You could distribute posters around campus based on the topics you plan to cover in class. Another suggestion is to have students present a humorous skit at orientation or on the first day of class based on the course, its content, and format. Present students with flyers at registration describing the course. Again, pique their curiosity with fun anecdotes, tidbits from the material, and even quotes from past students.

Suggestion: Present Other Student Perspectives

Many of the books mentioned in the section on *Incorporating Pop Culture* can help you present the perspectives and experiences of other students with regard to the value of a college success course. Some of the books simply have wonderfully written and very appropriate excerpts, such as Harlan Cohen's *Campus Life Exposed: Advice from the Inside.* The introduction offers a blunt, no-holds-barred look at many of the issues students will now be facing and be completely personally responsible for. His latest book *The Naked Roommate and 107 Other Issues You Might Run Into In College* is filled with tips, stories, and quotes from college students around the country about the most popular issues faced by students today. The book *Been There Should've Done That* offers quotes on numerous college success-related topics. These are words of wisdom from students ranging from freshmen to graduates that demonstrate the value of hindsight, and present a variety of regrets and lost learning opportunities.

To expose your students to those that have come before them (and wished they had learned what your students will have the chance to learn), consider creating transparencies of the excerpts to put on the overhead projector. Students can then discuss them in small groups, as an entire class, or write about them in their journals. The truth is, regardless of *our* qualifications and past college experience which validates our ability to emphasize the importance of this course to them, students respond with much greater enthusiasm to other students! If you don't choose to use material from text sources, consider inviting older students to your class early on in the semester. Let them tell your freshmen just how important the course is – particularly as they get further along in their college career.

Suggestion: Make Analogies

The point to be made with the analogies is that there are many major life transitions such as getting married, having a baby, and starting a new job, and for each one it is readily acknowledged that the individuals need and can benefit greatly from advice, guidance and skill development. The life transition of the college freshman is probably one of the most dramatic anyone can experience. A course offering just such preparation at this juncture in no way intimates that students are not capable of handling college or need special tutoring; it simply demonstrates the recognition of the incredible challenges ahead.

Teaching A First Semester Course

Another difficulty in teaching the vital information necessary for college freshmen is having to teach it to them during their first semester. As I mentioned in my personal summary of the course, students definitely need a great deal of the lessons immediately. The sooner they can apply the reading strategies, study tips, and time management techniques the better. But in many ways we're introducing concepts to them that they can't yet relate to. They have no understanding of the difficulty level and performance standards of college exams until they actually experience one first hand. They can't truly relate to the critical need for time management until they get into their semester full-swing, and sometimes not even until mid-terms. We can tell them all we want about what they will be up against, but to a great extent, it is lost on deaf ears. They often begin the term full of self-confidence, and believe you are only warning *other* kids.

Suggestion: Acknowledge "The Gap"

We can't make them truly understand something they have yet to experience, but we can communicate in ways that can close the time-lapse gap. First of all, *acknowledge* the discrepancy to yourself and to your students. Approaching your students with the knowledge that they are not fully prepared to understand what you share will enhance your teaching methods because:

- It will dispel your expectations that they react to the lessons with vigor, determination, and acceptance of their importance, and enable you to respond more sensitively to their inability to really "get it".
- It will prompt you to design your lessons according to their schedule of experiences.

For example, although theoretically inaccurate, it may make the most sense to wait and cover the chapter on test taking strategies *after* midterms when everyone has experienced true college exams. They may be much more likely to pay attention and apply the information when they know what they're really up against. There is no required order for use of the textbook. Other than chapter one, which is designed to be presented first, each chapter can stand alone, and thus be presented at any point during the semester, enabling this kind of customization for your students' particular needs and wants.

Share some personal examples of "eye opening" experiences *you* had your first semester in college. This will help them to see that you have been there and do know of what you speak. They will enjoy the personal aspect of the lesson, and may take your advice more seriously with the recognition of what you went through. Of course, you can always bring in older students to "back up" the lesson you're trying to teach.

Varied Student Class Make-Up

Whether or not your course is required by the institution, one challenge can be found in the variety of students gathered together in one class. This variety can be based on ability level, need, and/or major chosen. In each case, you have students requiring differing levels of input in some of the major areas of the class. Given that this course is designed and offered for their benefit, the last thing that you want is for them to feel like they've wasted their time.

Suggestion: Assess Student Needs

Begin, if you can, by assessing their needs. There are several ways in which you can do this. Obtain a class roll prior to the beginning of the semester that lists students and their declared majors. From this you can gain an awareness of how many from each curriculum or department are represented, and how many remain undeclared. You may then consider grouping students as such for particular aspects of the course. Reading, writing, and study skills are addressed in the text with regards to different disciplines. Learning styles are presented as they relate to individuals' choices of a field of study. Academic and career planning are covered, with relevant information for both those who have chosen a major, and those who have yet to do so. For these areas of focus, group students with their similar peers and they can more meaningfully discuss, explore, and work on projects related to the material.

Another means of assessing your students' backgrounds and needs is by using the *Know Yourself Checklist*, located at the beginning of each chapter. Have students fill these out, then write a one paragraph summary of what they think they have to gain from the chapter, as well as what they already feel confident about. Collect them, and as you compile your students' responses, plan how you will approach the chapter. You can do this chapter by chapter, or you can have them do the checklists for all the chapters at the beginning of the semester, and you can plan your entire course.

Suggestion: Give Choices

If you are faced with an incredibly diverse group of students, or simply want to make sure everyone feels their time in the course was well spent, you can design your course so as to enable the students to be in charge of what they cover. If you do not wish to require coverage of the entire text, determine the number of chapters students must read, and let them choose which ones they do and in what *order*. You may require that they turn in one each week, but which one is entirely up to them. This way they may address topics relevant to them at the time they feel they can benefit from them the most. The amount of work assigned for all chapters should be the same, but everyone works on what they want to at any given time.

As to what they feel will benefit them during class time, take a poll. Hand out a list of possible lecture topics, skill building activities, demonstrations, guest speakers, on campus service tours, etc. and have them indicate their top 3-5 choices of interest. Compile the responses and plan accordingly.

If you have certain topics you'd like to focus on for a longer term project, enable them to make that choice as well. Give them a list and identify the purpose of each and have them determine which they will pursue. Possible topics (suitable for one month to semester long projects) include: time management, creating a budget, and career exploration. All projects should begin with the student writing the reason he/she has chosen the project, and end with a brief paper about what they learned and how they benefited from it.

The Quiet Class

College success courses should be interactive in nature. They provide a forum for students to meet with peers and a college faculty or staff member to ask questions, discuss their experiences, and share their comments and concerns about college life. Although this sounds like a fun and interesting opportunity, many students don't take it. Worse than that, sometimes those that don't all end up in the same class! It's very difficult to create an effective course for students when the students don't participate. You may ask them questions to no avail, and sit facing a mute group who won't take the bait.

Suggestion: Create Intimate Groups

Many times, students won't speak in a large group, but you can get them talking when either paired with one other student, or placed in a small group of three to four. This is a good way to begin dialog between students, and often enables a large group discussion later on. After students talk among themselves for a period of time, reconvene the class and see what happens. You can even have a representative from each group share the ideas discussed earlier.

Suggestion: Develop Good Leads

Be specific with your prompts and questions. Even as college freshmen, students can have a difficult time with wide, open-ended questions, such as "What do you think about college so far?" When the topic is too broad, they don't really know where to start, and are most likely still too self-conscious to decide. More specific inquiries, such as "What has been the most difficult area of adjustment for you since starting college?" or "What has been your biggest surprise academically?" will provide them with a more concrete starting point. Another way to prompt discussion is to give students a few minutes to write their answer to the questions first, then they will be more prepared to share their thoughts and ideas.

Suggestion: Get Them Interested

Present topics that interest them. I stumbled upon this amazing activity in an attempt to cover relationships in a unique manner. I had each student e-mail me three questions they had for/about the opposite sex. I assured them complete anonymity, and I compiled the list prior to the next class period. The seating was arranged men on one side, women on the other, and I sat in the middle to moderate the discussion. I simply presented the questions one at a time to each group, and the fireworks began! Discussion and debate exploded from a class that was previously speechless. They didn't want to leave, and they wanted to continue the activity the following week. Every one of my classes, and of my colleagues' classes, that have experienced this "Gender Face-Off" reacted the same way.

Inspire Critical Thinking

Another way to inspire interesting interaction and promote critical thinking is to make use of questions found in a number of books full of thought-provoking, introspection-inducing queries. There are the more benign questions, such as "If you could add any new course to our nation's school curriculum, what would it be?" and "What is your all-time favorite commercial jingle?" from the book *The Conversation Piece* by Bret Nicholaus and Paul Lowrie. Then there are deeper, more personal explorations found in the series of *"If…"* books by Evelyne McFarlane and James Saywell. From the one in the series subtitled "How Far Will You Go?" you'll find: "When have you been *most* honorable?" and "Who is your *greatest* hero from history?" *The Book of Questions* by Gregory Stock, Ph.D is another rich source of conversation starters, with questions such as "If you could spend one year in perfect happiness, but afterward would remember nothing of the experience, would you do so?"

For each of these, choose your favorites and have students draw items from a hat. They can address them individually or as a group. It often leads to lively responding from many students, not only with regard to their own question, but to others' questions as well.

Effective Problem Solving

Challenges will always arise, as that's the nature of teaching. Yet every semester should be a new attempt to achieve the "perfect" method (and if you figure it out, let me know!) When trying to solve the problems at hand, if not for the current semester, but for the new one around the corner, try to identify what lies at the root of the problem. Consider if your methods are effective or ineffective for learning. Consider the types of students you have in the class: are they monopolizing or too reserved? Evaluate if students are satisfied with the amount of work assigned and the class format.

Suggestion: Student Critique

One of the best ways to find out what might be wrong and to get the answer to these and other questions you may have is to ask the students. Remember, this class is for them. If they don't see it as beneficial and effectively serving their needs, it has no value.

Assign a critique of the course at the end of the semester. You may want to attach a fairly significant grade to it so that students take it seriously. Your institution may have its own course evaluation for students to fill out, but this is something different. This is for *you*. The feedback will not only enlighten you as to what students thought of your class, but will give you the feedback necessary to improve your class for next time. Make this last point very clear to your students – tell them why you are having them do this. I actually title my assignment: "Do a New Freshman a Favor". I let them know that what they tell me about their experience in my course will have a direct effect on next year's incoming class. The things I find that most people liked and benefited from I incorporate into my future class. Negative feedback from a large number of students will prompt me to reconsider those issues.

I make it very clear that their critique should focus on what worked for them and *constructive* criticism. I warn them that pointless whining will be viewed as exactly that. They need to specifically tell me what they didn't like, or what didn't work for them and *why*. I also encourage them to offer suggestions in any area they see fit: topics to cover, activities to engage in, format of the class. They are assured that their grade is based on their time, effort, and thought put into the critique and not whether they report liking the class or not.

Another option along these same lines is to have students create their own class syllabus. Tell them to imagine that they are the instructor assigned to teach college success. They are required to use the text book (and include any other university requirements), but that the rest of the course is up to them. Have them be specific with regards to topics covered, assignments for grading, grading scheme, and class format. They enjoy doing this, and you can gain a tremendous amount of information as to what they would like to see in this course.

CREATIVE APPLICATIONS OF THE TEXT FEATURES _____

Your Guide to College Success includes a wide range of features, all of which have a number of potential uses. What follows are the descriptions of each feature contained in the text, and ideas for implementing them in a variety of ways.

The Learning Portfolio

Designed specifically to be used as the primary source for activities and assignments, the learning portfolio contains a variety of experiences for students of college success. It begins by offering several *Self-Assessments*. Each assessment provides students with the opportunity to learn about themselves relative to the topic at hand. Some of them are followed up with further questions for students to address, but you can help them make further use of what they find. Have students write in their journals about their reactions to what the Self-Assessment revealed. What did they learn about themselves? What might they do to change areas in which they need help? You also might have students choose several topics over the course of the semester to plan and carry out specific things to improve an area that an assessment indicated they need improvement in. Have them keep a record of their progress, and write a summary at the end of the semester.

You can also make use of students' responses yourself. Reviewing their responses is a good way to recognize areas in which your students need extra guidance, and you can address them either through topics emphasized in class, or on a one-to-one basis.

Reflecting the findings in experiential learning of David Kolb, the *My Journal* options include journal entry topics in the categories of *Reflect, Do, Think Critically,* and *Create.* The focus of each category of exercise is different and enables students to work the material from the chapter in unique ways.

The Learning Portfolio is a wonderful tool for helping you design your course. Each chapter offers a variety of possibilities for you to choose from, or to have your students choose from. The activities are clearly described and fully presented in the textbook so that no preparation or copying is required, ideal for those whose schedules limit the ability to plan ahead. However, for those who would like to get even more of out of the existing Learning Portfolio, it has numerous possibilities.

Many of the journal topics and critical thinking topics make very good topics for in-class discussion. You may find there are issues that, although beneficial for students to ponder on their own, would be even more effective for students to talk about with each other.

Many of the action and personal vision activities, although written with one student in mind, would work well assigned to pairs or groups of students. There are several suggestions for students to seek out several places on campus and gather information. It will increase their self-confidence and promote student bonding to have them go with others to explore their school. Some of the projects requiring the development of public service announcements and presentations to future freshmen will simply be more enjoyable and result in greater creativity if students work on them as a team.

The Six Strategies for Success – Linking College to Real Life

This model represents the fundamental theme of *Your Guide to College Success.* It communicates the interconnectedness of the six basic life elements relevant to college students. You can begin with any element and proceed in any direction and the relationship among the six points is the same. *Clarify Values* is both a driving force behind, and a result of *Know Yourself.* Both of these are inherent in the process it takes to *Create Your Future*, which can lead to, and derive from the need to *Build Competence.* All the elements play a role when you work to *Expand Your Resources*, and are imperative in order for you to successfully *Manage Your Life*, which, when done carefully and thoroughly, contributes to the individual achieving all of the other elements.

You will find this hexagonal diagram in whole, and in part, repeated throughout the text. This is to demonstrate the significance of the material in the book as it relates to these fundamental life elements. Often, college life is believed to be "different" – a unique time filled with experiences somehow removed from the real world. We know however, that this simply isn't true. Almost all aspects of functioning successfully in college – from the high level of commitment and responsibility required, to working cooperatively with diverse others – can be found as significant to success in life in general. Even skills such as reading for specific disciplines and understanding test-taking techniques generalize in some way to the information processing necessary in a future career.

As the text makes continual reference to the model to illustrate the significance of the information presented, you can further its impact by drawing the connection between the elements and other activities students participate in. In fact, it makes a very effective theme or sub-theme for a college success course. Mapping the experiences of college onto those of real life – now and in the future – will not only make your course more relevant, but all of their other courses and course requirements as well.

There are numerous ways to encourage thinking about the model of success. First of all, for any particular assignment, activity, or discussion topic, have students identify which elements drive the purpose of what they're doing. You can also have them expand on, or suggest variations of, assignments to incorporate additional aspects of the model. As they begin to see the connections, frequently take them through the dynamics of all the interrelated elements.

Focusing on the model may prompt you to specifically incorporate experiences with the sole purpose being to demonstrate its role in their lives. An enlightening and enjoyable experience for students is to work with the music they enjoy. Have them analyze the lyrics from their favorite song (a search on the Internet can lead to sites that provide song lyrics). Ask them to write out the song in its entirety, and to discuss what it means to them. Have them make direct reference to things such as the values it espouses, what it leads them to think about, and how this might influence their goals and motivation. Do they find their music is uplifting and supports positive functioning, or does it convey the opposite message? If the latter is true, what is it they get from such music? Does it in any way impact their thinking? You might also choose a couple of currently popular songs and discuss these issues in class. There may be a surprising number of different interpretations!

There are many opportunities to take students down this path, and as they recognize the role each of these six factors plays in their successfully reaching their goals, they will attend to the material more fully, and respond with greater purpose.

Each success strategy is further explored in highlighted features throughout the chapters. While they stand alone as excellent sources of information relating chapter material to the concept behind the strategy, you can help your students gain more from them. Consider engaging students in the following ways with your favorite stand-out strategies.

Personal Relevance – Prompt students to make connections between the information presented in the strategy feature to their own lives, or the lives of friends and roommates. Either through the class blog or journal, or simply through class discussion, encourage students to see the relevance of the example provided to personal experiences, then expand on ways in which they can make good choices and adapt their behavior accordingly in order to achieve success.

Adapt it to Your Institution – Have students consider the information, tips, strategies, or story elements presented in the strategy feature in the context of your college or university. While the strategies may present more generalized information about successful ideas, circumstances to avoid, and helpful hints, students can gain more by applying the information to the particulars of their school, living arrangements, classes, instructors, and college town. Conduct class discussions, assign journal entries, post a class blog, or have groups of students work together to hone the strategy features to reflect their college experiences.

Develop a Rubric – For strategy features that share vignettes of challenges faced by college students or general tips for success in a certain area, have students develop a step-by-step rubric for dealing with the challenge or carrying out the suggestions for achieving goals. Encourage them to transform the general into specific actions they can take.

Create a New Strategy – After reading and discussing the strategy features in the chapter, have your students select a topic and create their own strategy feature. You can assign the format (vignette, tips, etc.) or allow them to select the way in which they feel their feature can best benefit others. For both the students-created strategies and the rubrics mentioned previously, create a notebook or online site that future students can refer to and learn from their predecessors' perspectives and input.

Here are the general descriptions of the success strategies features contained in the text.

Know Yourself

This feature was designed to introduce students to material in the upcoming chapter in the context of their own personal experiences. As students read through the statements, they indicate whether or not it applies to them. This highlights the issues that will be addressed and lets them know where they stand with regards to what they'll be learning. At the end of the chapter there are several *self assessments* that enable students to more thoroughly explore elements of the chapter relative to themselves.
Although originally designed to benefit the student, instructors can use the checklists and assessments to their advantage as well. Have students fill them out and write a one paragraph summary as to what they hope to gain from the chapter, as well as what they seem to already know. Collect them and compile the responses. With your class' profile, you can then design your approach to the unit, not only emphasizing the topics students particularly need, but making use of student "experts" from the various

areas in which they feel confident. This can be done on a chapter-by-chapter basis or with the text in its entirety for the purpose of mapping out your entire semester.

Images of College Success

Each chapter begins with an inspiring true story of an individual's personal triumphs and their experiences in college. We enjoy reading about others' lives and stories of achievement, especially against the odds. They often provide great motivation for conquering our own challenges, and reaching our own goals. These success stories serve as an effective jumping off point for each chapter. They lend a personal perspective and illustrate the real-life application of the topics presented in the chapter. Using these "images" as the topic of an in-class discussion, or personal journal entry, can get students thinking about the issues from a positive and introspective perspective. Ask questions such as

- How did this story make you feel?
- Can you relate to the individual in any way?
- How is this story relevant to your life and circumstances?
- Do you have your own hero or idol with regards to the issues faced by the person in the profile?

More ideas for exploring *Images of College Success* can be found in the section on *Chapter Features*.

Quotes

The power of an eloquent phrase can be tremendous. A few well-placed words can speak volumes and communicate ideas of profound significance. Of course, some are just plain funny! The quotes located in every chapter throughout the book reflect a wide range of ideas, all relevant to various aspects of the college experience. You can sit back and hope your students take the time to read them and reflect on their meaning, or you can make certain that they do. Choose your favorite quotes and bring them to your students' attention. Have them write in their journal, discuss on the class blog, or bring them to the fore in a class discussion. Consider the following:

- Present students with a quote and have them talk about
    - What it means in general.
    - What it means to them personally.
    - How they might apply it.
- Have students debate the meaning, moral, and/or relevance of a particular quote.
- Have students identify their favorite quotes.
    - Which quotes are most relevant to them?
    - Which quotes serve to motivate them the most?
    - Which quotes do they take issue with?

You may also ask students to bring in quotes from people in the public eye: celebrities, musicians, politicians, etc. Explore and analyze them along the same lines, as well as with an additional focus on their relevance to current societal trends and values, and their influence on young adults.

More ideas for incorporating the quotes into your class are provided in the *Chapter Features* section.

Expand Your Resources

People, places, and services that can assist students in achieving their goal are presented, as are strategies for helping them take advantage of their benefits. Suggestions include tips on how to find such resources, how to engage and develop relationships with others who can help them during their college experience, and specific actions they can take both in and out of the classroom to get the most out of college and prepare optimally for their future.

Build Competence

Students are presented with stories of what not to do in college, how to recognize potentially problematic behavior (in themselves and others), how to deal with such challenges, and specific actions they can take to improve their approach to dealing with particular situations.

Manage Life

Stories in this feature highlight student responses to problems they encounter while adapting to college, and many features share tips for dealing with pitfalls and taking on life's challenges frequently faced by college students.

Create Your Future

This feature focuses on helping students prepare for their future after graduation, including expanding their resources, relating personal interests to an academic major, and pro-active choices for successfully paving the way to achieving their goals.

Clarify Values

The role that personal values play in college and life success is highlighted through vignettes about students losing – and then finding – their way in certain situations. Areas in which it is particularly important to use personal values as a guide and acknowledge their significance are illustrated, along with prompting students to turn their attention inward to develop strong self-awareness, and how to relate college challenges to what students find important academically and in life in general.

Tables and Figures

These features convey some of the most interesting and useful information in the text. Be sure to point them out, discuss them in class, and have students actively apply and respond to what they find here.

Review Questions

Traditionally, review questions are used for the purpose of helping students to prepare for a quiz or an exam. These certainly work well for that, yet they can also be used to prime students for what they will be learning. Have students look over the questions and highlight those they most look forward to discovering the answer to. They might also see if they can answer any before reading the text, and then compare their original ideas, to what was presented in the chapter. A great class discussion would be to compare what students believed initially about the material, to what they learned with regards to achieving college success. The *Review Questions* serve as a perfect prompt.

Resources for Mastering the College Experience

Many supplemental materials are mentioned in this *Resources* section. Books and websites are listed for students to explore on their own, should they so choose. However, you may wish to bring in some of these additional resources, assigning them to students or groups of students to investigate and report back on. Group students by interest – having them designate topics they'd like to read more on. Each group can then peruse a website or two, or take a few weeks to read a book they select from the list. Devote some time in class to hearing from students on the value of the resource they explored. From this you can compile your list of favorites to recommend to future students. Oprah had her book club; you can have your college success recommended reading list! Outside readings can be a great basis for larger, long-term projects, or an option for extra credit.

SUPPLEMENTAL TOOLS _____

Multimedia Manager 2007 Edition: A Microsoft PowerPoint Tool

Organized around 14 College Success topics, this easy to use tool will help you assemble, edit, and present tailored multimedia lectures. Create a lecture from scratch, customize the templates provided, or use the ready-made PowerPoint slides as is. The CD-Rom also includes video clips and web links.

ThomsonNow! Website

For instructors, this integrated testing, tutorial, and class management system saves you time and provides interactive learning support for your students. It offers assignable exercises with student's test results flowing automatically to a grade book. It can also be integrated with WebCT or Blackboard.

For students, it contains assessments, electronic journals, interactive exercises, and practice tests. No instructor set-up or involvement is necessary; students can simply log-in and go!

MENTOR'S CORNER

One way to really get excited and motivated about teaching your college success course is to talk to other college success instructors. Most people who teach this course really enjoy what they do, and sharing ideas with colleagues is nearly as much fun! Problem-solving becomes easier and creativity takes off when you get together with others who share your experience. Within each chapter of the *Chapter Features* section is a *Mentor's Corner* section. There you will find the names and e-mail addresses of experienced college success instructors and their areas of expertise. These individuals from across the country are available to answer your questions and discuss issues regarding teaching this challenging and exciting course.

    As your first mentor resource, I encourage you to contact me with any questions or comments regarding this manual, or any aspect of teaching college success. I wish you much success, enjoyment, and enthusiasm in your students!

Cynthia Jenkins, Ph.D.
Director of Undergraduate Advising
The University of Texas at Dallas
cynthia.jenkins@utdallas.edu

The College Success Factors Index: An Instructor's How-To Guide

Developed by Gary J. Williams, Ed.D. Long Beach City College, Long Beach, CA

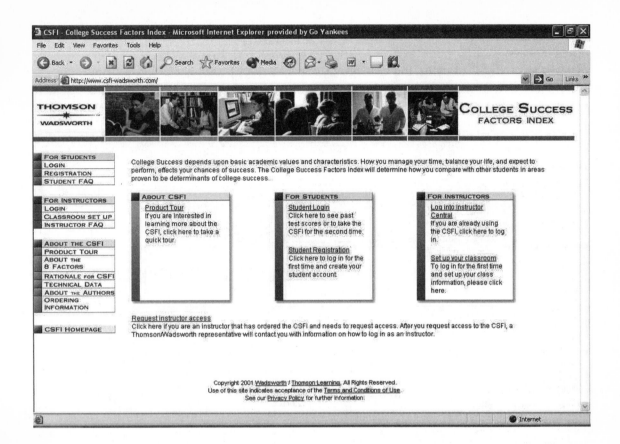

This guide is designed to be a simple how-to guide on how to get started using the College Success Factors Index (also known as the CSFI). In this guide, you will receive step-by-step instructions on:

- How to register your own instructor account on the CSFI website.
- How to set up your class on the CSFI website.
- What your students need to know and do in order to complete the CSFI on the Internet.
- How to access the CSFI results for your class, and what your next steps should be.
- Developing intervention strategies for your class using the CSFI, including a few brief examples.
- What to do if you or your students lose their access codes or passwords.
- How to contact Thomson Wadsworth's College Success Division if you have questions or need assistance.

I. Getting Started: Setting up your classroom on the CSFI Website:

Getting started using the College Success Factors Index is easy. Simply visit http://success.wadsworth.com/gardner7e and follow the link to the CSFI website.

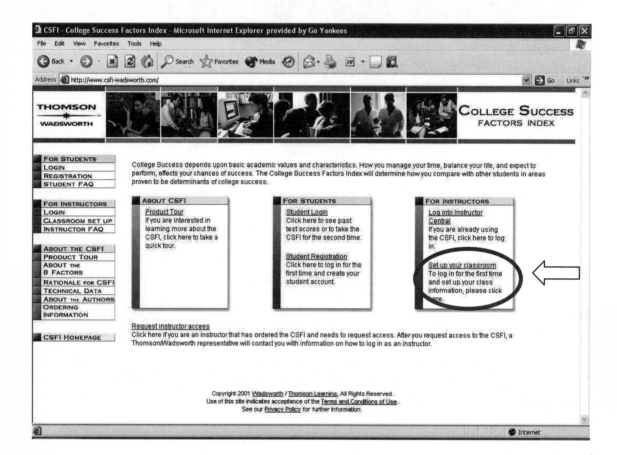

Your first task is to set up your own personal instructor account. To do so, follow these steps:

1. Click "Set up your classroom" link as indicated in the illustration above.
2. You will then be asked for a "School Password" as shown below. You can request a school password by e-mail at csuccess@thomson.com.

3. Next, you will be asked to provide the following registration information:

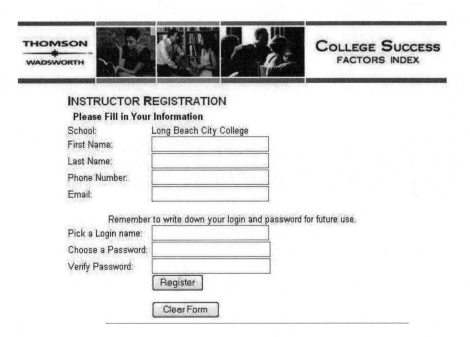

Be sure to write down your login name and password, as you will use this to access the CSFI website from this point on.

4. Should you forget your login or password, you can request them by e-mail at csuccess@thomson.com.

II. Instructor Central

Now that you have registered as an instructor, all the resources you need are located in one place on the CSFI website. Instructor Central is where you will go to set up your classes, to take the CSFI, access student results, and to find information about each of the 8 Factors, as well as strategies to address student needs.

To access Instructor Central, you must first log in by using the login name and password you just created. Navigate your browser to the CSFI website and click "Log into Instructor Central" as shown at the top of the next page.

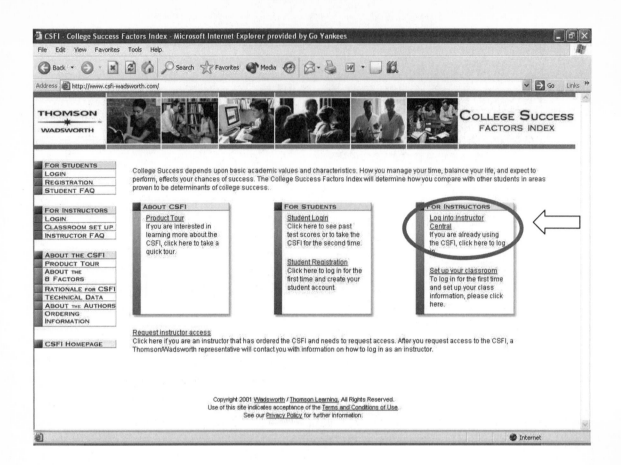

Next, provide your User Name and Password:

LOG IN TO INSTRUCTOR CENTRAL
Enter your username and password.

User Name	
Password	

Login

Before you can log in, you must register and set up a new classroom. To register and set up a new classroom, please click here.

You are then taken to the "Instructor Central" page, which is shown below:

THOMSON   WADSWORTH   COLLEGE SUCCESS FACTORS INDEX

VIEW SCORES
BY STUDENT
BY COURSE
BY SCHOOL
AS GRADEBOOK

MANAGING CLASSES
MANAGE CLASSES
SET UP A NEW CLASS
EDIT PERSONAL INFORMATION

TEACHING THE 8 FACTORS
RESPONSIBILITY VS. CONTROL
COMPETITION
TASK PRECISION
EXPECTATIONS
WELLNESS
TIME MANAGEMENT
COLLEGE INVOLVEMENT
FAMILY INVOLVEMENT

INSTRUCTOR CENTRAL

CSFI HOMEPAGE

CSFI
INSTRUCTOR CENTRAL

The rationale behind the CSFI system is that an understanding of the criteria for success will help the student move from being unaware of why he/she is not successful, to being a prophet of his or her own success. The College Success Factors Index can save instructors, counselors, and administrators valuable time in helping students find their areas of strength and weakness.

View Scores
- By Student
- By Course
- By School
- Grade Book

Click on these links to view individual student scores, class averages, and your school's average score. You can also view a table of scores for all students, to determine how your students have improved on the CSFI.

Managing classes
- Manage registered classes
- Set up a new class
- Edit personal information

Click on these links to set up a new class, or manage the classes you have set up. Click on "Edit personal information" to edit your contact information (phone number, e-mail, etc.).

Teach the 8 Factors
- Responsibility vs. Control
- Competition
- Task Precision
- Expectations
- Wellness
- Time Management
- College Involvement
- Family Involvement

Click on these links to find advice and suggestions for teaching students how to improve in each of the 8 factors for College Success.

From this page, you can view student and class scores and results, set up new classes and manage existing classes, and read all about strategies you can use to help your students get the most from their experience using the CSFI.

In the following section, we will cover how you can set up your class to take the CSFI.

III. Setting up a new class to take the CSFI

From the Instructor Central page, you can easily set up your class (or as many classes as you wish) to take the CSFI.

1. Click on "Set up a new class" link, which is located under the Managing Classes heading, as indicated below:

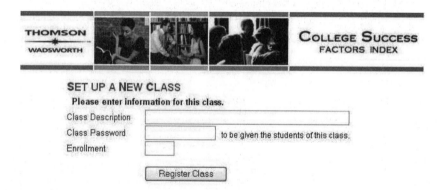

2. You will then be taken to the "Set up a new class" registration screen:

3. Provide a brief description of the class you are registering, and the number of students in that class under the enrollment screen. If you wish to register several classes, register each separately, using a separate description for each class.

4. **The Class Password is very important**. You will be providing this password to your students in each class section you set up and the students will need it when they register to take the CSFI. Make sure it is not a personal password that you do not wish to disclose to others. Also, you will need a different password for each class you set up. It helps to make them easy-to-remember for the students. Provide this password to them in writing, such as on a note card or in the syllabus.

The class password is also important because it is what uniquely identifies your student in the CSFI website database as part of the class you set up. If students were to use a different class password than the one you establish for your class, their results would not appear when you attempt to access student scores from the Instructor Central page. It is vital that you ensure that students use only the class password that you give them.

5. Once you've clicked on "Register Class," your students can take the CSFI.

IV. Administering the CSFI to your students

Because the CSFI is a web-based assessment, students can access the instrument in a number of settings - in a computer lab, at home, or wherever they can access the Internet. As an instructor, you have the flexibility of choosing to assign the CSFI as an out-of-class activity, or have students take the instrument all at once in a computer lab setting. Whether students take it individually or together as a class, the steps to completing the CSFI are the same.

1. Students will navigate their browser to the CSFI website: http://www.csfi-wadsworth.com and click on "Student Registration" as shown below:

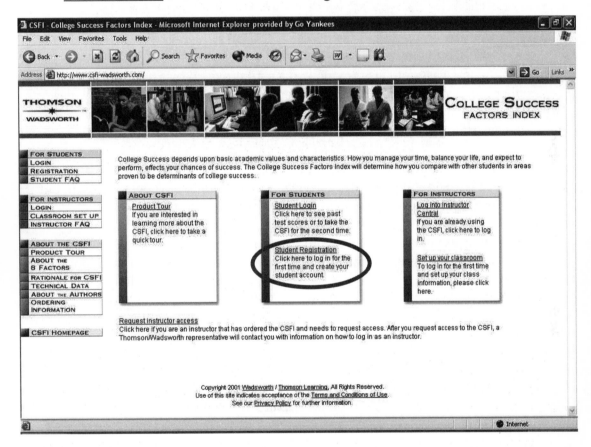

2. Students are required to enter two passwords to access the CSFI on the web:

STUDENT REGISTRATION
Please your access password and your class password

Your **access password** can be found on the back of the card that came with your textbook. Enter your access password in the text box below.

Your professor should have given you a unique **class password** to enter the CSFI. Enter your class password in the text box below.

If you do not have your class password, please see your instructor.

Enter

The "Access Password" is provided on a card provided by Thomson Wadsworth, either bundled in the student textbook or sold separately by Thomson Wadsworth. (For information on ordering Access Password cards, see your Thomson Wadsworth Campus representative, or e-mail csuccess@thomson.com)

The Class Password is the one that you established for the class in the previous step and have provided for them. Students are instructed to contact you should they lose their Class Password.

3. Once students enter the two required passwords, they are taken to a registration screen to input their name and other identifying information prior to taking the CSFI:

STUDENT REGISTRATION

You Are Approved for taking "Student Success/Transfer Services Center "

Please fill out this form and submit it for our records

First Name   [_____]

Last Name   [_____]

Gender   Male ○
        Female ○

Birth Date   [____] / [____] / [_____] (mm/dd/yyyy)

Ethnic Background   [African American (not of Hispanic origin) ▾]

Other Ethnic Background   [_____]

What was your high school Grade Point Average (GPA)?
[A to A- (4.0 - 3.5) ▾]

How many college credits have you completed?
[None ▾]

What is your college Grade Point Average (GPA)? (If this is your first semester in college, select "First semester.")
[A to A- (4.0 - 3.5) ▾]

Who asked you to take the CSFI?
[Course Instructor ▾]

What is your degree goal?
[Associates ▾]

Remember to write down your login and password for future use.

Please Choose a login name   [_____]

Choose a Password   [_____]

Verify your Password   [_____]

[Enter]

Students are asked to choose a login name and password, which will serve as their access to the CSFI website from this point forward. In other words, the access and class passwords are no longer required once the student has completed the student registration form. Emphasize to students that they must write down their login name and password.

4. Once students have successfully registered, they are given access to the CSFI assessment.

CSFI
STUDENT CENTRAL

Take the CSFI assessment
If you are ready to begin the 80-question assessment, click on the link above.

5. To begin the assessment, they click on the link to "Take the CSFI assessment," and after reading the test instructions, they can begin the assessment.

6. The assessment consists of 80 items, where students are asked to indicate their response by clicking on the bubble that most closely matches their view of each statement as it pertains to their attitudes and practices as a student.

#	Statement	Strongly Agree	Agree	Undecided	Disagree	Strongly Disagree
	CSFI ASSESSMENT					Page 1 of 10
1.	I involve myself with a lot of school or college projects.	○	○	○	○	○
2.	People should stand up for what they believe.	○	○	○	○	○
3.	I can handle examination stress.	○	○	○	○	○
4.	Competition at college is necessary for success.	○	○	○	○	○
5.	I know why my career choice requires a college degree.	○	○	○	○	○
6.	I am a strong competitor when I need to be.	○	○	○	○	○
7.	My family will definitely attend my graduation.	○	○	○	○	○
8.	My life rarely gets out of hand.	○	○	○	○	○
#	Statement	Strongly Agree	Agree	Undecided	Disagree	Strongly Disagree

Next →

7. Once students have answered item 80, they will click on the button titled "Score Test" and their results will be displayed on screen as shown below:

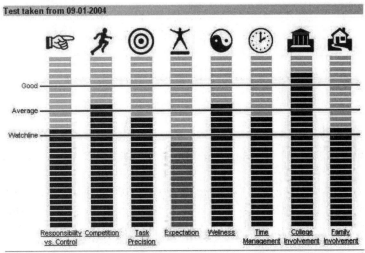

Test taken from 09-01-2004

The graph above shows how you stand in each of the eight factors that constitute the College Success Factors Index (or CSFI). The CSFI is not a test you pass or fail, but it does represent a set of characteristics critical to college success.

Look at the red areas where your score falls below the watchline. These are the areas that need improvement first.

At the same moment, the students' results are stored in the CSFI website database under the class associated with the class password that you provided. Simultaneously, an e-mail is generated to your e-mail account (the one you provided when you registered as an instructor), indicating the name of the student who just completed the CSFI assessment. You are now able to view the students' scores by logging into Instructor Central using your own login and password.

Toll-Free Academic Resource Center for CSFI
Please call (800) 423-0563 if you have any questions or concerns regarding the College Success Factors Index.

CHAPTER 1

MAKING CONNECTIONS

I. CHAPTER OVERVIEW

There is so much more to college success than intellectual ability! Sometimes students don't realize how important it is to make connections around campus and have a good understanding of where they are now and where they are going. This chapter begins by highlighting the new environment students will encounter once they start college. It is filled with a variety of resources such as academic advisors, personal counselors, and computer centers. Most campuses are aware of the scope of the transition many students are experiencing, and offer tremendous support systems to aid in their scholastic and personal success and satisfaction.

Freshmen are typically so caught up in the newness of their experience and adapting to the demands of college courses that they don't look to the future. It is imperative for them to consider their academic future – whether they have declared a major or not. Those who believe they know what they want to do and have an area of focus picked out need to be fully aware of the scope of their degree plan and the sequence of courses required for graduation. They must be on top of prerequisites and the acceptable categories from which they may choose electives. Students who are undeclared have even more to consider. Knocking out core courses is advisable, but it is important that they do so in a manner that will serve them well once they actually choose a major. Taking a variety of particular electives, or only taking certain courses while putting others (like math or lab science) off, may actually hinder them down the road. They may find that it is not possible for them to be as far along as they'd like and have to backtrack. Familiarity with the college catalog is imperative, as is mapping out a plan for achieving their academic goals.

To avoid these problems, students must meet with their academic advisor as soon as possible and establish a working rapport. It is necessary that they become aware of what their advisor can do for them, and how they can make use of their knowledge and experience with different courses and instructors, to map out the best academic plan.

We live in a world where being technologically savvy is no longer an option. Even art, dance, and theater majors will be required to use a computer and possess an understanding of basic software programs such as Word or Excel, and connect with the Internet to do research and communicate via e-mail. Most college campuses offer computer labs with technical support and student fees may cover a campus computer account, providing access to online databases and an e-mail address. If students are computer wary, they should be encouraged to take a basic computer course – they may find it is one of the best things they do! Of course, students who are already very techno-oriented may need to learn how to control their computer use. There is a new category of addiction – computer addiction – that is very real. With their newfound freedom and excessive free time, students often spend untold hours playing games, surfing the Internet, e-mailing friends, and even developing relationships in chat rooms.

The exercises in this instructor's manual for this chapter should be very fun and interesting for students to complete. Not only will the exercises prompt students to go on a campus scavenger hunt, but they will also tell students how to think about and develop an academic game plan. As you prepare to help students discover and apply the information in this chapter to your own campus situation, begin by determining whether or not these topics have already been addressed in pre-term orientation meetings. If so, what was the depth of coverage? Were all the areas considered? Were all students present? If all of your students have already been involved in an intensive and thorough orientation program that addressed most of the topics in this chapter, then you may be able to cover these subjects in a review session rather than in depth. A brief pre-test to assess students' recall of the information will assist you in selecting those areas that require elaboration during your class time.

II. IMAGES OF COLLEGE SUCCESS

Meg Whitman's story illustrates the value of having a well-rounded college experience. She succeeded academically, while staying in tune with what her intellectual interests were – and she didn't hesitate to make a fairly dramatic change in her career direction. To follow up on her newly discovered interest, she spent the summer working in the field of business. Meg also invested her time and energy into extracurricular activities, showing that even the best students have fun along with devoting time to their studies. It was undoubtedly this multitude of decisions and experiences that led Meg to state, "The university inspired me to think in ways that have guided me throughout my life."

Have students begin by thinking about their extracurricular activities in high school. Can they find something similar on campus that interests them? If they were not involved during high school, have students identify areas of interest either related to or separate from their major that they might be able to pursue while in college. Encourage them to find useful skills and experiences in their extracurricular interests that might benefit them in their future career.

After their general interests have been explored, have students identify any general skills that they believe are important to possess, particularly for career success, such as public speaking, computer software skills, and the ability to network and make interpersonal connections. How might they be able to obtain these skills while in college? What kinds of opportunities can be found on campus to provide such experiences?

Finally, have students brainstorm a variety of different avenues their careers might take, based on their acquiring a variety of different skills, as well as discovering their interests in different disciplines.. Help them to recognize that one major can take many directions, and that even once their career has begun, there are numerous possibilities as to how it can develop.

III. CLASS ACTIVITIES _____

Break The Ice!

1.   Academic Advising
If your students are eligible to meet with an academic advisor before the end of this term, ask two or three first-year advisors to visit your class and discuss the advising process. Request that the advisors make brief opening statements covering the most generic of the following questions and then be prepared to answer questions from the class regarding other advising concerns.

- What services do advisors on your campus offer students?
- Are advisors available as career counselors in addition to academic advising?
- Are advisors for first-year students specially trained in particular fields, or do they advise all majors?
- Do faculty members serve as advisors for first-year students?
- Are first-year students advised in groups or individually?
- How can students prepare themselves for a productive and efficient advising session?
- What materials should students bring with them to the advising appointment?
- After advising, how do students select and enroll in classes?
- As appropriate to your institution, ask the advisor panel to discuss requirements in general education in addition to specifics of particular majors. What general education course choices are available to first-year students?
- Why are general education/liberal arts courses valuable for students who already know their major field of interest is outside a liberal arts core curriculum; for instance, why do business or engineering majors need to complete general education requirements?

Leave enough time at the end of the panel presentation to allow students to address questions to the guests. However, prepare your students for this presentation by suggesting that questions be limited to those that address generic problems rather than a particular situation unique to a particular individual. Those questions are best left to an individual advising appointment. Following the presentation, ask students to write a brief note of thanks to each of the presenters. Remind students that sending a prompt note of thanks is a good idea both for job interviews and for times when a college staff person or faculty member assists them in a particular career search.

2.   Extracurricular Activities
Place students in small groups to share some of the extracurricular activities that they enjoyed in high school and address the following questions: Which of these activities was most important and why? Do students plan to continue their involvement during their college career? If not, what other interest might they like to pursue in college?   As groups share their lists of proposed college extracurricular interests, try to match students who share common interests and form teams to investigate clubs, organizations, and events. It is often more comfortable for a new student to explore an activity with a friend or classmate who agrees to attend as a partner.

Discuss reasons why extracurricular activities are considered to be important in the life of a college student. What advantages are offered to students who participate selectively in clubs or organizations that offer no academic credit? What are some of the potential hazards of such involvement?

3. Catalog Search Challenge

This activity works to get the students interacting with each other and to introduce them to the college catalog – a critical tool for successful matriculation and knowledge of institutional policies. Develop a list of questions on important university policies and procedures such as:

- What is the policy for dropping classes?
- What if you want to take a required course off campus at another institution?
- What are the requirements to study abroad.?
- What gets you placed on academic probation and what are the requirements if you are on probation?
- What is the university's grading system?
- Is it possible to take a class pass/fail?

Put students in groups and tell them they must find the correct answer and note the catalog page number on which they found the answer. Even if students know the answer without looking it up, they still need to find where it is stated in the catalog. The first team with all of the correct answers and page numbers wins! It's often fun to provide a token "prize" for members of the winning team – school stickers, pens from your department, etc. If your catalog is only on line, bring students to a computer lab for this activity, and if possible, incorporate a larger search of your institution's website.

Discussion and Reflection

1.   Campus Resources Scavenger Hunt

If properly prepared, this search will not only be fun for your students, but will also help them locate and visit some essential resources on your campus. The example included here is specific to a large, public university where all first-year students live on campus in residence halls. It is adaptable to commuter campuses as well. Students have two weeks to complete the assignment in teams of two. In addition to completing the search, each team is assigned a particular office to investigate in depth and then report their findings orally to the class. The instructor contacts each office unit listed in the search prior to the beginning of the term so that office personnel will know how many students to expect, when to expect them, and what validation method will be required. Personnel in these offices tend to be very cooperative and often give students extra assistance that translates into bonus points during their oral reports.

The assignment is graded either as complete or incomplete, and the oral reports are also evaluated either complete or incomplete. A three-minute time limit is given for each oral report. The search is constructed so that students can start from their residence hall and proceed on a systematic route to locate all the buildings and offices. Although it is possible to complete the search in one day, the instructor encourages students to make a few visits per day and to view this assignment as an exercise in planning ahead as well as in locating important campus resources.

Campus Search

BUILDING	OFFICES INSIDE	PHONE	CONTACT PERSON	ASSIGNMENT
Residence Halls	1. Mouse House Tower W 1st Floor	3569	Desk Tech	Activate your e-mail account & send an e-mail to: meatsu.edu
	2. Housing Learning Center Tower M Lobby	2452	Director Jim will stamp this space	Name four free services for students and hours of Center operation.
	3. Honors College Tower S, B Wing	5291	Dean Morgan	Pick up a copy of the the Honors brochure.

BUILDING	OFFICES INSIDE	PHONE	CONTACT PERSON	ASSIGNMENT
Cross Main Building 1600 S. George	CLEP Office Room 101	1921	Secretary Jerri	What does the acronym CLEP mean? Get a copy of the CLEP brochure.
CCE Admin Building	Intersession Office Room 209	2899	Coordinator Leslie will stamp here.	When are intersession classes held?
Fitness Center 1400 Birch	Main Entrance Lobby	3053	Director Paul	Get a copy of the intramural sports calendar of events.
Robert Hall 820 Elm St.	1. Financial Aid Room 104	4521	Director Matt	Get a copy of the FAS booklet.
	2. Parking & Transit Office Room 311	3311	Director Dempsey	Get a copy of the CART schedule. What does the acronym CART mean?
Health Center 611 Elm Street	1. H.E.A.T. Office Room 206	4611	Director Holmes will stamp here.	What does the acronym H.E.A.T. mean? [Health Education Awareness Team] Get a Hot Lines card.
	2. Counseling &	2911	Receptionist	What three types of

	Testing Office Room 210		will stamp here.	tests are available here? Name 2 types of counseling provided.
Sciences Building 614 Elm Street	1. Writing Center Room 209	2936	Director Judi will stamp here.	How do you schedule an appointment? What services are provided?
	2. Project Threshold Room 517	6261	Director Simmons will stamp here.	What services are offered and who is eligible for services?
Old Hall 620 Elm Street	1. Commuter Center Room 111	1031	Director Dan will stamp here.	Get a copy of the apartment guide.
	2. Student Government Offices Room 214	1001	Receptionist will stamp here.	Who is the student government president?
Library Main Campus Plaza	1. Circulation Desk Front Lobby	3967	Desk Staff will stamp here.	Use your student ID to validate your circulation privileges.
	2. Reference Desk Center Lobby	3957	Desk Librarian	Get a list of library tour hours and starting locations.
	3. Copy Shop Lower Lobby	3947	Desk Assistant	Get info about debit copy cards.
Brand Hall 603 Main	Study Abroad Office Room 213	1693	Director Mills	Get a Study Abroad brochure.
Bell Hall 610 Main	Affirmative Action Office Room 102	3546	Director Jensen will stamp here.	Give 3 reasons why a student might access this office.
Vance Theatre 400 Elm St.	Box Office Main Lobby	4101	Box Office Assistant will stamp here.	Get a schedule of the fall productions.
Art Museum 510 Main	Reception Area Main Entrance	3272	Docent on Duty will stamp here.	What are the Museum Hours? What is a Docent?
Freshman Building 620 Main	1. Assessment & Learning Center Room 200	4336	Director Jane will stamp here.	Get a schedule of the free Student Success Seminars.
	2. Advising Center Room 100	3521	Receptionist	Get a degree sheet for your major or a

				major that interests you.
Student Union 410 Birch	1. Center for Student Life Room 212	6873	Director Hall will stamp here.	Name at least five student groups served by this office.
	2. Career Services Office Room 316	1976	Director Marshall will stamp here.	Get a brochure describing services for freshman students.
	3. Learning Center Main Lobby West Wing	6542	Director Hodges will stamp here.	Get a test file request form.
	4. Volunteer Office Main Lobby East Wing	6541	Director Nance will stamp here.	Get a copy of the service project brochure.

Carson Building 411 Birch	Personnel Services Office Room 214	1826	Director Smith will stamp here.	Locate the student job board and get a copy of an application for employment.

2.   **Alumni Speakers**

If your class is organized by academic major specialization (all engineering students, all business students, etc.), invite alums who have degrees in this field to speak with your class about career opportunities following graduation. "What can I do with this degree?" is a common question for students who have a vague idea that this is the field in which they want to major, but who are quite unsure as to exactly what one does when one graduates with this degree. Often students have glamorous but hopelessly unrealistic ideas about what particular professional people do. You may be able to arrange a short series of speakers who will assist your students in discovering whether or not this particular major is, indeed, the degree field that matches their interests and abilities.

3.   **Playing it Safe**

Personal and property safety are often critical issues for new students and their parents. Contact a representative from your campus department of public safety or the community department of public safety if your campus is served by a community police department rather than a separate campus unit. Find an officer who concentrates on campus safety issues and preview a presentation that might be appropriate for your class. Students need to learn rules for personal and property protection. An officer who is a capable speaker and who can back up safety advice with local statistics is a very useful addition to the resource personnel pool for your orientation students.

Words of Wisdom

Call students' attention to the quotes placed throughout this chapter (and others). Consider having one on the board or on an overhead projector each day when they walk in to class. Begin each day with a brief discussion based on the quote. You can also end class in the same way, letting students think about the quote and discuss the next day.

Major Themes

1.   A Great Source for Information: The Campus Newspaper

Provide a copy of your campus newspaper for each student. Ask them to work individually, in pairs, or in small groups to discover what campus resources are listed. Are there special sections for academic resources? Is there a weekly advertisement for meetings of all student clubs and organizations? Are extracurricular special events publicized in a particular format? Are special topic guest lectures or regular course study sessions listed? What kind of information is provided about accessing resources? Office locations? Phone numbers? The name of a contact person? Requirements for participation? If the paper has regular weekly features that promote extracurricular events or resources, ask students to bring a copy of the paper to class each week and to assist each other in looking for opportunities to become involved in campus activities or in accessing resources. Encourage students to read the campus paper daily and share information with their classmates about important dates and events.

2.   A Guided Campus Tour

If your campus has a visitor's center or other office that provides guided tours, arrange for your class to take a walking tour with emphasis on locations of resources available to new students. This exercise combines an introduction to campus history and traditions with the practical activity of locating resource offices. It is important that you accompany your students on this and other tours and visits that are outside your classroom. First, you need to know that accurate information was provided to your students. Second, most instructors pick up additional information that will add to their own store of knowledge about campus resources. Third, each time that you accompany your students outside the classroom, you gain credibility as a trusted and responsible partner in their efforts to achieve their educational goals.

3. Looking into Mental Health Counseling

College is often a stressful personal time as students adapt to living away from home for the first time and relating to others in ways that are new. If mental health counseling is offered through your campus health center or other source, arrange for a brief visit from a professional counselor who can inform your students about services offered and how to take advantage of those services. Some colleges have student peer groups that work in interactive theater presentations to demonstrate solutions to personal problems. Financial worries are sometimes overwhelming for new students. Invite a financial aid officer to provide information about emergency loans or other sources of immediate help for students who find themselves in financial crisis. Are religious counselors available on or near your campus? Ask a student team to construct a list of campus ministers, their phone numbers and addresses, and office hours available for personal counseling with students.

4. A Library Tour

Arrange a class library tour with a professional library staff person. If possible, do this early in the term so that students will begin to be comfortable using the library. If student status verification is necessary before accessing library facilities, ask that this process be completed during your visit. By the time your students finish the tour, they should know when the library is open, how to find materials, the location of information and reference desks, and how to check out materials. What is unique about your library? Is there a library computer lab that is open to all students? Are rooms available for study groups? How do students reserve these spaces? Is there a library copy center? Are special collections open to first-year students? Are tutoring sessions offered in the library? These and other questions are important to answer early in the term before students begin to work on research papers and long-term assignments. Even if students have had an introductory tour, it is usually helpful to encounter information about a new library system more than once before patrons feel secure about policies and procedures. The point is to make the library a welcoming place to satisfy intellectual curiosity rather than an intimidating building to be avoided.

Online catalogs are wonderful and exciting resources, but they are absolutely worthless if students are not proficient in using the system. A hands-on presentation with students at individual terminals and a professional library staff person as the instructor is an ideal way to overcome reservations about using the library. Orientation instructors who have access to such a presentation do a great service to their students as well as to their colleagues who assign research papers to entering students. A word of caution is in order concerning presentations where only the library staff presenter has access to a keyboard terminal. Our students are hands-on learners. Watching someone else access online services is a frustrating exercise and may result in students who deliberately avoid using the library.

After touring the library, make a follow-up assignment so that students have to immediately use what they learned during the tour. Enlist the assistance of a professional librarian in constructing a library assignment that will help your students recall the information presented during the tour and provide practice in locating resources. Students who are enrolled in a common core of English composition and American history courses might follow up their library tour by working on an assignment from their core course syllabus. Coordination with the instructors in these courses will help produce a library assignment that has immediate practical value for your students.

If you do not have class time to devote to a library tour, have students do this as a homework assignment. Encourage them to go with classmates, and provide a list of questions – developed with the library staff – for them to answer after they have completed the tour. This, along with arrangements made with library staff, will serve as proof of attendance.

5. The Student Health Center
Contact the student health facility on your campus to arrange a tour during class time. Ask for a guide who will meet you and point out specific locations during the tour where students can make appointments to see a physician, file insurance forms, have lab work done, or attend non-credit health and wellness classes. Ask the guide to speak to your students about common health problems faced by entering students and what the health center can provide to assist students when they are ill. What happens in case of serious accident or illness after hours? Is there additional health insurance available to students? If a student has no health insurance, are health facilities still provided? What specific services are offered by your health center? Are peer health education groups open to entering students who are interested in volunteer service or future careers in health fields? Ask your students to take notes during the tour and then to create a booklet that lists all the services provided by the health center and what students must do to access them.

6.   Becoming Over-involved
One potential problem with extracurricular activities is that of maintaining an appropriate balance between academics and outside activities. Horror tales abound that describe students who majored in activities and neglected their classes. This scenario often results in academic failure with a terribly long and depressing prescription for regaining academic health, if GPA can be salvaged at all. If you have access to a student who fell into this trap and who is willing to speak to new students about the dangers of becoming over-involved, this kind of peer testimony is worth a thousand of your words as an instructor. Often student leaders will be able to speak to this – or their close call with this scenario. They are ambitious and want to be involved in many things – fully aware of how it can boost their college resume or med-school application. But they don't realize until too late that they have bitten off more than they can chew, and ultimately they limit their involvement to the things that mean the most, and successfully maintain their good grades as well.

7.   Using Cultural Activities to Engage Students
Cultural enrichment activities abound on most college campuses. If your campus has a music department, assign a student team to contact the department and bring a list of concert or recital dates to class. Then negotiate a convenient date for the entire class to attend a performance and if possible, arrange for group tickets. It may be possible to make arrangements to attend a dress rehearsal at no cost if your students attend as a group. Ask the conductor or member of the performing ensemble to visit your class before the concert and talk with your students about the music that they will hear. When students know what to expect, they are more likely to enjoy and learn from the event. If program notes are available, ask students to make their own set of notes about their reactions to the music and to the performance.
As an alternative, schedule a tour of your art museum or gallery. Many art museums provide group tours guided by a docent. If your campus museum has an admission charge, ask a student team to negotiate a reduced fee or free admission for a class tour. Encourage a student team to research the current exhibit and permanent collection by collecting brochures and informational guides from the museum prior to the

class tour. If any of your students took an art history class in high school or have studied painting or sculpture, ask them to brief the class on ways to best appreciate this experience.

You can also explore the drama department and the possibility of having the class attend a campus production. Assign a student team to contact the director, producer, or principle actors and invite one or all of them to come to your class to give a preview of the production. If the production is from the standard repertoire, some of your students may have participated in a high school production of the same play and can give an introduction to their peers. If feasible, arrange a brief discussion immediately following the production. Invite a member of the cast to attend as well. If your classroom management budget allows, conduct the discussion over pizza or dessert.

8.   The Culture Around You

Explore cultural opportunities unique to your campus or community. Arrange for out-of-state and/or international students to attend one of these cultural events and then share their experiences with the class. Does your community sponsor special events or festivals that would introduce college students to the local culture? Are there community mentors who would be willing to invite a student to share in one or more of these cultural events? As an example, students in Oklahoma colleges and universities have opportunities to attend Native American tribal powwows. Native American college students are paired with out-of-state or international students and serve as guides and hosts for these cultural events that are a unique part of their heritage.

9.   Your Route: Finding Out What Courses to Take

How many of your students have in their possession a degree check-sheet that outlines specifically and in detail the courses they must take and the electives open to them for a particular degree? Even if a student has not yet made a decision as to a degree field, ask each student to pick up a degree sheet in a major field that interests them. Review the sheets in class to discover any common core courses.

What happens if a student changes majors? Will courses already completed count toward the degree in the new major? What happens to students who take a heavy course load and also work part-time? What are your campus statistics regarding students who work? Are they usually successful academically? What about those students who are working full-time and also attending college classes? What is the success rate for these students? How carefully do advisors monitor students' enrollment? For instance, do advisors encourage students who have difficulty with heavy reading courses to enroll in no more than one such course per term? How does high school academic performance influence college enrollment? Is CLEP (College Level Examination Program) credit offered? AP (Advanced Placement) course credit? Are advanced standing exams available for any courses? Is there a penalty if the student doesn't pass the advanced standing exam? Is there a limit to the number of CLEP, AP, or advanced standing exams a student may take? Are correspondence courses offered? Are there intersession, J-term, or summer school courses available?

As a major assignment, ask your students to plan their own four- or five-year schedule using the degree check sheet and the college catalog. Remind students that they are ultimately responsible for their own degree progress and that this exercise will help them plan an appropriate schedule and stay on track. Ask academic advisors to read through the completed plans and comment on the feasibility of each one.

10. Using the College Catalog for Academic Guidance

Make sure that students understand the contractual nature of the college catalog in relation to their degree plans. What happens to this relationship when a student changes majors? Again, a professional advisor may be the best resource for questions related to the catalog. However, it is at this point that students need to realize that they are ultimately responsible for their own degree plans and graduation requirements. As changes in each term's degree plan enrollment are suggested by advisors and faculty members, students should get a copy of these changes *in writing* with the date of change and the advisor's or faculty member's signature on the form.

11. Looking Into Tutoring

Academic support services are often located in both the academic side of an institution and in the student affairs division. Assign teams of students to research both sides and discover not only what academic support services are available but where they are located and how a student gains access. Is free tutoring offered? How do students make appointments for tutoring? If tutoring is not free, how do students locate approved tutors? Are there departmental lists of recommended tutors? What is the normal fee for a tutoring session? How long is a normal tutoring session? What can students expect from a tutor? What can a tutor not do? Is peer tutoring available? If so, how do students access this service? Are peer tutors reliable? As an alternative, are tutoring services available on the Internet? Ask a student team to research this question and report any Internet sites that purport to offer tutoring services. Would this be a reliable source? Why or why not?

12. Finding a Mentor

Finding a mentor may be one of the best links your students can have to a successful college career that leads directly to a successful first job search. Some colleges specify that orientation instructors serve as mentors for their students. If this is the case at your institution, then you will want to develop a network of helpers who are willing and available to assist the students that you might refer to them when your own expertise is insufficient. Often it is only the orientation instructor who knows the student well enough to write the first official recommendations necessary for employment during the college years. And in some cases, this mentor relationship lasts far beyond the time of the first-term class.

Encourage your students to find a mentor among the faculty members in their chosen academic major field. Most faculty members expect to mentor students who are in their junior or senior years of study, but some are willing to take on the additional responsibility of mentoring a younger student if that person is a very serious and dedicated scholar. Students find faculty mentors by various means: enrolling only in the classes or sections taught by that faculty person, working on extra-credit projects in each of those classes, offering to assist in lab experiments for the experience rather than pay, achieving outstanding grades so that the student's quality of work rises to the top of the class, applying for student positions in that department or academic office.

Some students find peer mentors among upper-class students. If your institution is among those who assign a peer mentor to incoming students, monitor that program to see that your students are making the kinds of connections the program was designed to foster. Most peer assistants take their jobs seriously and offer good advice to younger students as well as the daily example of a good role model. However, if you perceive that a change would be in the best interest of the younger student, make contact with the office that coordinates this program and offer to assist with a change.

13. Exploring the Technology Center

Does your campus have a technology center that provides student services? Ask a team to investigate this and report to the class. What services are offered? Are computers available for purchase by students at discount rates? How do these rates compare with commercial vendors? Does the technology center supervise all computer labs? Where are these labs located? What are the hours? Is there an additional fee to use the computer labs? Is there a fee for printing and/or copying? What are peak lab hours? When are first-year students most likely to find open computers?

Novice computer users may require additional assistance before their skills are good enough to save time by using word processing software and other computer programs. Does your college offer beginning computer courses? If not, are there classes available at another institution within commuting distance? At a nearby vocational-technical center? For students whose major fields of study will eventually require extensive computer skills, concurrent enrollment in a short-term beginning computer class may be sound advice. If beginning computer classes are not available, inquire about the possibility of peer tutoring. Pair a student expert in computer word processing with a beginner. Monitor the time spent in this kind of peer tutoring so that the student teacher doesn't neglect personal study time commitments and so that the student receiving help is actually making progress rather than depending solely on the tutor to do all the work on the computer while the other student watches.

Instructors whose institutions provide free e-mail accounts for all their students have an additional resource for assignments, journals, bulletin board announcements and other projects. As an incentive for your students to use their e-mail accounts, assign at least one e-mail journal, and return your comments via e-mail. This is also a way of checking whether or not the students' e-mail accounts are working properly. Assign a student team to construct an e-mail distribution list for your class to post assignments, due dates, and important academic deadlines.

Summary Projects

1.   If extensive published resources that describe extracurricular activities are not readily available to new students on your campus, individuals or teams in your class could construct a comprehensive list of student clubs, organizations, and regularly-scheduled extracurricular events open to new students. This report might include annotated entries describing each group or event, requirements for participation, location of the office responsible for sponsoring the group or event, phone number of the office or sponsor responsible, and other pertinent information. Your students may have access to a

campus Internet website where this resource list can be posted and updated by students from the following year's class.

2.   Another very successful project, as recommended by past students, involves constructing a personal degree plan using the college catalog, printed degree sheets and check-lists, and personal interviews with the advisor responsible for degree checks in that major. Students annotate the degree plan by writing a brief paragraph defending the course selections necessary to complete the degree. This annotation includes all the general education core course selections with a rationale for each elective selection. A professional advisor can consult on each completed degree plan to verify that it is complete and correct. Students then use this plan to assist in enrolling for subsequent semesters. Those students who change majors have an effective model to follow to construct a new degree plan and then check their progress as they work through the plan each term.

IV. CAMPUS CONNECTIONS AND RESOURCES

Connecting with campus resources is what this chapter is all about. As an orientation instructor, one of your responsibilities is to know the resources and visit the sites to verify what students will find. Build up your personal pool of campus resource talent, and don't forget upper-class students who are valuable models. Access student peer assistants and student panels for current commentary on campus resources. Office locations and personnel can change quickly. Update your information bank each term to ensure that you are giving students accurate information. Students who become frustrated with finding the location of an office may give up rather than see the situation as an opportunity for creative problem-solving.

1.   The Library

Most librarians will be more than happy to provide your students with a tour and orientation to the resources available. They may review the different ways to research journals, periodicals, and books. They may also discuss how to process intercampus book loans or how to retrieve books from other colleges and universities. Many libraries have study rooms that may be reserved for study groups. Discussing the library and computer lab rules are also important.

2.   The Learning Resource Center

The Learning Resource Centers on campus provide students with a variety of resources to help them achieve academically. Have a representative for the tutoring center, math lab, writing center, and computer lab discuss the services provided with the students. Have the students visit the tutoring center to retrieve a schedule of tutors. Having them actually go to the center itself increases their likelihood of returning for tutoring. It helps reduce the anxiety and intimidation of asking for assistance.

3.   **The Counseling Center**
      The Counseling Center provides a variety of services on campus such as career assessment and development, academic and transfer planning, disability testing and accommodations, personal counseling and referral system, and mediation services with faculty or peers. Have a representative from counseling visit the class to discuss all the services provided. Another idea would be to have the students actually visit the center and pick up brochures relating to services so they won't be so intimated to go there to ask for assistance when needed.

4.   **Campus Career Center or Student Employment Office**
      Most campuses have a Career Center or Student Employment Office. Services provided include assistance with resumé writing, interview skills, job search skills, volunteer and internship opportunities, and employee referrals. Have a representative present to the class the different resources available.

5.   **Student Activities**
      Student activities differ on each campus; however, many schools have Student Government, Honor Society, Intramural Sports, Clubs and Organizations, Greek Life, and a variety of activities. Provide the students with a list of activities available on campus in addition to a calendar of college-wide activities. Require students to attend at least three different activities during the semester. Ask them to keep a journal on their experiences.

6.   **Gathering Information**
      Provide students with a Catalog, Student Handbook, and Course Schedule book. Develop an Information Search assignment consisting of important questions relating to these publications. Discuss the differences between the degrees offered, full-time status, rights and responsibilities of students, teacher expectations, grade appeal procedures, important dates, withdrawal and incomplete regulations, policies on repeating courses, academic standing, financial aid, different types of instruction offered, graduation requirements, general education requirements, department heads, names and offices of deans and administrators, student civility, etc. This assignment is one of the most important because it gives the students the information they need to succeed. Each campus has its own culture and set of rules and norms. These publications provide the students with the resources they need to survive college.

7.   **The School Website**
      Websites are taking the place of printed material on campuses. Bring a multimedia cart to class and review the school's website. Teach students use online resources to enroll, view academic transcripts, make payments, check grades, etc.

V. COLLABORATIVE LEARNING SUGGESTIONS _____

1.   **Campus Resource Commercial**
      Put students in groups of three to four and have them sign up for a particular

15

campus resource or service (Counseling Center, Learning Resource Center, Career Center, etc.) Make sure there is only one group per service. Have students create a "commercial" for their service that is designed to "sell" their classmates on taking advantage of what the service has to offer. They should include the logistics of using the service (times available, fees, student ID required) along with the benefits to students that the service provides. Encourage creativity and a dynamic presentation in the form of a skit, video, song, etc. Invite staff from the various services chosen to watch your students commercials!

2.   Campus Safety

Ask students to form investigative teams of two to four to research safety issues on campus and then report to the class. Report format may include a written summary, an oral account, or both. Some of the teams might concentrate on residential hall safety standards, policies, and practices. Ask them to research the availability of personal property insurance for residence hall dwellers. Other groups could study issues regarding protection of personal property while students are attending classes such as safe parking areas for vehicles, availability of bicycle racks and locks, and location of book or backpack lockers. Still others might examine campus crime statistics and crime prevention policies, including safety precautions recommended for students who have late night classes some distance away from parking or housing facilities.

2.   Mentoring

If there is no formal student mentoring process in place on your campus, suggest that your students work with student success programs, student government representatives, or campus organization officers to establish a pilot project matching incoming students with upper division students whose study habits and community service make them good role models. Research will suggest institutions of like size and mission who already have such programs in place. Contact the office responsible for the peer mentoring program on a selected number of those campuses and compile a list of suggestions for starting and maintaining this kind of program. Among the questions necessary to ask are the following, although not listed in priority order:

- What kind of support network is essential for the success of such a project?
- What is an appropriate budget to establish and maintain such a program?
- Which campus office would be the sponsor for this program?
- What are the criteria for selecting peer mentors?
- How would peer mentors be selected?
- Who would directly supervise the program?
- Who would monitor the success of the program and compile statistical evidence of success or failure?
- How would peer mentors be trained?
- How would new students and peer mentors be matched?
- How would new students and peer mentors be introduced?
- What were the problems and challenges involved in establishing this program at the peer institutions in the research group? What solutions were discovered? Are any of these applicable to our project?

16

These and other questions should form an extensive part of the research necessary to complete this project. Students may wish to pursue this project to completion if the opportunity arises to continue work throughout the academic year.

3.   Library Resources
In collaboration with the librarians, have students break into groups and complete a library scavenger hunt. Require them to search for certain publications, journals, full text articles online, and books. Require them to register for a library account, order a book from another campus, and complete any other tasks that are essential.

4.   School Website
In a group, have students review the college's website. Have each group research a separate section and present what they learned to the class. They may research different departments, distance learning opportunities, student services, chat rooms or discussion boards, and many other resources available online.

VI. ALTERNATIVE TEACHING STRATEGIES _____

1.   Make Use of Technology
Making connections via electronic technology may be available on your campus now. Assign student teams to discover department websites on your campus. Is it possible to make resource connections by first accessing websites and then making a personal visit to the campus offices? What are the advantages and disadvantages of making connections over the Internet? Ask students to share some of their favorite campus websites and compare the information available at each site. What is appealing about each site? The graphics package? The presentation style? Ease of accessibility? Links to other sources?

Check out the website for your main campus library. Is a library tour available on the Internet? How does the electronic tour compare with the live one?

Are your institution's academic departments represented on the Internet? Do particular professors have websites? Can students download a course syllabus from the Internet? Are tutorials available as links from departmental websites? They can even check if their advisors and instructors have a space on Facebook.

Add an online component to your course in which students would log in to your school's distance learning program. Students may review documents, join in discussion groups, e-mail homework, take tests, and participate in many other activities online. Having a little experience with distance learning is a great addition to in-class instruction because it provides the students an opportunity to check out the process of online learning.

2.   Bibliographic Resources and Journal Work
Ask each small group to select a book from one of the four print resource sections of the bibliographic resources for this chapter. Make sure all of the resource sections are represented by at least one book selection. Tell each group to search the library for their book, check it out from the library, and set up a schedule to do a team book report. This

will involve scheduling time for each group member to read the book, finding a study group room in which to work, matching time schedules to do the review, and writing the review using a word processing program in a campus computer lab. Although this will be a time-consuming project, it incorporates many of the essential learning goals of this chapter.

3.   **Chapter Quiz Suggestions**
        In a two-minute timed quiz, name and provide location information for at least ten different campus resources and/or organizations that provide assistance, facts, or advice for new students. Include at least one resource for academics and at least one for extracurricular groups. Give extra points for more than ten, but be sure that students give accurate locations for each resource listed.

VII. LEARNING PORTFOLIO

1.   **Self-Assessments**
        Self-Assessment 1, "Campus Resources to Meet My Needs", on page 24 of the text is an excellent opener for new students. Some of them will already have discovered many of these locations listed in this activity. Ask small groups to share what they already know before you make a search assignment. Compare answers among groups and then note which resources are not covered on the students' lists. Assign these resources to groups or partners to discover and report at the next class meeting. Part of the assignment will be to find general information sources that will help locate the specific campus services on the list. Ask students to brainstorm ways of accessing this information. Campus phone books? Visitor's information center? Residence hall information desks? Student union information booths or bulletin boards? Student government offices? Others? The object is for every student to complete Self-Assessment 1 as a permanent personal reference tool.

2.   **Your Journal**
        Have students complete the journal activity "Only the Best" on page 29. Then collect students into small groups to compare answers. Have the groups report back any common responses or particularly helpful "best" resources that have been discussed.

VIII. CHAPTER QUIZ SUGGESTIONS

1.   Use the Review Questions as a short-answer quiz. Points may be assigned equally at 25 points per question, or points may be divided unequally depending on the amount of class time and assignments devoted to various areas of the chapter. In short-answer quizzes, complete sentences are not always necessary as long as the essential points of the answer are present.

2.   In a two-minute timed quiz, name and provide location information for at least ten different campus resources and/or organizations that provide assistance, facts, or advice for new students. Include at least one resource for academics and at least one for

extracurricular groups. Give extra points for more than ten, but be sure that students give accurate locations for each resource listed.

IX. QUIZ _____

Multiple Choice. Choose the one best answer.

1. Participating in extracurricular activities
   A. is discouraged if you want to do well in college.
   B. improves your chances of meeting people who share your interests.
   C. can enhance your academic success.
   D. should not be included on a resume.
   E. both B and C.

2. Probably the most important person to offer you help on campus will be
   A. the reference librarian.
   B. your academic advisor.
   C. the book store clerk.
   D. the dean of your department.
   E. your favorite teacher.

3. The set of courses distributing your study across the social and natural sciences, humanities, and the arts are called
   A. general education courses
   B. fundamental element courses
   C. global university courses
   D. guided education courses
   E. educational exploration courses

4. Which of the following does your book *not* mention as being an important basis for your major?
   A. Your intelligence.
   B. Your values.
   C. Your interests.
   D. Your skills.
   E. Your abilities.

5. The best starting point for working with your academic advisor is
   A. your preferred times for scheduling classes.
   B. your favorite subjects.
   C. your most dreaded subjects.
   D. your career goals.
   E. your four- or five-year plan.

6. The college catalog is most helpful for information on the following:

A. The best restaurants and take-out options around campus.
B. Prerequisites, core courses, and electives required for various majors.
C. Employment opportunities on campus.
D. Extra-curricular activities.
E. Instructions on how to access resources in the campus library.

True or False

7. _____Librarians are often incredibly busy cataloging and managing the vast amount of information available to the campus community. They expect students to ask them for help only if they are desperate for assistance.

8. _____Once you select your major, it is always a bad idea to change direction.

9. _____Even if you are a very good student and familiar with your degree requirements, you should work with your academic advisor to ensure successful progression toward graduation.

10. _____There are many campus-based extracurricular activities that you can enjoy with family and friends that are free to students.

11. _____The Internet is a strictly managed source of information, all of which is carefully screened and filtered to assure validity and authenticity.

ANSWERS

1. **E** 2. **B** 3. **A** 4. **A** 5. **E** 6. **B** 7. **F** 8. **F** 9. **T** 10. **T** 11. **F**

X. TEST QUESTIONS_____

Multiple Choice. Choose the one best answer.

1. College campuses often have which of the following?
   A. Health center.
   B. Campus ministry.
   C. Mental health services.
   D. All of the above.

2. You should plan to meet with your advisor
   A. at the beginning of your freshman year and the semester before you graduate.
   B. once a year.
   C. regularly.
   D. only if and when changing majors.

20

3. More than _____ of first-year college students change their intended majors in the first year.
   A. 1/5
   B. 1/3
   C. 1/2
   D. 2/3

4. Which of the following is *not* a problematic reason for choosing a major?
   A. To please your parents, who have knowledge and wisdom as to productive, worthwhile majors.
   B. To follow your friends, who will always be there to study with and offer moral support.
   C. To have a relatively light course load, which will ensure optimum success in college?
   D. All of the above are problematic reasons for choosing a major.

5. In your text's advice to "ask the 'pros'" for advice on choosing the best courses and instructors for you, who are the "pros"?
   A. The professors in your major.
   B. Advisors in the department of your major.
   C. Students that are further along in your major.
   D. Your parents, who know your personality and habits.

6. One problem that can occur with word processors is
   A. they require a habit of frequent saving or you're likely to lose a great deal of work.
   B. they encourage procrastination due to the professional look of first drafts.
   C. their inclusion of features such as spell-checkers can encourage a lack of proofreading effort.
   D. All of the above are problems that may result with word processors.

7. A highly dynamic and powerful computer presentation tool is known as
   A. PowerPlus.
   B. PointPower.
   C. PointerPlus.
   D. PowerPoint.

True or False

8. _____Nothing will help you more than knowing about and using your campus resources.

9. _____It's important to have a good spell-checker with your word processing software so you can eliminate lengthy proofreading.

10. _____Computer addiction is only a concern for people who are majoring in a high-tech, computer-based field.

Essay Questions

1. Present an argument for the importance of a liberal arts education founded on a set of general education courses.

2. Computers are a wonderful tool, particularly for college students. However, there are some negative aspects to using them. Describe several problems associated with computer use, and ways in which to avoid them.

3. What are some important factors to consider when deciding upon an academic major? Also list some less important issues that should not impact this decision.

ANSWERS:

1. **D**   2. **C**   3. **D**   4. **D**   5. **C**   6. **D**   7. **D**   8. **T**   9. **F**   10. **F**

XI. MENTOR'S CORNER _____

Bonnie Garrett has been teaching Student Success at Anne Arundel Community College for three years. She most enjoys teaching students how to navigate college policies and procedures, and is continually amazed at how unaware they are and how much their lack of knowledge affects their academic record. Each semester she makes up a series of questions based on information in the current college catalog. She provides the page numbers on which the answers can be found. Students are required to obtain a current college catalog and to answer the questions as homework. She requires them to highlight the answers in the catalog and to briefly record the answers on the handout. The following class meeting the students play a game that combines the rules from Jeopardy and Who Wants to Be a Millionaire.

Students get in groups of three. Bonnie tapes sheets of paper on the board; each has the answer to one of the questions printed on the backside. She draws a grid around the papers. Rows are labeled A,B,C, etc. and columns are numbered 1, 2, 3, 4, etc. Students choose a question by providing coordinates such as A-3. Bonnie then removes the sheet from the board and reads the answer. The students must then provide the corresponding question (like Jeopardy). If the students do not know the answer, they are permitted to phone a friend (like Who Wants to be a Millionaire). The friend must be one of the members of their group. If the group gets the question correct, Bonnie throws them three pieces of candy and the next group of three gets to give coordinates and choose a question. If the groups do not answer the question correctly, then the next group attempts that same question.

Bonnie has found that students enjoy the relaxed interaction of the game. She tries to do it the second or third class session because it helps them get to know each other and to become comfortable with her. She believes that accidental learning is very important and tries to provide some sort of activity each class meeting. For more great ideas on accidental learning projects and how to make students feel connected to campus, contact:

Bonnie Garrett,
Retention Coordinator,
Anne Arundel Community College
410-541-2503 or e-mail: bjgarrett@mail.aacc.cc.md.us

Gloria Jones teaches a three-hour freshman orientation course class each semester that is designed for the student that is enrolled in two or more remedial classes. She finds that teaching this class is both rewarding and challenging. She says, "Keeping my students in school is my primary focus. The foremost emphasis that I continually commit to is communication, asking questions and networking. By encouraging students to network with students in all of their classes, a student will stay informed and stay involved with campus issues, study groups, and what teachers meet their learning style."

She finds that students who are involved in school are successful. Walking tours are a part of her class, and she does many exercises in class, including reading the school newspaper each week and keeping a journal. She also leads students on a library tour. Each student is encouraged to choose a career, and as part of the final exam, each student must do a research paper on his or her chosen career. Choosing a career does not mean that the student cannot change his or her mind; it just helps him or her to begin thinking about careers. You can contact Gloria at gjones@accd.edu. She looks forward to helping new instructors with any questions concerning how to get students involved on campus.

Jane Hession is the Freshman Advisor/Assessments Coordinator for the School of Business Administration at Gonzaga University in Spokane, WA. She has both her undergraduate and graduate degrees from Gonzaga, and has been involved at GU in a number of different capacities, including Assistant Director of Admissions, Graduate Director of the School of Business Administration, and academic advising. Her current roster of undergraduate business students numbers approximately 200 students; she works full-time as their academic advisor as well as directs a number of assessment projects in the School of Business. Additionally, she teaches a freshman seminar each fall semester to a classroom of new freshmen; at Gonzaga they limit the size of each seminar section to 22 students.

Jane gets the most enjoyment in her seminars from the interaction with her students, getting to know each one of them individually. She also finds it very rewarding to let them in on some of the special aspects of Gonzaga's history, its campus, and its Jesuit priests. She feels that the connection that is made in the seminar experience between students and the campus community is very important, so she underscores this part of the course. Of particular merit is the evening that students spend at Jane's home with her family, having dinner. She wants to encourage faculty to invite students into their homes so students will feel comfortable with their teachers. Feel free to contact Jane at:

Jane M. Hession
Freshman Advisor/Assessments Coordinator
School of Business Administration Ad Box 9
Gonzaga University
Spokane, WA 99258
509-323-3425; hession@jepson.gonzaga.edu

CHAPTER 2

MASTER COMMUNICATION SKILLS AND BUILD RELATIONSHIPS

I. CHAPTER OVERVIEW _____

This chapter presents a lot of information! Not only will students be asked to evaluate how they communicate with parents and friends, but they will also be asked to see how they view people of other races and sexual orientation. Some students may have had little exposure to other racial groups; other students may be homophobic. Dealing with the issues in this chapter and seeing students respond to the exercises and suggestions can be deeply rewarding. Be open to student questions and strive to cultivate an environment where every student is honored for his/her strengths and abilities. Journaling is especially important while discussing issues involving race and gender. Some students may be full of anger; others may have trouble digging deep and try to keep things light.

Among the most distressing experiences for first-year students are those that involve negative communication issues: misunderstandings involving roommates, harsh words with family members, confusing or broken relationships with significant others, lack of comprehension in classes. Part of the difficulty lies in the fact that many traditional-age students in transition often hear only what they want to hear and find it almost impossible to listen to advice that urges patience and caution. Especially for students who are living away from home for the first time in their lives, honest communication may pose problems. Communication in this chapter means dialog between or among parties where careful listening and thoughtful speaking opportunities are equally shared and respected.

Students are reminded of all the different kinds of relationships which they must, at the least, manage, and at their fullest, enjoy and thrive from. This includes getting along with instructors – something you can offer your personal insight on as to the incredible value this has for students – as well as continuing strong, positive ties with parents and children (for non-traditional students). More "voluntary" relationships are also discussed – those that students may perceive as playing a larger role in their day-to-day lives: roommates, dates/partners, and friends. Each one of these relationships requires a unique set of abilities to develop and maintain at a positive level, and they are the ones students may particularly want to explore and discuss in class.

Although not all campuses are ethnically and racially diverse, they are most certainly diverse in terms of gender. As surprising as it may seem, some students may be faced with viewing members of the opposite sex in a whole new light, through their choice of majors, functioning in the classroom, lab partners, and study groups. Newly independent freshmen of both sexes begin to really learn a lot about the other when they experience how the other half lives and the choices that they make during this transition into adulthood. They may not always like what they discover. Helping students understand the differences between male and female functioning and communication styles at this stage can help them to more effectively deal with each other as partners – whether romantic or business – in the future.

II. IMAGES OF COLLEGE SUCCESS

Most, if not all, of your students have watched Oprah Winfrey's television show. The fact that she is a successful and wealthy master communicator should not eclipse the circumstances of her early years. Oprah overcame a very difficult and abusive childhood; at some point in her teenage years, she turned her life around and discovered a professional field in which she could excel. Ask your students to watch Oprah's show and take notes with a specific focus on her communication style. How does she get guests on the show to talk freely to her? What kinds of questions does she ask to elicit good responses? Observe her body language. How does she communicate non-verbally? What gestures help guests on the show relax and open themselves to sharing their stories on national television?

Ask students to work in small groups to create a list of other famous people who are considered to be excellent communicators. What attributes do these people have in common? Encourage students to look for good communication models outside the entertainment field. Ronald Reagan was also considered to be a good communicator. Research the library video files to find clips of Reagan's speeches. What made him a good political communicator?

Make a master list of good communicators; try to find at least one example in several different fields, such as religion, education, business, public service, politics, fine arts, and others. Compare the qualities that make each person a good example of a communicator in that field. What are the five most important characteristics common to each person?

III. CLASS ACTIVITIES

Break The Ice!

1.   Humor and Communication

Charles Schultz often comments on communication issues in his cartoon features. What do the cartoons in this chapter say about communication? Why is humor often used as a vehicle to address communication problems? Schultz uses his cartoons to explore differences in communication among characters of particular personality types. What personality types are represented by the characters in the Peanuts cartoon in this chapter? How does personality type affect communication preferences?

2.   Non-Verbal Communication

Non-verbal communication is an area that many students will not have explored in depth previously. An exercise called "Mirror the Mime" allows students to concentrate on following non-verbal directions. In pairs, ask students to face each other. One student is the Mime, and the other is the Mirror. The Mime always faces the Mirror. No verbal communication is allowed, and no physical touching is permitted. The exercise is timed at 90 seconds, at which point Mime and Mirror exchange roles. The Mime displays physical gestures (moving a hand, foot, arm, or head) or facial expressions (smile, frown, etc.) one at a time in fairly rapid sequence. The Mirror must "mirror" those gestures or expressions exactly. The Mime is responsible for demonstrating as many gestures/expressions as possible within the allotted time without confusing the Mirror. The Mirror must concentrate on following the Mime, practicing the arts of observation and replication without benefit of any verbal communication. Following the exercise, ask students to comment on why the exercise is beneficial in learning about communication strategies.

3.   **Exploring Roots**
      In small groups, ask students to discuss their family roots. Where did their families originate? When did their ancestors come to America? What is their personal ethnic and cultural background? Does someone in their home speak more than one language? Have any of them lived in another culture that was different from their own? When, where, and why? Students who come from military families often have rich and varied experiences that have resulted from multiple duty transfers. Also, be aware that some students may not have answers. If some students are adopted and do not know their birth heritage, ask what they know about the history of their adoptive family. Perhaps those students can research their adoptive family background and report at the next class meeting.
      After small groups have shared this information, ask a leader from each of the groups to summarize the various background cultures represented in each group. Then ask all students what family traditions are celebrated within their close family circles. What makes each family different from other families in the class? Search for commonalties among the cultural and ethnic origins of your students. It may be more productive to approach diversity from a perspective of common ground.

4.   **Diversity on Campus**
      How well do your students know their peers? Prepare for this exercise by gathering answers to the following questions from your institutional research office. Before you share the correct answers, ask small groups to guess the answers to the following questions.

- How many diverse student population groups are present on your campus?
- Are there African-American students?
- Asian students?
- American Indian students?
- Hispanic-American students?
- International students?
- Students over the age of 35?
- Students younger than 17?
- What is the ratio of men to women?
- What is the percentage of students on your campus who come from out-of-state?
- Are there students who are differently-abled physically?
- Students with documented learning disabilities?
- What is the ratio of residential students to commuter students?
- Students with children to those who do not have children?
- Establish other categories as necessary to describe your campus.

After each group has had the opportunity to guess about specific populations represented on the entire campus, record the answers on the chalkboard. Then tabulate another set of answers based on the population of this class alone. Compare the population sub-groups in your class with the "correct" answers obtained from the institutional research office pertaining to the entire campus. Are your students representative of the student body as a whole? Suppose they want to find information about another population group. Where would they access accurate information? Is it appropriate to ask one member of a cultural, ethnic, or specific population group to speak on behalf of the entire group? For instance, would it be appropriate and/or accurate to ask one male in your class to generalize about all males on campus? What is the danger in such a proposal?

Discussion and Reflection

1. Diversity on Campus

Ask an administrative official on your campus to speak to your class about specific ways your institution deals with multicultural diversity issues, both opportunities and problems. Prepare both the speaker and your students by planning for an open question and answer period following the formal presentation. The speaker should be warned that students may ask tough questions that will require honest answers. Students should understand that they are allowed to ask penetrating but respectful questions about issues that may be troublesome for their institution. Then summarize the session by listing specific ways that your students can sample cultural and ethnic opportunities on your campus or in your larger civic community. Are there problems that this class can help address in a positive and culturally sensitive manner?

2. Issues Related to Date Rape

Contact the campus health clinic/department or the campus department of public safety and ask if the unit sponsors a presentation on date rape. Some campuses have peer education groups that present interactive theatre productions on this topic. If such a presentation is available on your campus, determine when your students might have opportunities to view or participate in the production. Some residence hall advisors schedule such presentations as a part of either their residence hall orientation or on-going educational activities provided by the housing units.

If this presentation is available and is not a regular part of housing activities, invite the presenters to your class during discussion of this chapter. Be sure to confirm the length of the production so that it will fit within your class time; it is also advisable to allow time for feedback or questions following a presentation of this nature. It may be wise for the instructor to preview the presentation before inviting the group to interact with the class. With regard to the subject of date/acquaintance rape, remember that peer education is often far more effective than lectures or videos that feature older adults.

Alcohol is often involved in cases of rape on campus. Contact student service offices to determine what programs, if any, are provided that link the topics of rape and alcohol. Some rape survivors groups provide speakers for student organizations or classes. Since this is a very sensitive subject, it may be best to introduce this particular type of presentation only after your students have developed a high sense of trust both

28

with the instructor and within their class. If such a speaker is available to your class, try to provide the opportunity for questions following the presentation. Questions written anonymously on 3x5 cards are often the least intrusive and provide the best opportunity for honest feedback.

Words of Wisdom

1.   Quotes for Discussion

Albert Camus writes, "We live to have relationships with people." What do your students think of this quote? Honest? What about when relationships fall apart? Is it unhealthy to put too much into relationships?

Look at all the quotations for this chapter and categorize them: ethnic, gender, age, culture. Will any quotation fit in more than one category? Do any of the quotations reflect stereotypical attitudes about diversity? If your class is comfortable enough with this discussion to continue, ask them to list stereotypical statements in each category to add to the quotation list. Then critically discuss each statement. Is the statement true? How do you know? Where did the statement originate? Why is this perception still a part of the common culture? Be sure to include statements about the majority group in your class as well. For example, is it true that "white men can't jump?" Ask students to be extremely careful in their research regarding these so-called truisms. Which sources can be trusted? Why are some sources suspect?

2.   Quotes and You

Look at the beautiful quote by Edna St. Vincent Millay, "Where you used to be, there is a hole in the world, which I find myself constantly walking around in daytime, and falling into at night." In order for students to practice their writing and creativity, have them write a short phrase about missing someone. Brevity is key here. Maybe they will want to send their phrase to someone back home.

Look at the quote by Alan Alda, "Be fair with others, but then keep after them until they are fair with you." Have your students ever accepted being treated poorly for any reason? Why did they put up with the treatment? Have they ever treated anyone else unfairly? You may want to have students fictionalize the experience in a short story. Have students write their story from the other person's point of view. Share stories with the entire class.

Major Themes

1.   Listening and Critical Thinking

Developing good listening skills may require students to exercise critical thinking skills as well. Ask students to explore the relationship between good listening and critical thinking. What parallels exist between the two? Is it possible to listen critically, organize what is being said without necessarily taking notes, and then be able to provide feedback that addresses possible points of contention?

2. **Barriers to Effective Verbal Communication**

Find some movie clips, or simply present a video of a television show that is currently popular with college students. Have them use the list on page 35 of the textbook to identify all of the instances of negative verbal communication. Have students do this individually, then discuss their examples in groups, and finally, with the class as a whole.

- Are all students in agreement with the examples of barriers to effective communication?
- Can some of the verbal elements/exchanges be interpreted in different ways? If so, how? (Students can employ critical thinking skills to make their arguments.)
- Do the communication exchanges viewed in the movie or in the show reflect realistic exchanges seen in everyday life, or are they more dramatic for entertainment value?
- Have groups of students try to re-write one of the scenes with the goal of keeping it compelling and the characters true to form, but with different methods of communication. How do the changes in approach to communication change the responses of the individuals involved?

3. **Solving Conflicts**

Some of your students may have been trained in conflict resolution in their public schools. If there are students in your class who have had this type of training and who also were appointed as mediators for their public school classmates, ask them to give brief presentations on their training. How was the training organized? How was their work supervised? What relationship does this training and experience from public school have to their current college experiences? Does the advice in the text match what they were told in conflict resolution training? Is similar training available on campus? In the residence halls? In specific classes? Are conflict resolution practices employed by resident advisors to solve roommate problems? Is there a mediation board for roommate difficulties? How are these conflicts handled on your campus? Ask a resident advisor or housing official to speak to your class on the policies that govern conflict resolution in residential housing.

4. **Away from Home—Family Relations**

How have relationships with parents changed since students left for college? For those who live at home and commute to campus, what differences have occurred between the time classes started and now? Are your parents less demanding or even more strict? For those students who can't go home often, what do they miss most about home? How do they compensate? Especially for international students who may not be able to go home even for holidays, how do they communicate with their parents and other family members who may be, literally, half a world away from campus? Have any students found substitute parents in faculty mentors, campus club sponsors, or religious advisors? Explore these new relationships in small group discussions. Sometimes it is easier to talk about being homesick with a small group rather than the entire class. Ask students to suggest positive ways to combat the homesick feelings common to all new students.

Even though students and parents may talk often by phone or communicate via e-mail, suggest that students write a brief note to a parent or relative who has been especially supportive during this first transitional period at college.

5.   Students with Partners

Students who have partners who are themselves students may find a great deal of support in their relationships. However, they may need to be aware of times of special stress during the term that might adversely affect these relationships. Students whose partners are not enrolled in classes may have to budget their time carefully to devote time to maintaining, if not strengthening, that relationship. Ask for suggestions from students about how students with partners can share their college experiences with their partners.

6.   Looking at Single-Sex Organizations

Are there student organizations on your campus in which membership is offered exclusively to either males or females? If so, what are these groups, and what is their purpose? Discuss with your students both the positive and negative aspects of single-gender organizations. What do your students know about current issues in common school education that relate to gender? Some high schools have experimented with education limited to one gender only. And some of these experiments have been invalidated by state or district court rulings. What do your students know about the colleges that have been historically all-male or all-female and have recently been forced to accept students of both genders? These issues are quite sensitive, and you will likely discover that your students have strong opinions on various aspects of the issue. Remind students that honest opinions formed from careful research need to be respected, although not necessarily owned, by each class member.

7.   Gay and Lesbian Student Panel

This topic area may be altogether too sensitive to address in your class. The issue is still very explosive for many college campuses where tolerance of, let alone respect for, gay and lesbian students is noticeably absent. If this is the case on your campus, you may wish to invite students to discuss their concerns with a counselor or advisor from a Student Affairs office on an individual basis or in small groups. If your students are open to this issue, gay, lesbian, and bi-sexual student organization officers are usually willing to be a part of a panel presentation that would address human rights concerns for students in these categories. Again, careful planning for this presentation is absolutely essential.

8.   Younger and Older Students

Are your first-year students primarily in the "traditional-age" (17-19) category? What is the percentage of the first-year student population on campus that could be classified as "returning adults" or first-year students over the age of 35? Are there special support groups available for older students? Are needs of older adults either returning to college or entering for the first time different from the needs of traditional-age students? What does it feel like to be a fellow student with someone who is old enough to be your parent? Or grandparent? What communication issues make it difficult for traditional-age students to interact with older students? Are there students on your campus who are enrolled concurrently in high school and college courses? What unique problems are faced by younger students who straddle the line between being a high school student and a college student at the same time?

9.   Eye Contact
        The president of one large public institution asked members of his campus community, faculty, staff, and students, to begin improving race relations on their campus by simply making eye contact and speaking to everyone they encountered while walking to class or work on campus. Although the president was criticized for suggesting a solution that was "too simple to work", the idea was implemented by several campus organizations and was found to be surprisingly effective. What ideas can your students add along these lines? Brainstorm in class about anything that might be helpful in improving relations with diverse others.

10.   Building Relationships with International Students
        If there are international students on your campus, contact the office that is responsible for assisting them and volunteer your class as mentors for several international students. Arrange for your students to share some or all of the following experiences with their international student partners:

- Meet for lunch once a week in the student cafeteria to talk about their home country, making sure to share information about the American students' home states and towns as well
- Attend a campus activity together, such as an athletic event, play or concert
- Attend a meeting of the international students' organization on campus, such as the Chinese Student Association, the Pakistani Student Organization, etc.
- Follow each of these activities by an informal discussion time at a local campus hang-out with soft drinks or pizza to help start the conversation
- If possible, invite your class members and their international student partners to your home for a traditional American holiday supper. Ask students to help with the refreshments or seek financial support for food costs from the international student office or another Student Affairs office.

Summary Projects

1.   Is there a local Women's Resource Center that assists women and their families who are in crisis? Students who are interested in Women's Studies, Sociology, Education, or related departments as major fields of study can use materials provided by a women's assistance center to begin developing a bibliography for a summary project dealing with self-assertiveness training for women. If volunteer opportunities exist at the center, students can add considerable credibility to their projects by volunteering to assist for a few hours each week of the term. A review of this volunteer work can be included as a section of the final paper or presentation.

2.   If your student support office for disabled students is equipped to handle this type of request, provide the opportunity for some of your students to serve as assistants for disabled students. The summary project could be a narrative journal describing this

experience and the learning opportunities it afforded both students. There is often a need for volunteer readers for visually handicapped or dyslexic students, volunteers to type class notes or reports for students who are unable to do so for themselves, or other types of volunteer services for temporary or permanently disabled students.

3.   Compile a comprehensive report on services and support offices designed for men only. Your campus may already have a department of Women's Studies. What comparable courses or programs are offered for men? What would be the difficulty of establishing a Men's Studies department? Include interviews with campus leaders, both students and faculty, on this issue. Would a Men's Studies department be seriously considered on your campus? Why or why not? Does this question lead to other questions regarding the value of organizations or groups that support one minority population only? Although a written report summarizing this research may be the most practical, are there other, perhaps more creative, ways that this information could be presented to the class or to a focus group?

IV. CAMPUS CONNECTIONS AND RESOURCES _____

Residence Hall Advisors: Most residence hall advisors have received specialized training in counseling and programming events for new students. Ask a team of students to interview several residence hall advisors and make an oral report to the class. How were residence hall advisors selected for their positions? What are their duties? What are their concerns? Is it difficult to be a student and a residence hall advisor at the same time? Who supervises residence hall advisors? Where do they go for help with difficult student problems? What are the limits of their authority?

Social Clubs: Social clubs provide a necessary and welcome opportunity to help students make friends and establish networks on campus. Ask a student team to obtain a list of all the approved student social clubs on campus. These may be fraternities and sororities or clubs based on special interests. The team should report answers to the following questions to the class. How does one join a student social group? What are the qualifications for membership? When do the groups meet? Is it possible to attend a few meetings before deciding to join? Are there financial obligations involved in joining any of these groups? Why is it important to be connected to some organization or club outside of class?

Academic Department Clubs: Academic clubs provide an opportunity for students with similar academic interests to join together and establish networks. These clubs may join competitions or be part of community services. For example, the Engineering Club usually competes in a variety of engineering contests. Psi Chi brings together psychology majors to discuss graduate opportunities, provide community service, and compete with other schools in psychology trivia.

Professional Counseling Centers: For students who find it very difficult to establish new relationships or for students who experience failed relationships or personal losses, professional counselors are available on most campuses to assist in making appropriate adjustments. Ask a student team to visit the professional counseling office and bring back copies of brochures or other printed literature describing those services for each class member.

Special Communications Courses: Investigate the possibility of special courses or brief seminars available to students who have difficulty with personal communication. What seminars or support groups are sponsored by the student health center? Are these services open to all students? Is there a fee involved?

Student Parents: Students with children may find a support group ready and willing to assist in the special problems that occur for parents who are enrolled in college classes while raising a family. Contact the commuter student office on your campus and ask about services especially for student parents. Is there a daycare facility on campus? If so, are students allowed to register their children? Is there a childcare cooperative? How does one join and what are the responsibilities?

Minority Student Advisory Groups: Are there offices on your campus devoted to the support and nurture of specific minority groups? If so, where are they located, and how would a student access these groups? What specific services are offered by these offices? Are the services limited only to members of that minority group? If so, are services comparable among minority group offices? Are any of these offices involved in academic support services? Retention support services? Are there statistical measures to indicate degree of success in retention and graduation rates?

International Student Clubs and Groups: What offices are responsible for support and nurture of international students on your campus? Where are these offices located, and how does a student access these offices? Are there special support services provided for international students that are not provided for American students? Why might these be necessary? Do international students come to your campus for academic work that leads to a degree? Or do the international students come primarily to experience American culture and to make network connections for future business concerns?

Women's Centers: Is there a Women's Studies department on your campus? Is there a degree program in Women's Studies? A women's center in your campus health facility? An active chapter of the Association of University Women? What other special programs or offices support women on campus? What is the rationale behind the establishment of such programs or offices? Ask a small group of men from your class to research these questions and then ask a group of women from your class to confirm findings. Are the answers the same? What might account for the difference in answers between men and women?

Advocate Offices for Students with Disabilities: The Americans With Disabilities Act has required colleges and universities to work diligently to come into compliance with accommodation requirements. Are there buildings or classrooms, including residence halls, on your campus that are not handicap-accessible? Is student transportation handicap-accessible? If not, what action is being taken to remedy these problems? Ask a team of students to visit with the director responsible for support of students with disabilities and report to the class about any lingering difficulties that your institution may have in reaching compliance standards. What are the plans to address persistent problems in this area?

Commuters vs. Residential Students: Is yours primarily a residential or commuter campus? If primarily residential, is there a support office or group for commuter students? What services does this office provide? Are there special study rooms reserved in either the library or student center for commuter students? Are there any student services that are not available to commuter students? If not, why not? How do commuter students learn about generic campus services? Are there any difficulties in communicating with commuter students? If so, what can students suggest to address these problems? If yours is primarily a commuter campus, what problems does this create in establishing and maintaining a sense of campus community?

Student Activities: Does your campus/college have student activities? What are some campus specific activities? What are some college-wide activities? How do students reserve tickets? Is there a specific number to call or office to visit? What is the calendar of activities for the current semester? Have students attend a student activity and write a couple paragraphs about their experience. Many schools have movie nights, theatre tickets, sporting events, weekend trips, and other fun activities for a student discounted rate.

Student Center: Many campuses have a student center or snack bar where students can come together and socialize while taking a break from classes. There are usually a variety of events held in this area throughout the semester, such as Fall Fest.

V. COLLABORATIVE LEARNING SUGGESTIONS _____

Exercise 1: Arrange for teams of students to interview recently retired faculty members on your campus. (Some of them may still be teaching part-time for special programs or emergency assignments.) Ask students to devise a generic list of questions that would help them become acquainted with this faculty person from an earlier era. How was the campus different when this person first started teaching? What were students like? How have students changed over the term of this teaching career? What was this person like as an entering college student? Brief oral reports, longer written interview summaries, or perhaps even an edited video of the interview could form the output of this project.

Exercise 2: Assign small groups to interview persons in your larger community (outside the campus) who are responsible for community ethnic or cultural resources. Is there a chapter of NAACP in your city? Are there advocacy groups for underrepresented minorities? Are there special community offices that help with transition for recent immigrants? You may find assistance in locating these offices or groups from your local Chamber of Commerce or city government ombudsman. Students who are interested in legal careers or social work may want to contact the offices of the city attorney to investigate what services are offered for victims of crime, juvenile advocacy, and other governmental assistance programs that impact minority populations. Work in small groups to construct an interview template that would address the primary issues covered in this chapter. Students should practice interview situations before they start this project; a role-playing exercise that tests the interview template during class would be helpful. Prepare students for the fact that interviews sometimes depart from the planned sequence of questions and lead to interesting topics that may not have been anticipated. Often some of the most interesting information comes about as a result of some of these departures. Students should be encouraged to present their findings to the class in creative ways, utilizing all members of their interview team, perhaps in a poster session or through video interviews with representatives and clients.

Exercise 3: Divide the class into two groups, one all male, the other all female. Ask each group to respond to the following scenario and then compare answers to see if gender plays a role in communication. Group process is important in defining the answers in this situation. How does each group determine their answers? Does this differ because of gender?

First-year students Sarah and Jim have been dating for several weeks. They enjoy each other's company and share common interests. They usually meet at the cafeteria each morning and walk to class together. One morning, Sarah tells Jim that she wants to wait for two other girls from her residence hall floor before she walks to class and that Jim should go ahead without her. Jim offers to wait with her, but Sarah urges him to go to class now so that he won't be late. Jim later sees Sarah come into the classroom just before the lecture begins; she is alone. She doesn't speak to him and sits at the back of the room even though Jim has saved a seat for her next to him. She hurries out of the room after class without waiting for Jim. What does Jim assume at this point?

Exercise 4: If participation in a club or organization is part of the requirements for this class, assign students to attend sample meetings in pairs. It's usually more comfortable for new students to attend a meeting of an unfamiliar group of strangers when a friend or acquaintance goes along for company and support. Ask the pairs to report to the class on their experiences at the first meeting. Was the group welcoming for new students? Were the purposes clear? What activities were planned for the future? Do your students want to attend again or would they rather try another group?

Exercise 5: Divide the class into a male group and a female group. Have each group come up with their top ten characteristics they look for in a partner. Also have them develop a list for the top ten characteristics they do not want in a partner. Have the two groups share their lists. Are they similar? Do men and women look for the same characteristics in partners? Do the traditional and non-traditional students seek the same things? On an individual basis, have the students write down the positive characteristics they hold and the negative characteristics they would like to change.

Exercise 6: After completing Self Assessment 1 on page 56, divide students into groups of four and have them discuss their conflict style. Are they assertive, aggressive, manipulative, or passive? Explain to them what assertive behavior entails and give them an example of how to deal with conflict in an assertive manner. To be assertive, one should first describe the situation, then explain their feelings using "I" statements. Next, one should specify what he or she wants out of the situation or person, and then finally provide a consequence if the behavior or situation is not changed. For example, if an assertive person lived downstairs from a neighbor who played the stereo too loudly late at night, then he or she would handle the situation in the following assertive manner: "When you are playing your stereo loudly at night (describe), I feel upset and irritated because I am not able to fall asleep and I have to work the next day (explain). I am requesting that you please play your stereo on a low volume after 10 p.m. on weeknights so I can get a full night of sleep (specify). If you continue to play it loudly, I will be forced to call the landlord or cops because it is affecting my performance at work and at school (consequence)." Have students practice being assertive by giving them different scenarios and letting them take turns role-playing how to deal with the conflict in an assertive manner using the example above. The students may critique and assist each other in how to be more assertive.

VI. ALTERNATIVE TEACHING STRATEGIES _____

Special volunteer communication opportunities exist on many college campuses with regard to crisis hotlines. Enlist the help of the coordinator of volunteer services for your campus or someone from the office of student affairs whose responsibility is to integrate students into campus life. Explore the possibility of new students being allowed to participate as crisis hotline counselors. What training is provided? Must students have had prior experience with this kind of activity in high school? What are the career exploration options for such experiences? Is this an appropriate way for students to discover whether or not majoring in counseling or social work is a good fit for them?

Some of your students may have been members of conflict resolution teams in their previous schools. Help those students explore ways in which they can continue to use the training they have already received. Are there similar team structures in the residence halls? Are there campus mediation boards on which they are allowed to serve? Ask an administrator for conflict resolution to assist in placing those students who want to continue this service during their college years. Some of these students may be able to volunteer to help local public schools organize peer conflict resolution teams. Look for connections with local public school guidance counselors to help facilitate this kind of communication.

Establish investigative teams to research living accommodations both on your campus and in the surrounding community. Search the campus and community news media for the past five years, looking for stories that deal with housing and minority populations. Are there recurring issues? Were some of the problems solved, and if so, what were the solutions? What difficulties remain in finding adequate housing for diverse population groups? Does your community have a fair housing act? Is it effective? Was school bussing ever an issue in the community? Was this issue clouded by housing patterns? Are there minority leaders in the community who will speak with your investigative teams about these issues? Is campus housing segregated, if not by edict, then by *de facto* policies? Are opportunities provided for students from diverse populations to live in close proximity? Are there housing programs that promote interaction among diverse student groups? Are these programs successful? By whose standards? Compile a research report that can be offered for publication in the campus newspaper and/or community news media outlets as either a single article or a featured series. If your campus or class has a web page, ask about the possibility of posting the report via this outlet.

As a class project, establish a service for the campus that would match international students with American students as mentors. Student teams can be assigned to visit with various campus support offices that might lend official sanction to this group. The international student support office might, for instance, provide funding for a pizza supper or get-acquainted function in the campus-wide student center. Organizing, directing, and implementing such a student group would be a time- and labor-intensive project that, if successful, could provide a service of lasting significance to your campus. Use some of the suggestions in exercise 3 of the section "Strategies for Improving Relations with Diverse Others" earlier in this chapter to begin the group activities. Assign specific duties to each small group. One group would be responsible for raising support from appropriate campus offices; another group would match American mentors with international students; another group would be responsible for recording events on video; another group would compile campus addresses, phone numbers, and e-mail connections so that each student involved in the project would have a directory of all others who were committed to the group; another group would keep a written history of the project and provide a master copy for sponsoring groups or individuals who volunteered to be a part of the project.

Mass media such as television and magazines have a great influence on college students. Have students pay closer attention to advertisements, TV programs, magazine articles, and commercials to examine how mass media portrays gender, racial, and age stereotypes. Have them discuss what the stereotypes are and how they influence society and discrimination.

Have students anonymously write down a problem they are having with their intimate relationships. Are they communication issues, sexual issues, financial issues, trust issues, or psychological issues? Read out several of the issues and have the class discuss resolutions to these problems. This will allow them an opportunity to seek advice about their relationships in a safe and anonymous manner. The exercise will also allow students to realize that they are dealing with similar issues, and they will feel empowered when assisting others in finding solutions to the issues.

VII. LEARNING PORTFOLIO

1.   Self-Assessments
Have students complete Self-Assessment 1 on page 56 and discuss the different approaches outlined here. What are advantages and disadvantages of each approach? What did students learn about themselves?

2.   Your Journal
          Have small groups complete the activity "Are Men Really from Mars…?" on page 59. Make sure groups include a mix of both men and women, if possible. Have them create a list of perceived similarities and differences between men and women. What items are consistent across groups? Why might this be?

VIII. CHAPTER QUIZ SUGGESTIONS_____

1.   Use the Review Questions as a short-answer quiz. Points may be assigned equally at 25 points per question, or points may be divided unequally depending on the amount of class time and assignments devoted to various areas of the chapter. In short-answer quizzes, complete sentences are not always necessary as long as the essential points of the answer are present.

2.   As you work through this chapter, be sure that your students discuss, either in class or in a residence hall informational meeting, answers to the following questions prior to quiz time. This is information that is crucial to the safety of your students, both male and female. In fact, students who are in command of this information may avoid a life-or-death rape or overly aggressive behavioral situation. This is also a quiz that may be repeated until all students can answer each question correctly.

<u>Short Answer Quiz:</u>

1. Name two offices or departments on this campus that assist students in issues of personal safety.
2. Where are these offices located? Be specific in your answer.
3. List five strategies to avoid settings in which rape most often occurs.
4. List at least one office or department on this campus where students can go to receive assistance in conflict resolution. Do not repeat any answer from the first question above.

IX. QUIZ_____

Multiple Choice. Choose the one best answer.

1. The most important skills employers report looking for in potential employees are
          A. intellectual skills.
          B. logic and reasoning skills.
          C. communication skills.
          D. skills acquired through experience in the field.
          E. technical skills.

2. The *Family Education and Privacy Act* states that
          A. the college can release your records only to you and your parents.
          B. the college can release your records only to you.

C. all family members are entitled to an opportunity for higher education.

D. family members' income will remain private when applying for education loans.

E. the college cannot release your records until you successfully graduate.

3. The best way to deal with conflict is
   A. assertion.
   B. aggression.
   C. manipulation.
   D. passivity.
   E. violence.

4. _____ of college men admit that they have *forced* sexual activity on women.
   A. About one-fourth
   B. One-third
   C. One-third to one-half
   D. Almost all
   E. None

5. All of the following are good ways to improve relationships with diverse others except:
   A. Taking the perspective of others.
   B. Seeking personal contact.
   C. Respecting differences while realizing similarities.
   D. Seeking relationships only with others like yourself.
   E. Treating people as individuals.

True or False

6. _____Many communication experts believe that most interpersonal communication is *nonverbal*.

7. _____The best solution to a conflict or argument is compromise.

8. _____Loneliness is only a concern of traditional-age first-year college students.

9. _____The American Psychiatric Association labels homosexuality as abnormal behavior and a mental disorder.

10. _____Hooking up is a good remedy for loneliness.

ANSWERS

1. **C**   2. **B**   3. **A**   4. **C**   5. **D**   6. **T**   7. **F**   8. **F**   9. **F**   10. **F**

X. TEST QUESTIONS

Multiple Choice. Choose the one best answer.

1. A critical skill for making and keeping relationships is
    A. listening to your friends, family, and significant others.
    B. opening up and sharing about yourself as much as possible.
    C. being available to help out when needed.
    D. providing frequent advice.

2. When the receiver goes through the motions of listening but doesn't really process any meaningful information, it is called
    A. ostracizing
    B. pseudolistening
    C. false interaction
    D. anti-auditory attention

3. The most appropriate style of dealing with conflict is
    A. assertion.
    B. passivity.
    C. insistence.
    D. All the above are equally appropriate.

4. Helicopter parents
    A. believe their college-age children are still seriously in need of their guidance
    B. are very involved in their child's school spirit, and become big fans of the athletic teams, typically attending every game and tail-gate party.
    C. essentially "drop" their child off at college and let him fend for himself.
    D. insist that their child attend school close to home.

5. *Rape*, as defined by the text, is
    A. sexual intercourse between individuals, at least one of whom is intoxicated or high on drugs.
    B. sexual intercourse forced on an individual who does not give consent.
    C. a legal term for an instance in which sexual intercourse took place and one individual claims afterwards that they were too incapacitated by alcohol or drugs to reasonably consent to the act.
    D. sexual intercourse that occurs when at least one of the individuals is a minor.

6. In a study of first-year college students, it was found that two weeks after school began, _____ of students felt lonely.
    A. 25%
    B. 35%
    C. 55%
    D. 75%

7. An individual who is *ethnocentric*
     A. is interested in individuals from different ethnicities.
     B. favors individuals from his/her own ethnic background.
     C. is of mixed ethnic heritage.
     D. is married to someone of a different ethnicity.

True or False

8. _____Employers rate communication skills as the *most important* skills they look for in who they want to hire.

9. _____According to the *Family Education Responsibility and Privacy Act,* the college cannot release your records to anyone but you.

10. _____Experts in gender studies believe that in order to truly be leaders, women need to stop caring for others.

Essay Questions

1. Explain the "gender controversy" discussed in your text. Have you had any personal experiences reflecting this?

2. Discuss ways that communication can be used to resolve conflict with others. List the four styles of dealing with conflict discussed in the text and why one type is considered more successful than the others.

3. Describe several specific behaviors that could be considered "sexual harassment" and explain why.

ANSWERS

1. **A**   2. **B**   3. **A**   4. A   5. **B**   6. **D**   7. **B**   8. **T**   9. **T**   10. **F**

CHAPTER 3

BE A GREAT TIME MANAGER

I. CHAPTER OVERVIEW _____

Do we really have enough time? You probably will say *no, I need more!* So will your students. Interviews with sophomore students applying for positions as peer assistants in freshman courses reveal very interesting information. When asked to name their most difficult problem in being a successful student, over seventy percent said, without hesitation, time management. That is why this chapter begins with the message: "Take Charge of Your Life by Managing Your Time." It makes the powerful statement that students have the ability to change and control this aspect of their life. Many misconceptions exist about time management; thus, we begin by helping to dispel the debilitating myths. Not only that, but it's exciting to realize that not only does good time management enable students to have enough time in their schedule to accomplish the things they want, it also reduces stress and improves self-esteem!

One necessary element to good time management is to first define personal values. Students need to realize that when they identify what is important to them, they have taken the first step in managing their time, as this serves as a foundation for making critical time-management decisions. Once values are acknowledged, it is time to focus on goals. A good schedule should result from what it is that students want to accomplish and in what time period. Achieving their goals is a great motivator for getting a handle on time management.

Effective time management is not done in your head (although some of us seem to think it works just fine – it's definitely not the best method!) Like any big project, the proper tools can help get the job done easier and more completely. Whereas in high school, much of their lives were scheduled for them, students now face many more decisions on their own. Encourage students to keep a day planner and semester calendar visible and ready for alteration. If students prefer high-tech gizmos, there are plenty of tools to accommodate them, from computer time-management programs to palm pilots they can carry with them. Even some cell phones now have programmable calendar functions.

Once students have located these tools, it is time to make use of them. Time management is not a one-dimensional task. Students should plan to map out long term (such as semester-length) schedules, as well as weekly schedules, and plan to review and alter them on a daily basis. This requires the ability to prioritize – something that can easily be related back to each student's current values and goals.

The planning is the easy part! Sticking to one's plan is the challenge, as freshmen are particularly bad with procrastination, viewing their newfound class schedules as allowing them a great deal more free time than they actually have. When students learn time management techniques that help them *create* schedules and *stick to them*, they will begin to learn how not to procrastinate and to find a balance between all of the elements of their lives.

II. IMAGES OF COLLEGE SUCCESS

Ask how many of your students know that Facebook was developed as a time management strategy – probably few, if any, are aware of Mark Zuckerberg's reason for creating the phenomenally popular cyber-social tool. Point out that it wasn't just students' complaint that they couldn't find a way to meet new friends, but that they couldn't find an *efficient* way to meet new friends – a big difference, highlighting students' desire to save time doing just about anything! Facebook is so popular because Zuckerberg was able to solve the problem and meet students' fundamental need, the ability to connect with others, get to know them, learn their background, discover their interests, meet their friends, and see what they look like – all in a single sitting! Students can spend as little or as much time as they would like (or have) to engage in social networking simply by sitting at their computer. Students with laptops and wireless ability can do it almost anywhere, capitalizing on a few free moments here and there.

Mark Zuckerberg's initiative, as well as other projects he has worked on, focuses on maximizing time spent in certain, potentially time-consuming activities. The response from users highlights the demand for tools and strategies for managing our time. Of course, Zuckerberg's story also depicts the fact that we can't do or have it all (at least not all at once!) as he has had to spend all his time managing Facebook – something he doesn't even have time to use himself!

III. CLASS ACTVITIES

Break The Ice!

1. Daily Calendar Essentials

Especially if discussion of this chapter occurs early in the term, ask groups to create a list of essentials that should appear on every student's daily calendar. Give each group two minutes to complete the exercise and then compare answers. Broad topic essentials should include:

- eating
- sleeping
- personal health and hygiene
- classes
- studying

As a prelude to further discussion, students should be aware that eating, sleeping and attending to personal health and hygiene are truly *essentials*. These may not appear on all lists! Some students will add job responsibilities; others will add family and/or childcare. Then ask students if they have *planned* time to include all of these in their daily schedules. Students who plan time for essentials are usually the most successful students.

2. Your Campus Calendar

If your institution provides a student pocket, backpack, or online calendar, investigate the contents. What events, activities, and academic dates are included? Some institutions provide small desk calendars that list important academic deadlines, final exam schedules, major campus events, and campus holidays as well as day-by-day space to list appointments and assignments. Some campus calendars provide additional information, such as lists of campus organizations, study resources, institutional unit flow-charts, and other helpful facts. Assign each group a section of the calendar to explore and then report on the contents to the entire class.

Discussion and Reflection

1. **Time Management and GPA**
   Check with your institution's office of research or the office of the Dean of Students to discover the average GPA of the freshman class last year. Tell each student to bring a pocket calculator to class. Provide calculators for those students who do not own one. Ask each student to:

- Figure the total number of minutes in a week. All answers will be identical. Emphasize that this number cannot change. Unlike money, we all have the same amount of time per week.
- Figure the number of minutes spent in class or lab for each person per week
- Using the standard formula, figure the number of minutes each student should spend studying outside of class for each credit hour enrolled.
[Credit hours x two = # of hours of study time required for an average grade. Convert study hours projected per week into minutes.]
- Add the number of minutes in class/lab per week to the number of study minutes projected per week.
- Subtract this total from the total number of minutes available per week.
- Write the average grade for last year's freshman class in large numerals on the chalkboard. Ask students if this GPA will be sufficient to meet their individual goals this year. Compare the average GPA to the number of study minutes required for this GPA. How many study minutes will be necessary this term for you to achieve an average GPA? What does this say about the need for time management?

   The exercise above may be replaced by an expanded version if time permits. The following instructions are more detailed and will result in an even more realistic overview. Using individual calculators, ask students to:

- Figure the total number of minutes in a week. All answers will be identical. Emphasize that this number cannot change. Unlike money, we all have the same amount of time per week.
- Figure the number of minutes spent in class and lab for each person per week.
- Using the standard formula, figure the number of minutes necessary for study outside of class for each credit hour enrolled. [Credit hours x two = # of hours of study time required for an average grade.]
- Convert study hours projected per week into minutes per week.
- Add the number of minutes in class/lab per week to the number of study minutes projected per week.

- Subtract this total from the number of minutes in the week.
- As applicable, subtract the number of minutes of job time per week from the last total.
- Ask students to estimate the number of sleep hours required each night to stay healthy. This number may vary from student to student, but the estimates must be realistic. Multiply hours per night by seven for a weekly sleep total. Then convert weekly sleep hours to minutes.
- Subtract the total of sleep minutes from the remaining weekly total minutes.
- Ask students to figure how many meals they will eat per day and to allot an average of 20 minutes per meal. Multiply this minute total by seven and subtract this number from the remaining total minutes.
- Follow the same process to estimate personal health and hygiene time requirements per day. Subtract this number from the total.
- For those students who have other obligations (childcare, other family responsibilities, religious and/or social obligations, etc.), figure those minutes into the total. What's left? Is there time for relaxation? Stress-reduction time? Are you out of time already? If so, how will you set your priorities? If you consider dropping a class to save time, will this result in less than full-time enrollment and endanger financial aid?

2. Exploring Types of Planners

Ask students to bring a personal planning calendar to class. Compare the kinds of calendar/planners within groups. Are any electronic? Are they all sized to fit in a backpack or purse? Why would this be an important qualification? Some students may have used a detailed planner in high school. Ask these students to explain the advantages of such a time management system. The point to stress is that time demands in college are quite different from high school.

Part II of this exercise involves scheduling essentials for the term *now*. Students will need to either use the list created in the first "Break The Ice!" activity or compile a list of their daily essential activities. They will also need a copy of the syllabus for each of their classes this term. An important instruction is to *use pencil*. Schedules often are tentative, and even exams are sometimes postponed. Successful students pencil in dates for the entire term at the beginning of the term.

- Using the syllabus for each class, list on your personal calendar all major assignment due dates, exam dates, and paper/project dates. Be sure to include the date, time, and location of each final exam.
- Some students list their classes each day, noting the times given on the syllabus when the class is canceled or meets in a different location.
- List required study halls or regular study group meetings.
- If applicable, write your weekly work schedule in your calendar.
- List all required meetings and events that are associated with your residence hall living arrangements. For commuters, include family responsibility times.
- After writing all these essentials in your term calendar, review a typical week. When can you schedule regular study times for each class? Remember that an average GPA usually results from at least two hours of study for every hour in class.

- Next, schedule regular times to eat and sleep just as you schedule classes.
- When will you relax? When are times available for social activities? When is there time to do laundry? What happens when unexpected events or activities make demands on your time? Determine your priorities now.

3. Create a list of at least 20 things that would reasonable reflect demand on a college student's time and the any related timeline for addressing them, for example:
   - History quiz tomorrow
   - Research notes due in two weeks
   - Homecoming float committee meeting tonight
   - Wanting to ask someone out on a date for Saturday night
   - Mom's birthday is next week
   - Hot new video game is released at midnight tonight
   - Cable bill and cell phone bill due in three days
   - Training for new job tomorrow morning

Provide a start day and time (it is now Monday, October 1st at 8:00 am), then have students prioritize items for accomplishing them. Once they have completed the task, begin by discussing how easy or difficult this was to do. What led them to make the decisions they did? Do they feel comfortable with their decisions or would their choices cause them stress if these were real things they had to deal with?

After spending time talking about the process, provide students with Covey's Time Usage Matrix from page 75 in the textbook. Have students work with the list again, this time with the matrix beside them. Has their approach changed? Do they find it much easier to decide what tasks to do when thinking about it along the two dimensions of Importance and Urgency? Continue the discussion about how such a simple tool can contribute so substantially to effective time management.

Words of Wisdom

1. **Quotes for Discussion**
    If you introduce time management with the quotations found in the body of the chapter, try reading them aloud and then reproducing them on an overhead transparency or writing them on the chalkboard. Ask students to discuss how each quotation relates to their personal time management goals. Does one particular quote appeal more than the others to individual students? Why?

2. **Quotations and You**
    Read the Alice Walker quote aloud: "time moves slowly, but passes quickly." Is this true or false? Do students feel that they are really aware of all the moments in life—the tastes, smells, and textures of the world, or are they too busy rushing to class? When they are at a party, does time move slowly because they are taking everything in or quickly? What happens when students drink or use nicotine? Does this affect time? Have students discuss these questions.

1.   Goal Tending

Ask students to write down a specific goal they want to accomplish and discuss their answers in small groups. Stress that such goals should be <u>challenging</u>, <u>reasonable</u>, and <u>specific</u>. Many students have difficulty writing specific goals, but time and money management are topics that lend themselves to very specific, short-term goals. Monitor student responses for those that are too vague to be measured. Assist students in re-writing those goal statements to be <u>specific</u>.

Demonstrate a time management goal in your own professional life; model what you want to see in students' responses by being challenging, reasonable, and specific. For example, your goal might state: I will read and respond to all student journal assignments before the next meeting of this class. This may be a very challenging goal considering your daily professional responsibilities! It is, however, reasonable for students to expect timely responses from their instructors and reasonable that instructors set aside time for grading. This goal is specific; it relates to a specific assignment and states what you as the instructor must do to meet the goal. You can then discuss how strategies can be planned to achieve the goal: grading so many assignments per hour until all are completed, reading all assignments within a designated grading time and responding via e-mail within a specific time frame, organizing the journals alphabetically before grading so that recording grades takes less time, etc. Then discuss obstacles to achievement of this particular goal and additional resources that would help achieve the goal. Mention the specific date of the next class meeting, and, even if it seems obvious, how you know that the goal was met.

2.   Exploring Procrastination

Have students list the ways they tend to procrastinate. Look at individual time management strategies for this term. Have favorite ways of putting off work on an assignment or goal been addressed? Work with small group team members to strategize specific ways to avoid procrastination by individuals. Make sure that these strategies are realistic, practical, and workable <u>personally</u> for each individual. The last question is the most important one for each student to address. What is the commitment level of each group member regarding the suggested strategies?

3.   Classroom Time Wasters

Ask your students to evaluate any time management strategies they have observed in this class and others. Is class time wasted by taking attendance every meeting? Is time saved by finding efficient ways to return assignments? Do you manage small group time by setting limits for responses and then firmly cutting off discussion when time is called? Does each small group manage class assignment time by monitoring the discussion to ensure that no one person dominates the conversation? Does your group need to appoint a time monitor to be sure that you get the group assignments completed in the assigned time frame? Ask students for suggestions about how class time can be used more efficiently. If necessary, remind students that although group work may appear to be more time-consuming, research indicates that lecture is the most inefficient way to achieve long-term learning.

Summary Projects

1. Top Ten Tips. Have each student create her own list of the top ten strategies that she uses to "manage" her time. Make copies of each student's list to distribute to all students in the class. Don't be surprised if you find some questionable strategies – working non-stop the night before (working best under pressure), foregoing other "minor" assignments for other classes, etc. For these unique techniques, have students explain how they employ them, then ask the rest of the class if they have done something similar with success – or negative consequences. Be prepared to offer scenarios which the students aren't likely to have considered, that would render these strategies ineffective at best, and disastrous at the worst. End by emphasizing the importance of learning new, effective ways to manage time, rather than relying on old, potentially dangerous habits that aren't likely to work in college.

2. Student teams may elect to create a time management booklet designed for incoming students. Ideas and tips can be garnered from class discussions and individual interview contributions as well as from published resources. Suggest they do a search of other institutions' websites. Often colleges and universities post valuable and unique information on time management on their websites, usually through their learning resource center, counseling center, or First Year Experience sites. Students must provide complete bibliographic citations when referencing published resources. If this project results in an interesting and valuable collection, students may want to offer it to campus orientation planners as a resource for the next entering class. At the very least, the project will provide additional information for orientation instructors to add to their teaching plans.

IV. CAMPUS CONNECTIONS AND RESOURCES _____

1.   Among the resources available at many institutions is an office whose purpose is to provide additional study skills assistance for students. Personnel in this office are usually highly skilled in helping students discover and practice time management techniques. An extra-credit assigned visit to this office with an individual appointment for counseling can be a life-saver for a student who is in academic danger because of poor time management.

2.   Academic planning is an essential factor in college success. It allows students to set goals semester by semester and provides them with a path to success. Have students bring in their curriculum guide or degree plan listing all the required courses and credits to achieve the degree. Once they check off the courses that have already been completed, they will need to decide what courses they will be able to take per semester and decide what is a good course load with their work schedule. If they have difficulty with this assignment, then have them visit an academic counselor or faculty advisor to assist them with developing a plan. Having an accurate idea of when they will complete their degree and graduate provides the student with a vision and a motivating factor to stay in school and succeed.

3.   Some students with ADHD, depression, or other types of disabilities tend to have more difficulty with time management. Refer students to disability services for more information and assistance with planning and goal setting.

V. COLLABORATIVE LEARNING SUGGESTIONS _____

1.   As a group, have students discuss what some typical obstacles are for college students when trying to set and achieve goals. Some of these obstacles may be peer pressure, friends who are not in school, work, family, significant others, lack of support, too many responsibilities, Internet or television addiction, depression, substance abuse issues, fear of failure, fear of success, people pleasers, control issues, and lack of focus. The students can then discuss ways to overcome the obstacles that may stand in the way of success.

2.   In collaboration with the English faculty, have students set up a plan for completing a term paper. Have them practice breaking the overall task into smaller tasks by setting short-term and long-term goals. Have them set up deadlines for choosing a topic, researching journal articles, reading the articles, developing an outline, writing a rough draft, completing the final draft and proofreading.

3.   In small groups, have students review their semester schedule and develop a study schedule. Remind them to set up their schedule so the more difficult courses are the highest priority and are set up at the most alert time. Studying for tests and exams should also be a priority. Easier courses with basic homework should be at the lowest priority and should be scheduled after the others. The three factors when deciding how much time to devote to a course are the grade one wants to achieve in the course, the difficulty of the course, and the student's ability in that course.

VI. ALTERNATIVE TEACHING STRATEGIES _____

1.   Share your time management needs and strategies. Begin by presenting an overview of your semester calendar, then show students your monthly calendar, your weekly schedule, then what you have planned for the day. Be sure to include all aspects of your life from your job to your family responsibilities, extra-curricular obligations, time for enjoying yourself, and relaxation (don't forget commute time!) Discuss your current strategies for keeping up with the daily demands of your life, and ways in which you try to work in time for yourself. If you struggle with time management yourself, perhaps your students could make some suggestions based on your schedule. The power of this demonstration is that students see that learning to effectively manage their time is not just important for college, but for succeeding in their career and enjoying their lives beyond college.

2.   A team of students can schedule an interview with a campus administrator to discuss time management techniques applicable to the professional academic world as

well as to students' everyday lives. The interview process can be extended to professionals in various positions within the community, such as city government officials, public school administrators, officers in commercial financial institutions, restaurant owners or managers, retail owners or managers, Chamber of Commerce officials, public safety officers, health care workers, and others. Interview techniques and etiquette should form an essential part of the preparation for this exercise just as a formal report, either oral or written, should form a part of the evaluation process.

During the prior week, students should keep track of how they spend every minute. Require them to carry a journal with them at all times and write down their different activities and how much time was spent on each one. Have them bring the journal with them to class so they can calculate where they spent their time. Actually seeing how our time is spent in this manner provides students with a realistic view. Many are surprised by how much time they waste on activities involving television, computers, games, phones, napping, commuting, getting ready, etc. They are also usually surprised by how little time was spent on studying, reading, sleep, and other important activities. Next, have them set up a schedule for the following week, revising how much time is spent on certain activities. Encourage them to follow that new schedule the best they can.

VII. LEARNING PORTFOLIO

1.   Self-Assessment
Have students complete Self-Assessment 1 on page 84. Afterwards, survey your students as to which items were checked most often as the ways in which students waste time. Discuss why such commonalities exist among students as well as specific strategies for tackling the most common time wasters.

2.   Your Journal
Discuss the *80-20 principle* as mentioned in the journal activity on page 87. Do students agree with this principle? Why or why not? Have them generate some specific examples.

VIII. CHAPTER QUIZ SUGGESTIONS

1. Use the Review Questions as a short-answer quiz. Points may be assigned equally at 25 points per question, or points may be divided unequally depending on the amount of class time and assignments devoted to various areas of the chapter. In short-answer quizzes, complete sentences are not always necessary as long as the essential points of the answer are present.

IX. QUIZ

Multiple Choice. Choose the one best answer.

1. Misconceptions about time management include all of the following except:
   A. Time management is all common sense.
   B. Many students work better under pressure, so they shouldn't worry about managing their study time.
   C. Time management skills are essential for success in college and your future career.
   D. If you are happy and doing well in your classes, you are managing your time most effectively.
   E. Managing time makes life less spontaneous and fun.

2. Good time management skills can help you
   A. be more productive.
   B. improve your self-esteem.
   C. reach your goals.
   D. achieve better balance in your life.
   E. All of the above.

3. Students who work full time are more likely to experience all of the following except:
   A. Being less likely to complete college.
   B. Having lower GPAs.
   C. Being less likely to go to graduate school.
   D. Graduating at the top of the class.
   E. Not graduating with honors.

4. It is better to work on campus because
   A. you are closer to your classes and can work out a more efficient schedule.
   B. campus jobs typically pay more than jobs elsewhere.
   C. your employer better understands reasons why you might need to miss work due to class demands.
   D. you are more involved in campus life and have a greater connection with students and faculty.
   E. Campus jobs tend to offer greater scheduling flexibility.

5. The time management approach in which you break a big task down into smaller tasks is called
   A. the set time approach.
   B. the multi-tasking approach.
   C. the Swiss cheese approach.
   D. the Roquefort approach.
   E. the less-is-more approach.

6. It is best not to work more than
   A. 5 – 10 hours per week.
   B. 10 – 20 hours per week.
   C. 20 – 30 hours per week.
   D. 40 hours per week.

E. In excess of 40 hours per week.

True or False

7. _____The most successful college students don't actually have time for play and leisure.

8. _____Effective time management reduces stress.

9. _____Truly successful people don't use daily "to-do" lists in their lives.

10. _____Everyone is most productive from 8:00 a.m. to 12:00 p.m.

ANSWERS

1. **C**   2. **E**   3. **D**   4. **D**   5. **C**   6. **B**   7. **F**   8. **T**   9. **F**   10. F

X. TEST QUESTIONS _____

Multiple Choice. Choose the one best answer.

1. Goals express your
   A. academic ability.
   B. personality.
   C. values.
   D. commitment to effective time management.

2. The *80-20 principle* refers to
   E. A. 80% of your day consisting of waking/productive hours and 20% of your day being necessary for sleep.
   B. 80% of students who don't manage their time effectively fail or withdraw from school, while 20% are able to achieve passing or successful grades.
   C. 80% of what you do should be scheduled, while you should spend 20% of your time spontaneously.
   D. what 80% of what people do yields about 20% of the results, while 20% of what people do produces 80% of the results.

3. Students who spend *less* time watching TV and partying are *more* likely to
   A. graduate with honors.
   B. feel stressed due to lack of leisure activities and thus drop out of college.
   C. have fewer social contacts and friends and thus drop out of college.
   D. There is no difference between students who watch t.v. and party and those who don't.

4. Students who spent more time studying and doing homework are more likely to
   A. stay in college.

B. graduate with honors.
C. get into grad school
D. All of the above.

5. The time management approach in which you pre-determine a particular period of time to work on a task is called
   A. the multi-tasking approach.
   B. the set point approach.
   C. the set time approach.
   D. the Swiss cheese approach.

6. Steven Covey recommends that for each of your tasks, you should determine whether they are
   A. Necessary, Immediate, Enjoyable.
   B. Vital, Important, Optional.
   C. Required, Demanding, Extensive
   D. Relevant, Related, Required.

7. When going to college as a full-time student, it is best not to work more than
   A. 5 – 10 hours a week.
   B. 10 – 20 hours a week.
   C. 20 – 30 hours a week.
   D. 40 or more hours a week.

True or False

8. _____Managing your time effectively can actually *increase* your self-esteem.

9. _____The idea of there being "morning people" and "night owls" – those who function better at particular times of the day – is a myth.

10. _____There are three basic types of planning tools.

Essay Questions

1. List at least three benefits of effective time management. Which would be most beneficial to you and why?

2. What role do values and goals play in time management? Provide some personal examples.

3. Describe some strategies for making efficient use of commuting time.

ANSWERS

1. **C** 2. **D** 3. **A** 4. **D** 5. **C** 6. **B** 7. **B** 8. **T** 9. **F** 10. **T**

XI. MENTOR'S CORNER _____

Vicki White is "delighted to help out if I can". She was one of the few brave souls to offer advice on teaching time management. Maybe instructors feel that they are making students feel inferior when they teach this subject. This is what Vickie has to say:

My teaching style has evolved over the years as I have become more comfortable with myself as a teacher and, therefore, am able to laugh at myself. Humor is a big part of my teaching style: silly stories to make a point, cartoons, games, etc. I am most comfortable teaching about time management, money management, and writing techniques. I also enjoy monitoring the discussions on integrity and diversity. I would be open to share what I do in the classroom on any of the topics covered in the text.

As background, I have been teaching since 1975: 3rd grade, 4th grade, 7th & 8th grades in language arts, 10th grade English, college freshmen (for 18 years) in English Composition and freshman seminar. Please feel free to contact me if you need more information:

Vicki E. White
Emmanuel College
Chairman, Developmental Studies/Coordinator, First-Year Experience
Program/Yearbook Advisor
PO Box 129
181 Springs Street
Franklin Springs, GA 30639
vwhite@emmanuel-college.edu
Phone (office): 706.245.7227 ext. 2632 (ext. 2631 yearbook)
Fax: 706.245.4424

CHAPTER 4

DIVERSIFY YOUR LEARNING STYLE

I. CHAPTER OVERVIEW

Most people have experienced the difference between visual and auditory learners when it comes to getting directions. Visual learners like maps—they feel comfortable with hand-drawn squiggly lines denoting trees or roads—who cares about the actual names of the streets? On the other hand, there are the auditory learners. They would rather *hear* directions. They don't care about the winding road or the gas station; they want to know the names of streets, the directions to turn. They will throw the hand-drawn map in the back seat, never to be seen again. What are *you* like?

Students fall into many categories of learners. According to Howard Gardner, individuals have varied learning strengths across eight different areas of intelligence. Although your students may learn best from primarily one particular approach, this chapter tells students that they should develop all the areas of learning in order to thrive in college, and even pursue learning contexts that *don't* match their learning preferences. There is also evidence that enduring personal characteristics play a part in how we learn. As students come to recognize themselves by learning the Big Five Personality Theory, they can begin to think about what classes they are best suited for, and which ones will likely pose more of a challenge.

The Myers-Briggs Type Inventory, long used to assess employees and the match between individuals and their jobs, can now be applied to student success. The type identified by the combination of Myers-Briggs categories can also provide insight into how a student is likely to function in different classroom scenarios. Students need to understand that what they bring to the learning environment will impact how they experience it. Having this awareness is critical to overcoming limitations they may encounter when a course or instructor clashes with their particular style of taking in and processing information. It is important to note, however, that a mismatch in styles does not excuse one from putting in the effort to succeed. In fact, it is just the opposite. When student styles are divergent from instructor styles, the student must actively work to adapt to the situation and rise to the challenge. Certainly not every course, nor every teacher can be a perfect match to our liking and way of learning. Taking on the challenge of a difficult learning approach can build our ability to be more flexible learners.

There is a big difference between thriving and surviving. Students who merely try to *survive* often view their experiences in an adversarial context, whereas students who plan to *thrive* already have positive images in mind. Positive images push students toward success. As you encourage students to interact in learning teams and to access resources (including their professors), your deliberate use of positive phrases will plant seeds of self-worth and academic success.

II. IMAGES OF COLLEGE SUCCESS _____

Mia Hamm is a world-famous athlete who many may not know, is also an accomplished scholar and highly socially skilled young woman. When considering our strengths and abilities, it is common to limit ourselves to only one or two descriptors, such as "athletic" or "smart" or "artistic" or "technologically savvy." It is not common to think of people as being all of the above – at the same time! Mia Hamm illustrates the diversity of skills that reside in a single person, but she certainly is not the exception. While she has incredible athletic ability, she also thrived as a college student at the University of North Carolina, and has been a strong contributor to many different teams of women – all of which have highly successful winning records.

Learning, intelligence, personality, and the abilities which stem from these are no longer viewed along a single dimension. The continuous study of human intelligence, learning styles and preferences, and personality traits indicates that we all have a multi-dimensional profile of strengths in a variety of categories, across a wide array of domains. Mia Hamm is just one example of an individual who has showcased her many diverse strengths throughout her different life experiences.

Have your students identify a variety of areas in which they see themselves as talented, skilled, and highly competent. They can then write about how their choices in life – along with their successes and challenges – reflects these characteristics, how they learn, and what drives their goals.

III. CLASS ACTIVITIES _____

Break The Ice!

1.   High School Experiences
Each member of the group talks for one minute or less about his or her favorite class in high school. The group recorder should keep a list of names and favorite subjects for comparisons. Once all have participated, ask the recorder to note if there were any favorite classes common within the group. Collate the responses of all groups and then ask students to re-group for five minutes according to their favorite high school classes. What learning behaviors do they have in common during re-grouping? If students read the chapter prior to this class, ask them to speculate about learning styles that might be common to the new groups. What might they gain from those whose learning styles are similar or different from their own?

2.   Modeling Bad Behavior
This one will really get your students going! Make arrangements with a colleague in the department of drama or theatre to have two or three sophomore students visit your class pretending to be late enrollees. Ask your drama department colleague to work with these students to demonstrate several highly negative behaviors at the beginning of the class. One might whisper loudly to students on either side something about "How do I catch up in here?" or "Is this teacher any good?" Another should enter class a couple of minutes late and walk to the front of the class looking for a seat, deliberately interrupting the start of the class session. Another should open a newspaper, rustle the pages loudly,

and never look at the class or the instructor, pretending to read. Another might enter wearing a set of headphones, moving to the (imaginary) music and not paying any attention to the instructor, nor to the class. After about three minutes of this behavior, the instructor should ask these visitors to leave the class and report to the Dean. Once the actors have left, ask the groups to discuss what they have seen and then report their reactions to the group. Following the reports, be sure to tell your students that this was a sting operation to introduce the chapter in a memorable way.

Discussion and Reflection

1.   Different Disciplines and Learning Styles
Invite a panel of instructors from various disciplines to speak to your students about learning styles. Try to ensure that both men and women are represented and that these instructors teach a freshman course. Tell students to take notes during the panel discussion. This not only helps them learn note-taking skills, but also will assist in prompting discussion following the panel presentation. Ask the panel to discuss how students thrive in their classrooms. Limit the panel remarks to five or less minutes per person, and then allow five minutes for questions. Compare what panel guests said with Table 4.1, "Linking Choice of Major with Learning Style Dimensions" on page 96. Ask a student volunteer to write a short note of thanks to each of the instructors who participated.

2.   Academic Etiquette
As a matter of campus etiquette, construct with your students a list of things to know about thriving in the classroom on your individual campus. For instance, does your institution rank instructors? If so, what is the hierarchy? Is this relevant for students to know about thriving in the classrooms of senior professors? What is *tenure*? If the year of tenure application is usually a stressful one on your campus, does this have significance for a student whose professor is up for tenure that year? What differences does this make in terms of student behavior? Do upper-level administrators have teaching responsibilities? Do any of them teach entry-year students? What, if any, difference does it make to your students if a Dean, Provost, or President is the instructor for a freshman class? Are there special rules for these people? What are the rules of etiquette when making an appointment with an instructor? Other questions will occur that relate to your specific institution, but the point is that students need to know what to expect, what are the accepted codes of common courtesy, and what could happen if one violates these codes.

Words of Wisdom

1.   Quotes for Discussion
If you use all the quotes, read them aloud and then reproduce them on an overhead transparency or write them on the board. Ask students to discuss how each quotation relates to thriving in the classroom. What do the quotations have in common, if

anything? Are there hints in the quotations as to how one can thrive in the college classroom?

2.   Quotes and You
Write David Gerrold's quote on the board, "Half of being smart is knowing what you are dumb about." In small groups, have student discuss what this is saying. Can you be both "smart" and "dumb"? How? And why is it important to recognize this? How can it make a difference in the college classroom? For studying? For managing time? For reading college texts? For writing papers? A simple quote can communicate a great deal about the essence of this chapter. Help your students discover how significant those words really are.

Major Themes

1.   Examining the Learning Portfolio
Spend time with your students exploring the Learning Portfolio feature at the end of each chapter of this textbook. Discuss how each section of the Learning Portfolio addresses one or more learning style. What are the advantages and disadvantages of focusing on assignments that are geared toward one's preferred style versus a less preferred style?

2.   Using the Myers-Briggs Type Inventory
If your institution has a counseling center, learning center, or career office that provides free services, arrange for administration of the Myers-Briggs Type Inventory, LASSI, Kolb *Learning Style Inventory,* or a similar measure for each of your students. Not only will this kind of instrument help your students discover their preferred learning styles, but it should also assist in major field of study and career decisions. A professional counselor may be available for individual appointments or a brief presentation overview of the instrument and outcomes for your class as a group.

3.   Do Groups Work?
Ask students in their small groups to share their experiences in working with teams as part of their high school courses. If team assignments were not a feature of their high school coursework, ask if any of them are currently enrolled in classes that employ small groups or teams as either study groups or for specific assignments. Among those that might be mentioned are lab partners in science courses, discussion groups in history or political science courses, and team projects in freshman English composition courses. Ask students to speculate about the advantages and possible disadvantages in such learning configurations, including grading schemes.

4.   Call Waiting
Propose the following scenario to the class: *You are assigned a discussion group that will meet throughout the semester, but one of the group members brings her cell phone. The phone usually rings throughout the meeting. She excuses herself to take the calls and usually misses half the meeting. What strategies could you and your group members develop to address this challenge?* After the small groups have time to work

through some strategies, share the results with the entire class. Discuss the merits or disadvantages of each strategy. This particular assignment may be all too relevant for some of your students!

5. **Bird's of a Feather.** Research a simple and free learning styles/personality inventory that you can quickly and easily administer to your students (one recommendation: The Paragon Learning Styles Inventory – PLSI. An MBTI – type instrument designed to look at learning personalities, yielding the same "personality" types as the MBTI. It can be completed in about 15 minutes and self scored.)

Find some interesting case studies (on any interesting topic) or develop some problem-solving puzzles. Without telling the students what you are doing, to the best of your ability, place them in groups of 5-6 with students of all different learning styles. Have them work through the problem-solving exercise and discuss how easy or difficult it was, note how long it took, was there conflict, different approaches, etc. Then create groups of students who share learning personality types and give them another problem-solving puzzle. Again, discuss what their experience was with the activity and see if they report any differences in the ease of working with the others in the group, etc.

Only after the discussions are complete (and they've had the chance to discover this on their own) should you reveal the different make-up of the groups. Are their observations any different now that they know the similarities and differences of group members?

6. **A Professor's Party**

If your campus has a Faculty-in-Residence program, it is often possible to arrange a visit to those faculty quarters for an informal seminar or discussion with the faculty member and perhaps even the faculty member's family. Some institutions provide a food stipend specifically for faculty-in-residence who entertain students in their quarters. Whatever the situation, a volunteer from your class or one of the small groups as a team could arrange the visit and then write a note expressing their thanks for this courtesy.

As an alternative, check your institution's policies on inviting students into your home for an informal discussion. Researchers tell us that faculty + food = motivation for students. Most students are very curious about where and how their instructors live. A pizza party, chili supper, or salad sampler in your home or apartment may be feasible, especially if your institution will assist with the cost of the meal or if your students are willing to contribute food or drinks. Instructors who are brave enough to invite students to take over the kitchen are sometimes astounded at the creativity and helpfulness of their students. Students are often astounded to discover that their college professors are real people and are approachable and interested in their students.

Summary Projects

1. A summary project utilizing materials from this chapter might be constructed from a case study of the interaction of a small group. If students stay in the same small group (or change only once in the semester), a weekly journal of the progress made in solving problems created by group interaction could then be summarized as a term project. The summary could contain a compilation of the problems encountered and a

statement of the solutions reached with evaluative commentary. Have students keep in mind how different learning styles may contribute to the problems they encountered, as well as the solutions.

2.   Have students bring the syllabi from all of their other classes to your class. Help them identify key elements within each syllabus that can help them gain an understanding into how well each course will or will not match with their preferred learning style. They should be able to pick out aspects of the class format, assignment protocol, timelines, amount of readings, number of exams, type of exams, professor's policies, etc. and assess them in terms of whether or not they are a good "match" with the way student feels most comfortable, or tends to be most successful in learning.

After students have gone through all of their syllabi in this way, lead a discussion based on the issues related to learning styles and classes (and professors, for that matter.) Point out that the best guide for students when choosing classes may be to find out the particulars about a class and how certain instructors approach a class. This way, they can assess whether it will likely be a good match with their learning style. It also highlights the pointlessness of asking friends and roommates whether a certain class is "good," "bad," "easy," "hard," and the same of instructors as well. These questions can really only be answered based on each student's individual learning personality and preferences, which may be very different from those of their friends (and this should be evident in the class discussion of syllabi.) Have students taking the same class discuss their individual interpretations of whether the class is good, interesting, boring, difficult, etc. and let them discover this for themselves.

IV. CAMPUS CONNECTIONS AND RESOURCES _____

Most institutions provide assistance to students who have difficulty in communicating with or relating to instructors. Students should know where to access help if they are having problems with a particular instructor, especially if there is a concern about fair and equal treatment under the policies of the institution or state/federal law.

1.   As an instructor, be prepared to offer specific advice about campus offices that deal with student complaints and concerns regarding instructors. If there are printed materials available from these offices, secure copies for your students and review the access routes. Often students will regard you as their most trustworthy advocate and may ask that you accompany them to meet with a senior official who will act on their complaints or concerns.

2.   Instructional development offices on campus exist to help faculty learn how to teach more effectively. If you have such an office on your campus, ask for assistance from that office in helping your students learn how to form study groups for specific disciplines. Coordinators of instructional development are trained to help faculty members in working with small groups; the process can easily work from the other side to assist students in forming their own study groups if such help is not forthcoming from their instructors.

3.   Some institutions have campus-wide convocations at the beginning of the term to help motivate students and give advice about making the most of their educational opportunities. Campus speakers at these events are often willing to address orientation classes in follow-up meetings that will discuss the details of how to connect with instructors and peers in academic inquiries.

4.   Most institutions have Student Handbooks that list the rights and responsibilities of the students and faculty. Review the handbook with the students, emphasizing student civility and expectations, student grievance procedures, final grade appeal procedures, and other topics that may be beneficial.

5.   Provide students with contact information regarding the division deans or department heads so students know where to go in case they have a problem with a faculty member. Also discuss the duties of the Dean of Student Services and the Provost.

6.   Have a disability counselor visit the class to discuss different types of disabilities and some recommendations on how to improve learning based on the variety of styles. Some examples might be discussing what works best with students that have ADHD or visual impairment, etc.

7.   Using the course schedule book, review the different formats of courses, such as online, tele-courses, hybrid, independent study, and in-classroom instruction. Discuss what course format works well with the different learning styles to achieve learning success.

V. COLLABORATIVE LEARNING SUGGESTIONS _____

1.   Ask each small group to create a list of three or four positive classroom behaviors that college instructors might expect of all students. Then make a similar list of negative behaviors that might irritate professors. Combine the group lists and see what positive and negative behaviors are common to all lists. How would each set of behaviors contribute to thriving or failing in the college classroom?

2.   Collaborative learning suggestions found earlier in this section form a significant part of the assignments in this chapter. These collaborative assignments may be evaluated according to the same criteria listed in the Chapter 1 *Collaborative Learning Suggestions* section. Another very useful collaborative learning exercise involves exploring the syllabus for this course.

3.   The Syllabus Assignment. With a partner from your small group or team, explore the syllabus for this class. Create a short exam that will show your mastery of the syllabus contents. Share your exam ideas with the other team(s) in your small group and combine the best ideas into one exam. Then trade exams with another group in the class. Using the open-book concept and a time limit of three to five minutes, take the exam that

another team has created. Did you pass? Could you pass a similar exam using the syllabus from each of your classes this term?

4.   After the students complete Learning Portfolio Self-Assessment 2, "Sensory Preference Inventory", divide the class into three groups based on their dominant sensory learning styles (auditory, visual, and tactile). Have each group discuss and present the different memory and study strategies that work best for that learning style, in addition to a summary of the advantages and disadvantages.

5.   After completing the three self-assessments in the textbook relating to learning styles, have the students come up with some suggestions to improve their learning based on all the recommendations listed in the text. Have them discuss if there are similarities and differences between the three assessments, and if the characteristics and suggestions of the learning styles are consistent with one another. Let the students develop their own individual learning style strategies and challenge them to try out the new techniques over the next two weeks. They can then write a journal about their experiences.

VI. ALTERNATIVE TEACHING STRATEGIES _____

Some orientation instructors have established shadowing exercises for their students. In such an exercise, the student shadows (or follows) an instructor through a working day, observing and recording events and activities and then reporting on those activities to the class. For students who are considering college teaching as a career, this exercise can be a very revealing one!

Another alternative teaching strategy involves mentoring or tutoring an elementary school student or junior high school student whose learning style is quite different from that of the mentor. Researching strategies to help the younger student is a significant project that may evolve into a term paper or significant case study paper.

Provide the students with an opportunity to perceive the classroom through the teacher's eyes by having them make a presentation on different parts of the chapters. Discuss the teaching styles they use and how it relates to the different learning styles. Did the students teach in a manner consistent with their own learning style? Did they use a variety of teaching techniques to reach all the students? Have them discuss the experience through a journal.

After completing the MBTI, have the students visit the Career Resource Center or a career counselor to explore different careers and majors that are best suited to them. Students can then write a report on the strengths and weaknesses of their personality type.

VII. LEARNING PORTFOLIO _____

1.   **Your Journal**
Use the journal activity, "Everything I Need to Know I Plan to Learn in College" as a discussion topic for small group interaction. After small groups have had an opportunity to come up with a list of "10 simple truths", compare answers among groups. What "truths" are held in common?

The journal activity, "Connect with a Special Teacher", is an extremely effective exercise for freshman students. Interviewing a teacher, while a frightening experience for some freshmen, may be one of the most productive assignments they do this term. Some helpful hints include:

- giving students a written guide for the interview
- reviewing the importance of scheduling the interview in advance
- expanding the list of questions so that shy students have ample materials from which to form their interview queries
- discussing some common courtesies such as removing baseball caps during the interview, leaving headphones and tape sets at home, being on time, and refraining from asking questions about the instructor's personal life.
- discussing the importance of writing or e-mailing a note of thanks following the interview
- giving specific instructions for the follow-up report: Will it be written? If so, how many words and in what format? Or will it be an oral report to the class or small group?

2.   Self-Assessments

Ask students to complete Self-Assessment 1 on page 114 before the next class meeting. What did they learn about their intelligence profile? How does this reflect their current course preferences and past academic experiences? How might it impact future academic decisions and what are some pros and cons of this?

VIII. CHAPTER QUIZ SUGGESTIONS_____

1.   Use the Review Questions as a short-answer quiz. Points may be assigned equally at 25 points per question or divided unequally depending on the amount of class time and assignments devoted to each area. In short-answer quizzes, complete sentences are not always necessary as long as the essential points of the answer are present.

2.   Especially in this chapter, construct a quiz using the syllabus designed for this class. Instructors who have experimented successfully with this model have given a timed quiz (with quiz time dependent on the length of the quiz and the length of the syllabus). Allow students to use the syllabus to find the answers, but assume that they know the syllabus well enough to use it quickly. Sample questions for the syllabus quiz include:

- What is the attendance policy?
- What is the date of the first scheduled quiz or exam?
- What are the instructor's office hours (days/times)?
- Is there a final exam? If so, when and where will it be?
- What is the policy for late assignments?
- Where is the instructor's office located (building/room number)?
- What is the grading scale?

Instructors may also prefer to assign this quiz in teams of two students, again with a short time given for accurate responses.

IX. QUIZ _____

Multiple Choice. Choose the one best answer.

1. Studying the minimum of what needs to be learned is called
   A. surface learning.
   B. superficial learning.
   C. skim learning.
   D. laziness.
   E. basic learning.

2. An instructor who runs his/her class in a highly structured way and who expects students to take careful notes is known as a(n)
   A. student-centered teacher.
   B. concept-centered teacher.
   C. content-centered teacher.
   D. concrete-centered teacher.
   E. instruction-centered teacher.

3. Which one of these is *not* an intelligence cluster, or domain:
   A. Technical abilities.
   B. Verbal-linguistic skills.
   C. Logical-mathematical skills.
   D. Musical abilities.
   E. Spatial skills.

4. Which is *not* a type of experiental learning preference?
   A. Learning by doing.
   B. Learning by practicing.
     F. C. Learning by critical thinking.
   D. Learning by reflecting.
   E. Learning by creative thinking.

5. The first thing you should do if you are upset by an instructor's conduct is
   A. talk to him or her directly.
   B. talk to the dean of his or her department.
   C. have your parents talk with the instructor and/or dean.
   D. nothing – instructors are the authority in class and you have no right to debate any issues related to class.
   E. drop out of the class; it is not likely to get any better.

True or False

6. _____The notion of "learning by doing" is one of Howard Gardner's domains in his theory of multiple intelligence.

7. _____Critical thinkers are usually more successful than creative thinkers.

8. _____The Family Right to Privacy Act (FERPA) ensures that how you do in your classes will remain a private matter.

9. _____Auditory learners may not need to actually take notes in order to learn from listening.

10. _____If you go to a large school, it is not really possible to get acquainted with your instructors.

ANSWERS

1. **A**   2. **C**   3. **A**   4. **B**   5. **A**   6. **F**   7. **F**   8. **T**   9. **T**   10. **F**

X. TEST QUESTIONS_____

Multiple Choice. Choose the one best answer.

1. Howard Gardner proposed a theory of
    A. multiple learning styles.
    B. multiple attitudes.
    C. multiple intelligences.
    D. multiple senses.

2. According to Howard Gardner's theory, abilities appear to cluster in _____ different areas.
    A. 3
    B. 5
    C. 8
    D. 10

3. The mnemonic OCEAN refers to the following basic personality dimensions:
    A. Open to experience, Conscientiousness, Extraversion, Agreeableness, Neuroticism
    B. Optimistic, Cognitive, Extraversion, Aptitude, Neutrality.
    C. Open to experience, Cognitive, Energetic, Attentiveness, Neutrality
    D. Optimistic, Conscientiousness, Enthusiasm, Assessment, Neutrality

4. Auditory, visual, and kinesthetic learning are
    A. different learning styles.

66

B. examples of sensory preferences.
C. Neither of the above.
D. Both A and B.

5. _____ students prefer concepts and theories, and
_____ students prefer emotion to logic.
   A. Extroverted, sensing
   B. Intuiting, feeling
   C. Thinking, perceiving
   D. Judging, intuitive

6. Surface learners
   A. rely primarily on rote memorization.
   B. tend to be motivated by grades.
   C. are less likely to be successful in class.
   D. All of the above.

7. The following is a description of a(n)_____.

Sets goals of truly understanding the course ideas; actively constructs learning experience; enjoys the process of learning for its own sake; uses more thinking skills; and remembers things for a longer period of time.

   A. visuo-spatial learner
   B. auditory-sensory learner
   C. older student
   D. deep learner

True or False

8. _____Your personality influences how effectively you learn.

9. _____If you aren't sure about how something works at your university, your best bet is to ask a friend or another student because they'll tell it like it really is.

10. _____Your learning style should have an influence on which career you pursue, and thus your related major.

   Essay Questions

   1. Discuss the personality types delineated by the Myers-Briggs Type Inventory. What are the characteristics of each and how might this knowledge direct a student toward a particular major?

   2. Describe some things that you can do in order to become a distinctive student.

3. What do you think Robert Bjork means by suggesting that it is not a good idea to pursue only learning contexts that are a good match for your learning style?

ANSWERS

1. **C** 2. **C** 3. **A** 4. **D** 5. **B** 6. **D** 7. **D** 8. **T** 9. **F** 10. **T**

XI. MENTOR'S CORNER _____

Dr. Tonnie L. Renfro has been teaching a college success course for the last six years. For the last three, she has been teaching at Spencerian College in Louisville, Kentucky. She believes that Critical Thinking and Learning Styles are two areas for which she has developed numerous techniques to enhance student involvement and understanding.

   In particular, she has students keep journals and complete various writing assignments. One assignment that students get emotional about is "The Bomb Shelter." The class is divided into several groups and each group has a scenario where they select individuals to be put out of the bomb shelter in order to survive. There are additional group activities that students participate in during the sections on Learning Styles. After they discover each student's learning style, they are then paired together based on opposites. These teams work together on various projects throughout the remainder of the course. They do many group activities to encourage critical thinking and to adapt to other's learning styles. For more information, contact Dr. Tonnie L. Renfro at TRenfro@Spencerian.edu.

CHAPTER 5

EXPAND YOUR THINKING SKILLS

I. CHAPTER OVERVIEW _____

College freshmen often learn rather quickly the different demands on their thinking made by college. They might recognize that more reading and better study habits will be required, but understanding that their mode of thinking needs to be refined is a new concept. For nearly their entire high school career, most students were limited in how they could mentally approach material – often being expected to take what instructors said without question or analysis. Suddenly they find themselves being asked their personal opinion on issues, and it can be a jarring new expectation. This chapter begins by highlighting how college courses expand one's knowledge and learning beyond simply providing facts, figures, and theories. Rather, they begin to stimulate one's thought processes like never before, and promote better thinking.

It is imperative that students learn to become critical thinkers as quickly as possible. The sooner they learn to open their minds, consider different points of view, tap into creativity, and think outside the box, the more beneficial and satisfying their college experience will be. Go over the comparison list between the three types of thinkers on page 123 of the textbook. Have them look for examples within themselves, as well as identifying the areas in their current classes which call for, and will benefit them through, critical thinking. Provide them with opportunities to question and criticize information in order to get used to the process. Demonstrating how this can heighten their perceptiveness and thinking processes will prompt them to become more active students.

Students may find that they enjoy the chance to argue with professors and classmates over ideas and issues. This book provides all of the basics for helping them recognize how to put together a successful argument. Focus on helping them develop their awareness as to how to attend to the proper cues in others' reasoning, whether or not to accept a claim, and how to logically evaluate those put forth by others and themselves.

Solving problems is also not something that one happens upon through luck or mere perseverance. There are systematic approaches to take which fundamentally involve evaluating potential outcomes and their consequences. Students will need to hone their observational skills, learn strategic approaches to problem solving, as well as understand the need for persistence and attention to detail. This section offers another good opportunity for students to assess their learning styles and most likely method of problem solving. They will have to recognize elements of the process that may challenge them due to how they work with information best, and subsequently learn to adapt the necessary steps to fit with their style.

The concept of mindfulness is often new to students, yet can be a very interesting and motivating idea. Students who keep a journal can use it to record their moments of mindfulness, and assess how they are incorporating it into their daily lives. You may even want to take your class for a walk, or meet someplace different, and have students practice mindfulness. Follow up their experience with a class discussion. Does the effectiveness of mindfulness vary depending on learning style? Do students who resist the notion have particular difficulties in areas of critical thinking, reasoning, or problem solving?

Decision making is common to all students, who have probably recently experienced making an important decision in their choice of school and living arrangements. Remind students of the role their values will play, in conjunction with their various thinking strategies, in decision making situations. Have them take an honest look at any personal biases they may have, and the role those perceptions have played in recent decisions they have made. College is a time of constant decision-making, often with potentially big consequences: becoming involved in extracurricular activities, what major to pursue, to experiment with drugs and alcohol, and enter into intimate relationships. Make the most of this critical section.

Last but not least, this chapter highlights the issue of creativity. Students are often surprised to learn that they can, in fact, increase their creative ability. Ending the unit examining the concept of "flow" offers a very positive way for students to consider their thinking abilities and what they can do when they put their mind to it.

II. IMAGES OF COLLEGE SUCCESS

Ann Swift epitomizes both critical and creative thinking at it's best and most practical. First, she develops an idea to solve the problem of commuting with her computer. To implement it, she decides to approach it on a larger scale – filing for a patent in order to bring the idea to others. During this process, a new problem arises – someone has beat her to it. From this problem, Ann gets creative and develops an organization to help others avoid such problems. Not only is this "creation" a tremendous success, but Ann continues to employ her strength of critical and creative thought through pursuing an advanced degree in decision science and share her experiences by consulting as a motivational speaker.

Have your students reflect on a time when they faced – and solved – a significant problem in their life. If they have difficulty coming up with a "problem", suggest it can be something like deciding where to go to college, what to major in, whether to go home or stay on campus for an upcoming weekend or holiday, etc. Ask them to identify elements of their thought process that illustrate critical thinking, and elements that reflect they were thinking creatively. While they may not be familiar with terminology from the chapter yet, see if they have a basic understanding of the concepts behind both powerful kinds of thinking – even if they just draw on the experiences and decisions of Ann Swift.

III. CLASS ACTIVITIES

Break The Ice!

1. Critical Thinking Across Disciplines
If you have not used a professor panel up to this point in the term, the topic of critical thinking skills is a good one for professors to address with your class. Invite three or four professors from different disciplines to talk with your students about critical thinking. Ask each panel member to define "critical thinking" with respect to their

particular academic discipline. How does each professor expect students to demonstrate higher order thinking skills on assignments or exams? Ask the panel members to concentrate on Bloom's highest level, evaluation. What pitfalls might occur as a result of inadequate preparation and practice in the lower level thinking skills when evaluation is expected? Encourage panel members to share their favorite critical thinking "warm-up" exercises with your students.

2. **Bloom's Taxonomy**

Give each small group a sheet of transparency paper and several non-permanent transparency pens. Ask each group to illustrate Bloom's taxonomy in a way that will remind others in the class how to recall each level in order. The instructions should include an admonition to be as creative as possible. Then show the transparencies and ask students to critique each one. Are they effective reminders of the taxonomy, particularly with regard to correct order of thinking skills? Did color play a significant part in any of the creations? Does each group's transparency relate to the individual learning styles within the group? Keep the transparencies and refer to them visually during the discussion of this chapter. As you conclude chapter discussions and exercises, return the transparencies to each group along with a clean transparency page and ask if they want to revise their original work. If so, keep the original version and compare it to the revision. Is the revised version more effective in helping students recall Bloom's taxonomy? Why or why not? Make the point that often even the most creative ideas get better when the creators allow them to simmer and then undergo an editing process.

Discussion and Reflection

1. **Critical Thinking in the Workplace**

Extend the professor panel idea by inviting several corporate employees to talk with your class about critical thinking skills required in their daily work routines. What kinds of problems must they solve? Does the employer provide specific training in problem-solving that is unique to that particular workplace? What problem-solving techniques did each of these employees learn while in college that transferred to the workplace? Are creative solutions to problems encouraged in the workplace? If so, how is this encouragement rewarded? Are problem-solving teams engaged in the workplace? What strategies are used by teams to discover effective solutions?

2. **Critical Thinking and Your Job Search**

If your campus has a career planning or career services office that schedules on-campus interviews for graduating students or for summer interns/apprentices, ask a career services officer to bring examples of critical thinking problems that are often used by interviewers as a way to test the critical thinking abilities of prospective employees. Experienced orientation instructors often compile collections of brain teasers, word-puzzles, or picture puzzles with which to challenge their students periodically. Add interviewers' critical thinking questions to your own collection for future reference.

1.   Quotes for Discussion
        Present students with this quote by John F. Kennedy: "Too often we . . . enjoy the comfort of opinion without the discomfort of thought." Through this and the quotes presented in the chapter, help your students explore reasons why both critical and creative thinking are hallmarks of human aspiration, motivation, and achievement.
        Think about the phrase "enjoy the comfort of opinion". Illustrate this phrase with specific examples in small groups and then share the examples with the class. Focus on the words "comfort of opinion" with regard to the definition of opinion stated above. Why would thinking be discomforting? John Kennedy was a politician who became President of the United States. How do politicians enjoy the comfort of opinion? Why would critical thinking be discomforting or uncomfortable for political leaders? What role does political compromise play in critical thinking processes? What factual evidence is offered by present-day political leaders on the legislative goals and policies they often state as opinions?

2.   Words and Thoughts.
        Have students read through the quotes in the chapter – and others – and identify the elements that relate to the three different kinds of thinkers identified by Potter. Discuss their perceptions of people who truly *think* about things and those that skate by on the words and thoughts of others. Do they feel more compelled now to engage information to a greater extent rather than accept it passively?

3.   Quotes and You
        What is opinion? Ask your students to define the word from their everyday usage. List some of the definitions on the chalkboard or overhead transparency. A definition specifically related to the use of the word in this quotation is that opinion is a confident belief not validated by proof. Spend a few minutes talking about instances in which students encountered someone who held a confident belief that was not validated by proof. "Because I said so." Did any of your students hear this statement from their teachers, advisors, or parents? Other than in regard to rules of safety, in what circumstances might the phrase "because I said so" apply to opinion? How could some of these opinions be substantiated with proof?
        Read Charlotte Perkins Gilman's quote: "To swallow and follow, whether old doctrine or new propaganda, is a weakness still dominating the human mind." Do students ever "swallow and follow" against their will? What about when they are at a party; do they ever behave in a certain way to please the group (ie: peer pressure)? Is it ever *good* to follow other people? Discuss.

Major Themes

1.   Observation Exercise
        Create an observation exercise outside the classroom. Be very precise and specific in your instructions and reflect on the facts collected during the exercise. Compare answers when students return to the classroom. Do the facts recorded during

the exercise depend upon the observer's perspective? What does this exercise reveal about learning styles and preferences? As students share their answers, let each group share one fact at a time, taking turns, until all lists have been exhausted. The following is an example of an observation exercise that elicited a healthy discussion of the powers of careful observation in obtaining foundational facts for drawing inferences.

1. Your small group has 10 minutes in which to complete this entire exercise, including travel time. You may find it helpful to elect one person as a recorder of information, one as a timekeeper, and one as a reporter for the class discussion which will follow.

2. Leave the classroom through the main exit door. Turn right and exit the building through the double entry doors. Go down the outer steps and turn right.

3. Follow the sidewalk past the adjacent building and turn right on the diagonal sidewalk on the north side of Monet Hall. Continue on the diagonal sidewalk, bearing left, until you arrive at the entry to the Fisher Garden.

4. Using your powers of observation, record as many facts about the garden area as possible in the time remaining. Do not leave the garden boundaries. Remember that you must return to class and be ready to report your findings exactly ten minutes after you exited the room. Do not share your findings with other groups.

Adapt the exercise to your own campus area, selecting an interesting site that is close to your classroom. What did your students learn from this observation? It is quite likely that each group will have observed different things. If these observations are accurate, how does each observed fact fit into the description of the site as a whole? Do all the facts complement each other?

After all the observations have been voiced, look at Bloom's taxonomy and talk about this exercise on higher thinking levels. Why is this particular site important on your campus? Is it a pleasing aesthetic experience? Why would this kind of experience be important on a college campus? Does the site commemorate a particular event or significant person in the history of your institution? Why is it important to remember this event or person?

2.   **Cartoons and Creativity**
Consider the cartoons sprinkled throughout *Your Guide to College Success.* Humor can often break down resistance to creative ideas. How do the cartoons in other chapters contribute to creative ideas about the chapter topics? Do they help students see chapter content in a unique way? Can they help break tension in class discussions?

3.   **Surprise!—For Creativity**
Csikszentmilhalyi's ideas on creativity include remembering surprises. What were the surprises in your students' lives since they began college classes? Share some of these with the class, noting those that were unpleasant or fearful as well as the pleasant ones that cheered the overall experience of starting college. Note that things that surprise

some students are considered routine by others. What advice would your students give to next year's class about avoiding unpleasant surprises?

4.   Solve It!
Have students identify a couple of problems or challenges that they are currently facing. For each one, have them ask – and answer – Ann Swift's "The Five Questions" in order to help them develop a solution to their problem. Follow the exercise with a discussion about this approach to problem solving. Did they find it helpful? How does it prompt critical and/or creative thinking? Did they view the problem in a different light once they begin to think about it from this perspective? Which questions lead to the greatest insight or prompted the most critical and creative thought? Do students have their own additional questions they ask when problem solving?

5.   Holistic Thinking
Langer suggests that students practice mindfulness by creating new categories among other possibilities. Borrow an exercise from early childhood math teachers to help your students re-think categorization. Collect small container lids of all sizes, colors, and shapes. It doesn't take long in an average American kitchen to save enough lids to make a plastic baggie full of them for each small group in your class. Give a baggie of lids to each group and ask the group to sort the lids in at least three different ways. Be sure that each baggie contains several lids that are identical. Award extra points to the group that sorts their lids in ways not discovered by the other groups. Explain to students that even this simple game can stretch their creative powers of redefining categories in new, unusual, and often very productive ways.

Summary Projects

1.   Analyze the exams in all your courses this semester according to Bloom's taxonomy. What thinking levels are required on the exams in each course? How do these levels compare from exam to exam within the same course, and how do levels compare from course to course? Which classes demand the highest levels of responses according to Bloom's taxonomy? Speculate why this is so. Be sure to include the exact wording of exam questions as you present your analysis.

2.   Some recent research has questioned theories about right- and left-brain thinking. Compile sources from the last two years that tend to dispute or support theories relating to right- and left-brain learning. Make a thorough study of these resources, compare the findings, and evaluate the results. How might this current research affect the way you are learning to think creatively, critically, and holistically? What strategies are suggested by this recent research that might have a significant impact on the way you are learning to think?

IV. CAMPUS CONNECTIONS AND RESOURCES _____

Thinkers' Clubs. What are the clubs and organizations on your campus that encourage critical or creative thinking? Review a list of approved campus organizations with your students and interview club leaders to determine which ones are purely social, which are oriented toward career exploration, and which are academically challenging. For instance, is there a chess club on campus? How does one join? What other clubs welcome students who want to practice critical or creative thinking processes?

College Bowl-Type Teams. Competitive teams for various academic games are often available to entering students upon application or interview. Residence hall teams for games such as Jeopardy or Trivial Pursuit often provide outlets for students who enjoy combining the social activities of games with mental exercises. Ask a student team to investigate opportunities for such interaction in residence halls and report their findings to the class.

Debate Club. Many campuses have debate teams or clubs where students set up debates to argue and counter-argue a variety of topics. Have your students either join the Debate Club or at least attend a debate on campus. This will be a great opportunity to view critical thinking at its best. Have them turn in a report on how the arguments presented related to the suggestions and techniques listed in the text book.

Critical Thinking Speaker. Many colleges and universities have a course in critical or logical thinking. Invite the professor to speak to your class about the steps of critical thinking. Discuss the advantages of critical thinking and how they apply to school, work, relationships, and life in general.

V. COLLABORATIVE LEARNING SUGGESTIONS _____

Community Service Project. As a class community service project, collaborate with a nearby elementary or middle school teacher and offer tutoring in reading, writing, and/or math. Assign pairs of students to an elementary or middle school student who would like assistance in learning how to work at a higher level. Plan a regular schedule so that your student pairs have at least one hour per week with the student to whom they are assigned. This association is ideal if it can be made in person; however, e-mail is a possibility for some elementary and middle schools that are equipped with the technology.

The cooperating teacher should talk with your students about specific objectives for this venture and should explain the expectations and limitations that affect your students. An exchange of journals is a good way to start a writing tutorial. Simple math games with pattern sorting and counting materials are often helpful for remedial math work with elementary students. Reading aloud to and with younger students can be a powerful incentive for progress. As your students learn how to tutor and teach, they will discover new and creative ways to stretch their own thinking processes.

Evaluation of the project may be accomplished by construction of a portfolio that shows beginning, middle, and ending samples of a student's work. Tape recordings that sample beginning, mid-point, and final reading sessions also demonstrate progress. Self-assessment narratives, either written or oral, both by the tutors and the younger students indicate effectiveness of the endeavor.

Quote Discussion. One of the reasons that some students don't offer creative solutions to problems is that they are afraid to take the risk of failing. Students who are hesitant to propose their ideas may not realize how many times very creative people toss aside ideas that don't work before finding an appropriate answer. Marva Collins, an unusual educator in Chicago, urges her students to test all possibilities and look for different solutions that may be out of the ordinary. She says, "If you can't make a mistake, you can't make anything." Ask small discussion groups to talk for a few minutes about this statement. Is it applicable to college learning? How does this statement relate to individual creative thinking processes?

Curriculum Review. Have students bring in a copy of their curriculum guide listing all the courses required to complete their degree. If possible, group students with similar curriculums together. (For example, group them as follows: business administration, engineering, science, social science, and liberal arts). Have the students review their curriculums and discuss which courses may require a deeper level of critical thinking, reasoning skills, problem solving skills, and creative thinking. How will the required courses relate to their careers and work experiences? How can they improve their critical and creative thinking skills, and their reasoning and problem solving skills, to help them succeed?

VI. ALTERNATIVE TEACHING STRATEGIES _____

Assist your class in opening and staffing a challenge room in a study area of the library or student union. Provide chess boards, cribbage boards, Mastermind® games, Trivial Pursuit® sets, and other board games that pique curiosity and challenge students to think in different ways. Spend a class day exploring the ways that some of these popular games stretch the mind and the imagination. Give extra points to students who bring unusual and challenging games to class or to the challenge room and who will teach other students strategies for mastering the game.

A great way to assist students with thinking and problem solving is to provide them with situations in which they have to provide advice to the solutions. Set up a variety of different scenarios relating to college success, such as "Mary and her psychology instructor do not see eye to eye. Tension is rising between the two in the classroom. What should Mary do?" or "Phil is taking Spanish 101 for the second time, but he is still not getting it. What advice would your give to Phil to help him succeed?" Students can play the counselor role to help with problem solving. This activity is also a great way to review different rights and responsibilities of students and to review the resources available on campus.

Most students love to give advice to one another and most are dealing with some kind of problems in their life. In an anonymous manner, without using any names, have students describe a problem they would like assistance solving on a piece of paper and have them turn it in. Review the problems and choose ten that would make great examples and are common problems for college students. Divide the class into ten groups and have them discuss the problems using the five step IDEAL method listed in the text. Have the groups present their solutions to the class reviewing each step. This hands on approach to problem solving not only provides the students an opportunity to practice the IDEAL method, but it also helps solve some of the students' problems.

VII. LEARNING PORTFOLIO

1.   **Self-Assessments**
Have students complete their "Creative Profile" on page 145. Which questions did they find most challenging? Easiest? Have a few students read aloud their most creative responses.

2.   **Your Journal**
Have students complete the journal activity "Question a Day" on page 146. How did they feel about asking questions in class? Gather responses about concerns prior to this activity. After students have been forced to practice asking questions, were they more or less anxious? What did they learn?

VIII. CHAPTER QUIZ SUGGESTIONS

1.   Use the Review Questions as a short-answer quiz. Points may be assigned equally at 25 points per question, or points may be divided unequally depending on the amount of class time and assignments devoted to various areas of the chapter. In short-answer quizzes, complete sentences are not always necessary as long as the essential points of the answer are present.

IX. QUIZ

Multiple Choice. Choose the one best answer.

1. The use of purposeful, reasoned thinking to reach your goals is the definition of
     A. conceptual thinking.
     B. contextual thinking.
     C. critical thinking.
     D. coercive thinking.
     E. creative thinking.

2. Interpretations that you derive from processing cues in a situation are called
     A. influences.
     B. inferences.
     C. intricacies.
     D. indicators.
     E. interpreters.

3. Generalizing from specific instances to broad principles is called
   A. induction.
   B. deduction.
   C. critical thinking.
   D. argumentation.
   E. specification.

4. All of the following will help you evaluate the credibility of information you find on the Internet except:
   A. Avoiding opinions that can't be substantiated.
   B. Identifying the author and his/her level of expertise.
   C. Checking the date of information.
   D. Tracing information to its original source.
   E. Accepting what you read as true.

5. The heightened state of pleasure derived from being completely absorbed in mental and physical challenges is known as
   A. creativity.
   B. mindfulness.
   C. flow.
   D. critical thinking.
   E. All of the above.

True or False

6. _____Asking questions is an important part of thinking critically.

7. _____Deduction involves moving from general situations or rules to specific applications.

8. _____Any and all questions are welcomed by college instructors.

9. _____Creativity is hard work.

10. _____Wikipedia is a new, highly – reliable Internet resource that professors hope to see among research citations.

ANSWERS

1. **C**   2. **B**   3. **A**   4. **E**   5. **C**   6. **T**   7. **T**   8. **F**   9. **T**   10. **F**

X. TEST QUESTIONS _____

Multiple Choice. Choose the one best answer.

1. A four-part strategy that can help you decipher what kinds of questions will be successful involves questions that

A. Read the lines, React to the lines, Read between the lines, Read beyond the lines.
B. Read the lines, Repeat the lines, React to the lines, Read between the lines.
C. Read the lines, Repeat the lines, Remember the lines, Review the lines.
D. Read the lines, React to the lines, Remember the lines, Repeat the lines.

2. What makes a question *unwelcome* to an instructor is that it
    A. detracts from the momentum of the class.
    B. focuses more on a student's self-concerns rather than the needs of the class.
    C. demonstrates that the questioner has failed to pay attention.
    D. All of the above.

3. A sign of a good critical thinker is that his/her inferences are
    A. practical.
    B. potential.
    C. plausible.
    D. laudable.

4. If an argument is *valid* it is
    A. weak.
    B. false.
    C. irrelevant.
    D. true.

5. When we try to make a good decision and we entertain too many options, we are engaging in
    A. overwhelmed thinking.
    B. sprawling thinking.
    C. unfocused thinking.
    D. diffuse thinking.

6. Psychologist Mihaly Csikszentmihalyi created the concept of
    A. flow.
    B. mindfulness.
    C. IDEAL.
    D. critical thinking.

7. The letters IDEAL in the five step IDEAL method for problem solving stand for
    A. Imagine, Decide, Express, Analyze, Learn.
    B. Insight, Develop, Explore, Assess, Logic.
    C. Identify, Define, Explore, Act, Look.
    D. Investigate, Decide, Experiment, Analyze, Link.

True or False

8. _____Your own knack for critical thinking will depend on your learning style.

9. _____ Inferences can produce biases in interpretation of the events around you.

10. _____ Potter's three critical thinking styles are *information avoiders, information approachers,* and *consumers.*

Essay Questions

1. How can you tell if a claim is valid? When should you accept a claim? When should you question a claim? Provide examples.

2. Explain IDEAL. What does it stand for? What is it related to? What does it consist of?

3. Describe the various ways in which you can foster creativity. How creative are you? How could you improve your own level of creativity?

ANSWERS

1. **A**   2. **D**   3. **C**   4. **D**   5. **B**   6. **A**   7. **C**   8. **T**   9. **T**   10. **F**

XI. MENTOR'S CORNER _____

For eighteen years, **Laynah Rogers** has taught study skills at Evangel University and teaches the course not only in person but also on the Internet. She especially enjoys teaching sessions on learning styles, but other skills are imperative to a student's success in college as well. Calculating GPAs, goal setting in eight dimensions of their lives, advisor/advisee roles, identifying resources to assist students with developmental academics, and career options are other fine topics to explore!

Additionally, at Evangel, college success teachers have launched a new Degree Completion program for adults. The adults will be linked up with study skills assistance as well, so that the spreading influence of technology will be easily accessible for nontraditional students. Contact Laynah at RogersL@Evangel.edu for more information about combining study skills with technology.

CHAPTER 6

TAKE IT IN: NOTES & READING

I. CHAPTER OVERVIEW

Commit, concentrate, capture, and *connect.* This model of efficient information processing is one of the unique foundational strategies offered to students in this chapter. When students *commit, concentrate, capture,* and *connect,* they may be assured of academic mastery. Each step, followed in the exact order stated, is necessary to achieve the desired outcome. It is also noted that information should be summarized in a manner that will fit the student's learning style, making the four C's more effective. It will be well worth your time to carefully review this model, step by step, as you and your students work through individual topic areas for the remainder of the term.

How students function in the classroom is key to how successful they are at taking in information. It should be a primary focus to emphasize the importance of attending class, being prepared, and overcoming any distractions. Listening effectively is a learned skill and students should be aware that they need to approach listening in a variety of ways, based on the demands of the course and the style of the instructor.

Once students develop effective listening skills, they will be prepared to take great lecture notes. Help them discover the note taking method that fits best with their learning style, and make the connection between the style of their lecture notes and their subsequent ability to recall the information.

Often students cite that the reading demands in college far exceed anything they could have expected. It is a task they feel overwhelmed by and typically don't approach in a very productive way. A good place to start when covering the section "Take Charge of Your Reading" is the logistics of when and where they actually do their reading. If this seemingly simple element is problematic, what follows – the important aspect of learning from the reading material – is certain to be as well. Once students have a clear understanding of the best places and times to read for their own success, they can be presented with techniques for reading for different disciplines and course requirements. Most students don't realize that one size does not fit all when it comes to approaching a reading assignment. Demonstrating and having students practice the basic kinds of reading – previewing, skimming, active reading, analytic reading, and reviewing – will help them to recognize the various ways in which they can tackle reading assignments, and make the most of the time they allot for reading.

Another area in which freshmen need several good pointers is marking and/or taking notes from reading. Many have established the bad habit of highlighting *everything*, leaving no indication of what's really important. Again, marking readings, or taking notes from readings, is a learned skill. Work with your students to help them discover what methods work best for them based on their learning styles.

This chapter covers a tremendous amount of important material and numerous skills that require a good deal of practice. Remind students that information processing is one of the most important and *necessary* skills – not only for their college courses, but for their later career.

II. IMAGES OF COLLEGE SUCCESS

Condoleeza Rice is one of the most accomplished women in the world – and in many different areas. Success over a lifetime in athletics (figure skating), music (piano), languages (she speaks 5), and academics (a doctorate in political science) has undoubtedly required Rice to master numerous ways of taking in, processing, remembering, and communicating information. Her determination has driven her to discover the ways which worked for her in order to achieve success across such a vast array of disciplines, to the extent of being chosen as national security advisor to the President of the United States.

Despite her current title and career demands, Condoleeza Rice had to master each step along the way to every accomplishment. She had to be able to effectively listen and discern important information from massive amounts of reading and lecture material. She had to be able to take effective notes in order to study the information and ultimately communicate it back to instructors (or play it back musically as she was instructed). She had to be able to concentrate and productively read material from textbooks and other sources, and she had to do all of these things across the different disciplines she encountered throughout her many years of education.

Point out to students that the lessons they are learning in this chapter – and throughout this course – are fundamental to anyone's success. The basics of active listening, effective note taking, productive reading, and focused concentration have been mastered by the most accomplished people in our society. This is not just material to give them "busywork" or rhetoric enabling us to say we are trying to help them. This is real. This works. It did for Condoleeza Rice.

III. CLASS ACTIVITIES _____

Break The Ice!

1.   Taking Charge of Lectures

Assign one group to read the section "Take Charge of Lectures" on pages 151-156 before class. Do not discuss the contents with anyone, and do not take notes on your reading. Tell the next group to elect a reader; all other group members must be listeners. The reader must read this section once to the other members of the group before the next class meeting. Do not discuss the reading, and do not take notes. Tell the next group that they may not, under any circumstances, either read or discuss this section with anyone. They must, however, interview a junior or senior student on the topic of "Classroom Listening". Do not take notes either during or after the interview. Duplicate these instruction sets until all groups have an assignment. Prepare blank transparencies and a different-colored water-soluble transparency pen for each group for the next class.

When class begins: Give each group a blank transparency and pen. Allow three or four minutes for each group to summarize what they learned about the topic of "Classroom Listening". Using the transparencies, compare and contrast the answers. Was it easy to remember the content without taking notes? Note the transparencies that mentioned the four C's information processing model. Compare the information discovered by the individual reading group to the information processed by the listening group and then with the outside information from the interview group. What differences resulted? If your evaluation grade is dependent on material from reading and lecture, how valuable is word-of-mouth information from upper-class students? Might that information be tainted in some significant way? How trustworthy is someone else's memory or empirical information bank? This exercise leads into a discussion of the importance of reading material assigned <u>before</u> hearing the lecture, taking notes on the reading, and then taking notes or at least comparing notes during the lecture.

Discussion And Reflection

1. Reading Specialists

Invite a reading specialist either from your department of education or a local high school to talk about college reading strategies. Some students are learning that they read too slowly to complete all the assignments in their college classes. Others find that although they read the assignments, they don't remember core concepts well enough to discuss them either in class or in peer study groups. Ask the reading specialist to suggest resources available on campus or the Internet that will assist students in increasing reading speed and enhancing comprehension

2. Taming Tough Lectures

Review *Build Competence* "Tame That Tough Lecture" on page 154. Without divulging the names of instructors, do any fit in one of these four categories? Are there other categories of tough lectures besides the ones mentioned? Are tape recorders allowed in any of these classes? Would a lecture tape be helpful in solving some of the problems encountered during a tough lecture? How many professors give permission to tape? Why might they allow or disallow for such taping during lectures?

Words of Wisdom

1. Quotes for Discussion

Read M Scott Peck's statement on page 153 about the limits of listening. Ask students to comment on their own listening skills. Is it hard to concentrate during a 50-minute history or zoology lecture? What things distract them in class? How much of their distraction comes from other students and how much comes from their own multitasking? Ask for suggestions about learning to do nothing but listen. What does it take to hold your concentration? Is this possible to do when the lecture doesn't particularly interest you? What are some techniques that students already know about forcing themselves to concentrate? List these on the chalkboard or transparency. Are some more reasonable than others? How does the four C's model presented in this chapter relate to listening skills?

2. Quotes and You

Read George Washington Carver's quote: "There is no short cut to achievement.

Life requires thorough preparation – veneer isn't worth anything." Do your students ever feel that some people don't have to work hard, that things are just handed to them? Have they ever worked hard at something only to fail? Was that really a "failure" then? Discuss in terms of Carver's quote.

Read the quote by Angela Carter, "Reading a book is like re-writing it for yourself. You bring to a novel, anything you read, all your experience of the world. You bring your history and you read it in your own terms." Do your students agree with this quote? Is there any way to "escape the self" and become an objective reader? Also, are students influenced by the cover of a book? What about this college success text. What does the cover say to your students? Are they drawn in or turned off?

Major Themes

1. Commit to Class

Ask students to think about the commitments they made before coming to college. Which were the most serious? Were they short-term or long-term? If long-term, have these commitments changed since arriving on campus? Are some no longer applicable to the current situation?

2. Exploring Syllabi

Ask students to bring a syllabus to class for each of their courses this term and review attendance policies at your institution. Is class attendance mandatory? For all classes? For first-year students only? Does the policy change from department to department? Within a department? Are the attendance policies stated clearly on each class syllabus? What is the attendance policy for this course? If attendance is mandatory for any class, what are the penalties for absences? Are any absences excused? What documentation is required for an excused absence?

If attendance is not required, discuss the consequences of missing class. What level of commitment is demonstrated by students who miss class often? When you make arrangements to copy a friend's class notes, can you trust them? Suppose you have someone tape the lecture for you. What are the disadvantages of this solution? What are the possible consequences of being late for class? Is it possible to travel between classes in the time allotted? If one instructor consistently dismisses class late, and if this makes you late to the next class, how can you solve this problem? Talk about what might happen when employees are always late on the job. What level of commitment does this demonstrate to an employer? Talk frankly with students about the necessity of commitment, especially in regard to class attendance and being on time. What habits are being built for a workplace environment after graduation?

3. Concentrate and Listen

Ask students to discuss their personal techniques for focusing on a particular task, such as concentrating on a difficult lecture subject. What successful and creative ideas do students bring with them from their high school experiences in concentrating? What is it about certain tasks that make concentration easy? What are the possible consequences of losing your concentration?

4. Capturing Key Ideas

In small groups, ask students to compare the lecture styles of their current instructors. Have students who have taken exams or completed graded assignments at this point in the term compare their class notes with exam or assignment outcomes. Were their class notes thorough? Effective? If your grade on the exam or assignment was not what you expected, can you revise your note-taking system to improve your chances of a better grade on the next exam or assignment? Use this opportunity to compare note-taking styles among students who are taking the same course from the same professor. What differences can be observed? Did the exam or assignment grades reflect these differences? Although note-taking styles cannot totally account for grade differences, this may be a significant point in making necessary grade repairs!

5. Connect Ideas

Students who paraphrase lecture content and reading assignments are usually better prepared for essay exams than those who do not. Translating content into your own words is an important skill for all college students. Those who need practice in this skill can paraphrase content of a television or radio news broadcast from a video or audio tape. Play a taped segment in class and ask students to share their translations. Did all students capture the content? Did students connect the content to their own personal information bank? Were there any words that were unfamiliar? If so, add those words to your weekly word bank and use them when writing class notes or assignments.

6. Note-Taking Strategies

As students look at their daily planners, see if time for reviewing class notes is included each day. Research indicates that students who review their notes immediately following a class often retain more information than those who do not. Ask students to find small blocks of time in their daily schedules for note review. If there are days when this seems impossible, strategize with members of the small group to find creative ways to schedule note reviews.

A common, and costly, mistake made by many first-year students is that of failing to date each page of notes. For students whose schedules don't permit instant review, this can result in a time-consuming repair process as they contact fellow students to try to discover a logical order to a set of notes. Make an occasional random check of the notes your students take in this class. Are they dated? Are they readable? Are they focused?

7. Note-Taking Formats

Compare favorite note-taking formats among your students. Are they most familiar with outlines? The Cornell method? Do any of them use concept maps or fishbone diagrams? Is there any relationship between preferred note-taking style and preferred learning style?

8. Commit to Reading

Students who have difficulty making a commitment to academic reading may also be reluctant to read for pleasure. Even students who are excellent academic readers may be hesitant to read non-class materials for their own enjoyment. Ask students to share in small groups the name of their favorite book in kindergarten or elementary school. Why was this book a favorite? What books were favorites in middle or high school? Did most students read for pleasure in high school? Do any of your students have a favorite book in common?

9. Plan to Capture and Connect

Connect class notes and notes made during reading sessions. What are the most prominent points of connection? Talk about ways students personalize the combining of their notes on readings and class notes. Does the instructor mention the assigned readings during lecture, or are the readings intended to provide amplification for essay exams? How can students connect reading and lecture notes to what they already know? Students who are fearful about their own academic capabilities often assume that they don't know enough to make connections. Part of the job of a good orientation instructor is to assist students in building their self-confidence and in putting their prior life experience and knowledge to use in the classroom.

10. Reading Primary and Secondary Sources

Ask a professional librarian or member of a research team to visit briefly with your students and talk about the difference between primary and secondary sources. Reassure students that you aren't trying to insult their intelligence, but that you want to make sure that there is a good working definition held in common about what constitutes primary and secondary source material.

11. Reading in Different Disciplines

Invite a panel of professors who teach, respectively, literature, history, science, and math courses to address your class on effective ways within their own disciplines to read assignments, take notes on readings and lecture, prepare for exams, and, as a review of earlier materials, what behaviors are expected in their classrooms. It lends credibility to the message if each of these professors teaches entry-level students. Ask your students to take careful notes as the professors discuss these topics, and then compare notes within groups. Share the most important points made in small group discussions with the entire class.

Summary Projects

1.   Some students who have excellent word-processing skills will find it reassuring and academically advantageous to type all of their class notes each day. A simple word-processing program will allow students to reorganize notes in logical order; highlight by underlining, bolding, or using italics, and leave room for additional handwritten margin notes as the student reviews notes for later exams.

2.   Some students need to bolster self-confidence before the first set of college final exams. To this end, a complete set of typed notes for each class in a 15 credit-hour term, personalized with the student's own sketches or graphs, and annotated just prior to final exams as a review unit for each class provides necessary and reassuring support throughout a successful exam season. A final project of this size and detail may be considered appropriate for those orientation courses whose primary goal is to build and

support study skills. The commitment to such a long-term project on a daily basis will give strong reinforcement to time management plans as well.

IV. CAMPUS CONNECTIONS AND RESOURCES _____

Test Files. Ask students to locate the test file office on your campus. If such an office exists, what specific services are offered? How do students access this material? What does the student grapevine say about unauthorized test files? What are the legal concerns regarding unauthorized test files? What are the advantages and disadvantages of an approved test file service?

Tutoring Services. Is free tutoring provided? If so, in what courses? Are these services provided at more than one location? What are the hours? Where are reading tutorials offered? If free tutoring is not available, how do students find reliable tutors in different academic areas? What is the average cost of a tutoring session? How long is a normal tutoring session? Will tutors work with more than one student at a time to reduce costs? Help students understand that advertisements on campus bulletin boards for tutoring services do not guarantee that the tutor is qualified to assist students in this field. Are peer tutors available? How reliable are the peer tutors on your campus?

Reading Instructors. Many community colleges and some universities require students to complete placement tests when they are first admitted. These tests assess students' reading levels and place them accordingly. Some students may be required to complete reading improvement courses before enrolling in intensive reading college courses. Invite a reading instructor to present different reading and note-taking strategies to the students.

Disability Services. Every institution has a counselor involved in disability services. Invite the disabilities counselor to discuss learning disabilities with the class. They may present different strategies to deal with these disabilities which may assist some without disabilities. They should also discuss accommodations available to students such as permission to tape lectures, longer times to take tests, etc.

V. COLLABORATIVE LEARNING SUGGESTIONS _____

An interesting project for student teams is to interview upper-class students who are on the Dean's Honor Roll. Ask these successful students what note-taking systems they use. Do their systems vary according to the type of course? How do note-taking systems and strategies differ among beginning zoology, introductory American history, English composition, beginning chemistry, or math courses? Report findings to the class using specific examples of successful note-taking strategies suggested by the academic all-stars interviewed. Compare the strategies. Are any of them workable for first-year students?

In the class prior to reviewing the present chapter, give students the assignment to take notes from the textbook. In groups, have students share their notes with one another for comparison and review. Have them discuss the different styles of note-taking such as outline, summary, and the Cornell method. What are some ways they can improve their note-taking? Are they writing down too much or too little? Are they using abbreviations? Are they hitting on the important points and ideas? After the group discussions, pass out a copy of your text book notes to demonstrate effective note-taking.

In the beginning of class, read a few paragraphs from a text book and have students take notes as usual. Have them trade their notes with other students to critique each other's note-taking style. Have them pay attention to the method they used, to the main ideas they caught or missed, to their listening skills, and other note-taking strategies listed in the chapter. This exercise provides them the opportunity to compare their notes to others' and gives them a realistic view of their own note-taking skills.

In groups, have students discuss issues with listening such as distractions, fatigue, boredom, and stress. Have the students discuss different strategies to improve their listening skills and then share their ideas with the remainder of the class. Encourage them to try out these strategies for a week.

VI. ALTERNATIVE TEACHING STRATEGIES _____

Work with individual students to help them set realistic goals to improve listening, reading, and note-taking skills. Be aware that many students have difficulty in writing goal statements that are specific as well as realistic, and that projected dates to accomplish these goals must also be specific. Invite several students to share how they will know that they have succeeded in accomplishing their goals. Help students express success statements that are specific and measurable. Individual help at this point in the term on this particular assignment may be one of the most important intervention strategies orientation instructors can offer.

Referring to Chapter 4, have students discuss how their learning styles and preferences affect their listening, reading, and note-taking skills. Are there different strategies for managing lectures based on learning styles? What about for different types of courses? Are certain learning styles more adaptable to lectures? What are some suggestions for the instructors to help in the learning process for students with different learning styles?

Many institutions provide different types of instruction, including in-class, online, televised, live broadcasting, and independent. Discuss what types of instruction work best with students lacking in listening skills, reading skills, and note-taking skills. Discuss the advantages and disadvantages of each type of instruction. If possible, bring in an example of each type of instruction for in-class demonstration.

VII. LEARNING PORTFOLIO _____

1.   **Your Journal**
The exercise "Analyze the Sixth Sense" on page 184 was enthusiastically recommended by students who previewed *Your Guide to College Success*. Refer to the Chapter 6 section "Capture Key Ideas" as your students work through this exercise.

VIII. CHAPTER QUIZ SUGGESTIONS_____

1.   Use the Review Questions as a short-answer quiz. Points may be assigned equally at 25 points per question, or points may be divided unequally depending on the amount of class time and assignments devoted to various areas of the chapter.   In short-answer quizzes, complete sentences are not always necessary as long as the essential points of the answer are present.

IX. QUIZ _____

Multiple Choice. Choose the one best answer.

1. The four C's as discussed in this chapter include all of the following except:
    A. Commit.
    B. Capture.
    G. C. Concentrate.
    D. Clarify.
    E. Connect.

2. Normal speakers talk at a rate of about _____ words per minute, while normal listeners can process about _____ words per minute.
    A. 75, 50
    B. 150, 75
    H. C. 150, 500
    D. 500, 150
    E. 50, 25

3. _____ learners tend to have an easier time extracting information from lectures.
    A. Auditory
    I. B. Visual
    C. Tactile
    D. Sensory
    E. All types of

4. Your course textbooks are
    A. primary sources.
    B. secondary sources.
    C. ancillary sources.
    D. periodicals.
    E. fiction.

5. The term for sounding out words as you read is
    A. subreading.
    B. subreferencing.
    C. subverbalizing.

D. subvocalizing.
E. subtracting.

True or False

6. _____A concept map is a helpful tool for visual learners.

7. _____Instructors are likely to include ideas on tests that they consider to be exciting.

8. _____It is important to erase mistakes when taking notes so you don't get confused when studying.

9. _____You should always tape a lecture if you're allowed.

10. _____If you find you're having problems reading, such as re-reading the same passage over and over, you should take a break and regroup.

ANSWERS

1. **D**   2. **C**   3. **A**   4. **B**   5. **D**   6. **T**   7. **T**   8. **F**   9. **F**   10. **T**

X. TEST QUESTIONS_____

Multiple Choice. Choose the one best answer.

1. The four C's in the model for getting the most out of your college classes stand for
   A. commit, concentrate, capture, connect.
   B. convey, convince, commit, connect.
   C. communicate, convince, capture, complete.
   D. convey, convince, commit, complete.

2. The signal words *first, second, finally, while, now, and then* indicate which kind of lecture pattern of organization?
   A. Cause-Effect.
   J. B. Sequence.
   C. Cycle.
   D. Both B and C.

3. The note-taking method in which you divide your paper into 2 columns with one column being for lecture notes and the other for personal comments, questions, and examples is known as
   A. the Cornell method.
   B. the summary method.
   C. outlining.
   D. a fishbone diagram.

4. It is most important to takes notes on
    A. the lecture.
    B. films and videos.
    C. questions and comments from other students.
    D. All of the above are important sources of information.

5. Autobiographies, speeches, research reports, and government documents are all examples of
    A. primary sources.
    B. secondary sources.
    C. official sources.
    D. required sources.

6. Although it can be beneficial, one problem with highlighting your text is
    A. overdoing with too much highlighting, resulting in having to re-read almost the entire text when studying.
    B. that just highlighting doesn't tell you *why* you highlighted, thus it may be meaningless when you review.
    C. it may cause your book to be worth less when you try to sell it back after the course.
    D. All of the above are dangers of highlighting.

7. The four reading strategies described in your text are
    A. assess, plan, start, comprehend.
    B. preview, skim, read actively, read analytically.
    C. prioritize, scrutinize, read analytically, review.
    D. preview, read analytically, review, skim.

True or False

8. _____Different kinds of reading require different reading speeds.

9. _____Your textbook can be a great source of support if you have a disorganized lecturer.

10. _____Subvocalizing is an effective technique when reading college texts.

Essay Questions

1. Describe the four C's as discussed in this chapter and key aspects of each step of this approach toward more effective learning.

2. What are the patterns of academic information? Discuss ways to recognize each and how you can benefit from being aware of the lecture pattern used in your classes.

3. Present the most effective approach to highlighting, and discuss other effective means of *working with* your textbooks.

ANSWERS

1. **A**   2. **D**   3. **A**   4. **D**   5. **A**   6. **D**   7. **B**   8. **T**   9. **T**   10. **F**

XI. MENTOR'S CORNER

Tami Eggleston, an assistant professor of psychology at McKendree College in Lebanon, Illinois, has been teaching the freshman seminar course for the past 3 years. She enjoys teaching the class, working with freshman, and believes in the importance of this class.

Along with another professor, Dr. Brenda Boudreau (assistant professor of English), she created a web page for the freshman seminar class. This web page includes the syllabus, a discussion page, announcements of important dates, and a page with web links. When she teaches the note-taking and test-taking section, students get into groups and find 5 good web pages that relate to these topics. The pages that the students find are then included in the links page on her website. Students could also find web pages about other important topics such as stress management, money management, health issues, etc. This web page links assignments, lets students find information, learn to evaluate web pages, and also encourages them to get onto the campus computer system early in the semester.

Tami and Dr. Boudreau also include diversity and community as a theme. Early in the semester they show the movie "Higher Learning" as an evening program for an entire week so students can select a night to watch the film. After the viewing, the class discusses issues such as race, class, gender, date rape, alcohol, and other important issues related to campus life. Tami says, "Many students enjoyed this movie night and it was a good way to begin a dialogue on difficult issues."

At McKendree, a small, liberal arts college, the freshman seminar class is very small (an average of 12 students). This allows Tami to do some activities that larger classes may not be able to do. At the end of the semester, most of the professors in the program have the students come to their homes for the final class session. After a semester of getting to know each other, she finds that it is important to take a little time to say good-bye. This could be done with a party at school, but most students seem to really appreciate the personal touch of coming to a professor's home. Tami says, "Personally, I know the students enjoy coming to my home, having pizza, playing games, and meeting my dog. Since I am not only their freshman seminar instructor, but also their freshman advisor, I think it makes the relationship with them even stronger."

Tami encourages new teachers to get in touch with her about web pages or how to engage students in the course. You can call her at: 618-537-6859 or e-mail her at: tegglest@atlas.mckendree.edu.

Pamela Anderson-Mejias does not teach a "college success" class per se, but rather she is involved with the "language of success," especially as it relates to non-traditional students. At the University of Texas—Pan American, she teaches courses in Language and Culture, linguistics, and she also trains ESL/EFL teachers both on campus and through their distance education center. She also trains teachers in curriculum design for language learners, including developmental readers and writers, freshman writers, etc. Because she has practice working with "remedial" readers, please contact Pamela with questions about teaching this chapter. Her e-mail address is: pandersonmejias@hotmail.com.

CHAPTER 7

ENHANCE YOUR STUDY SKILLS AND MEMORY

I. CHAPTER OVERVIEW

Studying gets a bad rap. Just the thought of having to do it puts most students off. They would rather do just about *anything* than sit down and study. This chapter is so important because it addresses the issues fundamental to effective studying, helping students recognize the active effort required to be productive and have their studying pay off. The first important point to be made is that studying has benefits more far reaching than simply helping them get good grades.

It is important for students to realize that the where's and how's of settling in with their notes is critical for success. The timing of studying is also relevant – have students take an honest look at the times of day they think the most clearly and are most in tune with their school work. They should also set goals for what they want to achieve during the time spent studying so that they are focused and productive.

Understanding the workings of memory is significant to making the most of study efforts. Learning the difference between short-term and long-term memory, how one encodes, retains, and recalls information, as well as what can disrupt their functioning will help students adopt more effective approaches to studying. Memorizing has a place in college learning, and students need to be aware of what that place is – and what it is not. Deeper learning is required for much of the information they must retain in college, and certain types of exams require a more in-depth *knowledge* and *understanding* of the material. Work to demonstrate the difference in effectiveness between deep and surface learning for your students, and they will be on the right track to better learning through studying. Bloom's taxonomy also offers a good paradigm for clarifying study techniques and outcomes.

As with reading, the demands of studying vary across disciplines. Since all students must take core courses which cover a wide variety of different kinds of informational learning, it is important to highlight these differences and introduce tips on how to approach each. It also offers another opportunity to emphasize the role of individual learning styles in a very practical manner.

Learning disabilities (or learning *differences)* impact a much higher proportion of the population than most students realize. In fact, people with learning disabilities have been found in all countries of the world. Many learning-challenged freshmen come to college not knowing how to work with their different ways of processing information. Introduce your school's resources to students and assure them that making use of special assistance is in no way problematic for their instructors or their degree. This book also presents some compensating strategies for minimizing the effects of some learning differences.

Study groups may be viewed by students as insignificant, and a means of socializing under the guise of studying. However, when organized and carried out correctly, study groups can be one of the most effective tools for learning. Help students understand the necessary elements to a successful study group, and encourage them to make this a regular part of their study routine.

II. IMAGES OF COLLEGE SUCCESS

This profile of Janeane Garofalo demonstrates the wide variety of ways that strong study skills and memory techniques can positively influence one's career – any career! Consider asking students to brainstorm aloud about different ways that strong study skills and memory techniques can benefit them now and in the future. Have them identify the ways in which these skills are necessary for Janeane to be successful as a comedienne (it's not just memorizing material, but understanding and staying current with the latest world events, fads, people, and being able to employ higher-order thinking in order to create prudent observations that can be presented in a humorous way.) This also demonstrates to students that a successful college career doesn't just lead to "boring" office jobs, but a limitless array of opportunities.

III. CLASS ACTIVITIES

Break The Ice!

1. Focus on Good Study Habits

In small groups, ask students to spend four minutes creating a master list of study habits sure to result in excellent grades for first-year students this term. Give each group a blank transparency page on which to transcribe their lists. Remind them that new leaders, writers, and reporters should be elected periodically. When time has elapsed, compare the lists to find points in common. Provide a few minutes to debate any parts of the lists that appear to be inappropriate or unnecessary. If essentials are missing from all lists, suggest that students do a quick preview of the chapter, revise their lists if necessary, and then compare again.

2. General Education Courses

Why are your students required to take general education courses? Study habits are often quite different among the vast area of general education courses. Why should a student be required to learn how to study topics that hold no particular interest for that student? Since this chapter helps students explore study skills appropriate to different academic disciplines, this is a good time to think about the value of a liberal arts education. Some required general education classes may be difficult for students whose primary intelligence areas lie in math and/or the natural sciences. One instructor invited the Dean of the College of Arts and Sciences to speak to his class on the value of a liberal arts education for all students.

During the question and answer portion of the presentation, several students were surprised to hear the Dean advise that since general education courses were required here, this particular institution might not have been the best choice for all students in the class. However, her next statement was that students who discovered that their abilities and interests did not match this college usually needed good grades in order to transfer to another institution. The Dean said that part of her job was to help ensure that students were academically successful so that they would continue to control their own academic options. Healthy grades ensure that students, rather than the institution or the Dean, control their own options. The discipline necessary to achieve good grades comes from learning how to study, regardless of the topic. Students reported that this presentation stirred their imaginations and helped them understand the importance of learning lifelong study habits.

Discussion and Reflection

1.   Making the Grade

This simple math exercise demonstrates to students the difficulties that are encountered when poor study habits lead to poor term grades. Ask members of small groups to work together to answer the questions posed by the following scenario.

Sally enrolled in 14 credit hours for her first college term. She worked at an off-campus job 15 hours weekly and was elected residence hall secretary. She went home every weekend to see her boyfriend and two of her best friends who did not go to college this term. Her course load was not considered difficult, so she scheduled only two hours daily to read assignments, review notes, and attend study group meetings. She usually stayed up all night to cram before major exams and didn't get much sleep during final exam week. Her term grades were:

English Composition I	3 credits	B
Beginning Math	3 credits	D
Orientation Class	2 credits	B
American History	3 credits	F
Beginning Psychology	3 credits	C

Review the formula for figuring grade averages. Although this is a simple process, some students are misinformed about details. For instance, do grades of F or D count when figuring grade point averages? If the institution has a repeat policy, be sure that this is also considered.

Figure Sally's grade point average. Note the following college policies:

- Students who make between 1.99 and 1.70 are placed on <u>academic notice</u> and enroll for the next term only with the understanding that the total GPA at the end of the second term must be at least 2.0
- Students who make between 1.50 and 1.69 are placed on <u>academic probation</u> and may continue for the next term only by repeating the courses in which they made D or F grades, receiving no grade less than C in the second term, <u>and</u> bringing the total GPA up to a minimum 2.0
- Students who make less than 1.50 are <u>suspended</u> for at least one term and considered for readmission only after completing a term at another college in which 12 hours of credit are earned with a minimum 2.5 GPA.

Into which category was Sally placed at the end of the first term? She pre-enrolled for next term in the following courses:

English Composition II	3 credits
Political Science I	3 credits
Math II	3 credits
Introduction to Zoology	5 credits

What grades will Sally have to make in these courses to remedy her current grade situation? Remember, her first and second term grades must average 2.0. What changes will she have to make to succeed? What advice would you give her about how to become a successful student?

Sally's major is English literature. She plans to apply to law school after graduation and understands that she will be considered only if she has at least a 3.25 grade average for all undergraduate courses. What grades will Sally have to make to have a 3.25 at the beginning of her senior year when law school applications are due?

The purpose of this exercise is to demonstrate how long and what kind of grades it takes to make up for a disastrous first term. Poor study habits in high school can easily translate into poor first-term grades in college. Many entering college students state on new student surveys that they studied less than 10 hours per week in high school and expect to study the same amount in college to receive the same 3.25 grade average. Reality has to set in soon for these students!

2.   Chunking Time
Ask students to bring their daily planners to class. After filling in all class times, work times, and other regular obligation times, what is left for study time? Are there large chunks of time? 15 minutes or less between classes? Ask small groups to work together to make reasonable study plans for each person's schedule. Of course, plans will have to be individualized to account for the particular way students need to study for specific classes, but what things may be studied or reviewed in 10-15 minutes chunks? Language vocabulary, math formulas, scientific terms and their definitions, rough drafts for a large end-of-term paper? What other ideas can your small groups contribute? What things will need extended time to study? Is it possible to study for too long at one time?

Words of Wisdom

1.   Quotes for Discussion
Share with your student the quote by Miguel de Cervantes: "For a man to attain an eminent degree in learning costs him time, watching, hunger, nakedness, dizziness in the head, weakness in the stomach, and other inconveniences." Oh, so learning is uncomfortable then? Is that what the quote is saying? Why is learning uncomfortable? What does Cervantes mean by *nakedness*? Have your students ever felt vulnerable when they have tried to learn something new? Have students share these experiences.

Indira Gandhi said, "My grandfather once told me that there are two kinds of people: those who work and those who take the credit. He told me to try to be in the first group; there was less competition there." Ask your students to comment. Has being studious lost its respect? Do they find more students are proud of finding ways to succeed with very little effort? How might this impact the decision to cheat? Also, do students report feeling pleased when they do well in a class that they labeled as easy? Would they prefer to have all "easy" classes so as to cruise through college having to invest less time and hard work? Do they have any sense of intrinsic satisfaction when they master difficult assignments or exams? Or do they just complain that it is too hard and a pain in the neck to deal with? Explore this in relation to the value they place on being educated and what earning a degree really means to them.

Major Themes

1.   **Alumni from the Business World**

Invite an alum from your college who is employed at a successful business in your community to talk about the kind of personal study necessary to keep current or advance in the business world. Ask the speaker to talk about the kinds of study encountered in that particular business. Are there reference manuals for new equipment that must be mastered? Is one required to read and learn company policy manuals on hiring, business etiquette, or standard presentation formats? How do professionals in this particular business field learn new information? What kind of professional development opportunities are offered? Is successful completion of an additional course of study required for promotion in the workplace? Are periodic exams or tests a normal part of keeping up? If professional licensing requirements must be completed following graduation, how do graduates prepare for board or certification exams while working at a full-time job? What study habits must be acquired in college that will make these tasks easier?

Certified public accountants, workers in medical professions, teachers, attorneys, architects, and others who are required to either update credentials on a regular basis or pass exams before professional status is granted are good candidates to speak with your first-year students about the importance of establishing good life-long study habits at the very beginning of their college careers.

2.   **Location, Location, Location!**

Great study habits include finding the right conditions in which to employ them. If the chapters are studied in sequence, your students will have been in class for a while by now. Have students individual create lists of the best places *besides their dorm* to study – on campus or off. They should be able to illustrate how their choices reflect the elements for ideal study places described in the textbook. Student can then share their favorite spots – those they've tried and use the most with their classmates.

3.   **Studying in High School**

When did your students study during high school? What *regular* study habits did they bring to college? Use the Chunking Time concept in this chapter to work individually with students to discover bits of time in their schedules in which to review class notes both immediately before and after class. Is this possible for all students?

4.   Bloom Where You Are Planted
        Have students bring in their syllabi from other courses and look through the content covered, the various assignments, and exam formats. Can they identify the levels of processing specified in Bloom's Taxonomy? Are they able to recognize in which areas they will need to employ higher-order thinking skills, and which ones may only require lower-order thinking? Have them try to specifically label various aspects of each class with each of Bloom's levels, then map out a plan for approaching the course requirements from this point on.

5.   Using College Notes
        Visual examples are potent teaching tools for today's college students. Construct or borrow sets of notes for a common first-year lecture course such as American history. Sets of two weeks' lecture notes are sufficient for this exercise.

- Set #1 notes should be dated, typed, and organized into outline form.
- Set #2 notes should be clear, hand-written, dated and organized on a concept map system.
- Set #3 notes should be undated and poorly handwritten in narrative style. Shuffle the pages so that they are not in the order in which they were written. Make sure there are no obvious outlines, mapping, or any other recognizable system of organization. Set #3 also might have phone numbers and/or grocery lists written in the margins. The object is to make set #3 very difficult to understand.
- Set #4 notes should be dated and demonstrate clear fishbone diagrams.

        Sets 1, 2, and 4 should also contain an upcoming exam date written or underlined in red. No exam date should appear anywhere in set #3. Distribute one of the note sets to each small group. Ask each group to quickly review their note set and provide a brief critique. Exchange sets until each group has seen each note set. At that point, state that a student has one hour to review notes for an upcoming exam. The student has access to these four note sets. What are the merits of each note set considering the time allotted for review? Keep in mind that the student has already studied for the exam and that this is a final review session. As groups, discuss the advantages and disadvantages of each note set. Remember that the plan to have a last review session is a good one, but also remember that *how* notes are taken will influence the *when* of a study plan. Will this student have time to decipher and place in order the notes from set #3? Will the student's learning style make a difference in which of the other three sets are used for the review session? Can all three of the other sets be valuable?

6.   Improving Your Memory
        Your students may already have experienced negative effects from memory decay. This is a more significant problem in some academic areas than in others. What kind of learning is most affected by memory decay? Mathematics and languages are two

answers that you might expect from students. With these two subject fields, the old adage, "Practice makes perfect," seems to hold true. What other subject areas can your students suggest that may require constant review in order to be readily useful in class or work-life situations?

7. **Sleep Deprivation**

A common problem for students as they develop study skills is that many of them are too sleepy to study. A rumor circulating among first-year students is that they can perform well academically on short chunks of sleep time as long as they can catch up occasionally on weekends. Ask students to compare their sleep needs in their small groups. To ensure good physical and mental health as well as good academic health, how many hours of sleep per night are necessary for each student? How many hours of sleep did each student get last night? On an average night? Is this enough to stay academically (as well as physically and mentally) healthy? For students who require more than eight hours of sleep per night to do their best work, how can waking hours be used more efficiently?

Summary Projects

1.   Students may be interested in compiling a handbook of memory enhancement techniques gleaned from interviews with professors in humanities, natural science and math, social science, and foreign language. Include lists of the professors' favorite acronyms. Add to the master list information from interviews with academically successful senior students in each of these fields.

2.   Recent experiments with gender-segregated learning environments at the elementary and/or middle school levels have generated a number of research reports that may be of special interest to some of your students. With assistance from a reference librarian, students may wish to compile an annotated bibliography of research in this area over the past five years. Internet and current periodical resources may be two of the most essential tools for students who elect to work on this project. A summary paper might relate findings to the Chapter 7 material on gender and learning.

IV. CAMPUS CONNECTIONS AND RESOURCES_____

Academic Support Services. Review the locations of academic support offices or departments on your campus. Ask a student team to investigate what specific services are offered by each academic support office or department. Are these services available to all students? Are fees charged? Must one be a full-time student to access services? Are appointments necessary? The student team report might take the form of a typed list including name and location of the office or department, phone number(s) for information or appointments, cost per hour (if any), and depth of service offered.

Disability Services. Review the disability services provided on campus. Is testing free? What accommodations are provided to students? What are some characteristics of students with disabilities? What are the different types of learning disabilities? How do disabilities affect memory and study skills? Who are the disability counselors? Where are their offices located? How does one set up an appointment to meet with them for screening? How can all students assist students with disabilities?

Professor Office Hours. Are professors required to keep weekly office hours? If so, what is the policy regarding academic assistance from professors during office times? Do certain professors hold special review sessions before exams? Are old exams provided by instructors as review help for students? If so, where are these exams located?   Ask your students to do a brief survey of their professors this term. What do professors expect to do during office hours? What preparation is expected of students before visiting a professor for help during office hours?

Tutoring. Does your campus have a learning center where free tutoring is offered to all students? How do students access these services? How are tutors selected? Are tutors available in all disciplines? If your students have not researched tutoring services on your campus, this is an ideal time to discover whether or not tutoring is available.

V. COLLABORATIVE LEARNING SUGGESTIONS _____

In groups, have students discuss their experiences with study groups. What are the advantages and disadvantages of study groups? What learning styles work best with study groups? What are some etiquette rules for study groups? What courses or disciplines do study groups work best for? How should one prepare for study groups? What are some suggestions to get the most out of study groups?

Divide the class into groups and have them discuss factors that hinder memory. What are some techniques to improve memory? What lifestyle habits improve memory? What are some mnemonic devices that work best for certain learning styles (auditory, visual, and kinesthetic)? Have them share different study strategies for specific courses or disciplines, including useful mnemonic devices.

In groups, have the students discuss the different study strategies relating to taking subjective and objective tests. What are the differences between the two types of testing? What are examples of the two types of tests? Is there a different level of learning? How should a student prepare and study for the tests? What are some ways to make studying for these tests more effective?

In groups, instruct students to discuss distractions to studying. What are the main distractions and what are some ways to overcome these obstacles? How can students break up the overwhelming task of studying for a test throughout the semester? How can students make boring courses more interesting to study?

VI. ALTERNATIVE TEACHING STRATEGIES _____

Every institution offers different types of instruction such as online learning, televised courses, live video interactive, in-class, and independent. Have students discuss what study techniques work best for each type of class. If some students have experienced one of these types of instruction, have them share their experiences including advantages and disadvantages.

To test memory, hand out a list of 20 terms to be memorized in order. Give students 5 minutes to study and memorize the terms. Instruct them to be aware of their study and memory techniques. After the 5-minute study period, have them write down the terms in order. Take a poll on how many terms students remembered. Then discuss the study techniques utilized. What mnemonic devices did they use (acronyms, visualization, acrostics, rhymes, diagrams)? Discuss the different ways to effectively memorize lists.

Divide the class into four groups to present on the rules, risks, resources, and remedies to mastering the four disciplines listed in the chapter (Humanities, Natural Science and Math, Social Science, and Foreign Languages). Have them discuss the information in the text in addition to providing personal examples of their experiences with these disciplines. Discuss how some disciplines are easier or more difficult for some based on learning styles.

VII. LEARNING PORTFOLIO

1. Self-Assessments

Have your students complete Self-Assessment 3 on page 210. Take a brief poll as to whether more students have already developed effective study habits or have many areas in which they could use improvement. In what areas do they seem to need the most help? What strategies can they implement now to improve these areas?

2. Your Journal

Have students complete the activity "Study-Group Savvy" on page 211. In small groups, have them gather a list of positive and negative talents and traits members bring to study groups. Discuss how students can make the most of such talents and improve such traits.

VIII. CHAPTER QUIZ SUGGESTIONS

1. Use the Review Questions as a short-answer quiz. Points may be assigned equally at 25 points per question, or points may be divided unequally depending on the amount of class time and assignments devoted to various areas of the chapter. In short-answer quizzes, complete sentences are not always necessary as long as the essential points of the answer are present.

IX. QUIZ

Multiple Choice. Choose the one best answer.

1. Important study techniques to implement immediately after class include all except:

A. Rewriting and reorganizing class notes.
B. Highlighting the most important ideas.
C. Putting notes away to clear your head.
D. Writing a summary paragraph of main ideas.
E. Identifying any ideas that are still confusing.

2. Successful students get to class
    A. about ½ an hour early to organize, study and review.
    B. about 10 minutes early to briefly look over previous notes.
    C. right on time - they know better than to waste valuable time sitting in an empty classroom.
    D. actually a few minutes past the official start time, since most classes begin with a review that they don't need.
    E. whenever is most convenient; it can change from class to class.

3. Short-term memory is also known as
    A. academic memory.
    B. weak memory.
    C. working memory.
    D. intricate memory.
    E. memory storage.

4. Long term memory is built through
    A. repetition.
    B. association.
    C. chunking.
    D. scientists do not know yet.
    E. memorization.

5. Your learning strategies should ideally be geared toward
    A. streamlining your short term memory.
    B. increasing the number of chunks admitted to working memory.
    C. developing as many mnemonics as possible.
    D. building long term memory.
    E. building short term memory.

True or False

6. _____When planning your study sessions, you should plan specific times to take breaks and relax.

7. _____Memorization is not necessary or recommended at the college level.

8. _____If you are taking two similar subjects, it is best to study them together to maximize learning.

9. _____ When using visualization, the most effective thing to do is make your images as ridiculous as possible.

10. _____ Studies suggest that traditional-age college students need 10 hours of sleep per night.

ANSWERS

1. **C**   2. **B**   3. **C**   4. **B**   5. **D**   6. **T**   7. **F**   8. **F**   9. **T**   10. **T**

X. TEST QUESTIONS _____

Multiple Choice. Choose the one best answer.

1. Short term memory has a retention span of about
    A. 30 seconds.
    B. 60 - 90 seconds.
    C. 3 minutes.
    D. 30 minutes.

2. The process by which you can enable short-term memory to hold more detailed information is called.
    A. chanting.
    B. changing.
    C. charging.
    D. chunking.

3. "Mnemonics" refers to
    A. memory systems.
    B. memory aids.
    C. memory structures.
    D. the study of memory.

4. The term for what happens when information crowds out other information, making retrieval difficult is
    A. interchange.
    B. exchange.
    C. interference.
    D. intermittence.

5. The term for what happens when ideas are not kept in use, making retrieval difficult is
    A. disappearance.
    B. denial.
    C. decay.
    D. delay.

6. Application, analysis, and evaluation are
   A. higher-order thinking skills.
   B. mnemonic strategies.
   C. more difficult for individuals with learning differences.
   D. only required when studying the sciences.

7. The two types of learning that college instructors differentiate between are
   A. imitative and actual.
   B. effective and superficial.
   C. deep and surface.
   D. intellectual and social.

8. Nearly _____ Americans experience complications in their learning due to a learning disability or learning difference.
   A. 1 in 10
   B. 1 in 15
   C. 1 in 20
   D. 1 in 35

True or False

9. _____Intelligence is the key to effective studying.

10. _____Individuals with learning differences often show greater motivation to succeed than those who do not have a learning difference.

11. _____Study groups are a poor use of time, as they often get off-topic and involve a variety of different people who may be difficult to communicate with.

Essay Questions

1. What is Bloom's Taxonomy? Discuss how it relates to studying and learning in college.

2. Explain the two memory systems and the role each plays in learning in college.

3. How should study strategies vary depending on the discipline and why?

ANSWERS

1. **A**   2. **D**   3. **B**   4. **C**   5. **C**   6. **A**   7. **C**   8. **A**   9. **F** 10. **T** 11. **F**

XI. MENTOR'S CORNER

Dennis Congos has been teaching and counseling in learning skills for 23 years. He developed a series of 60 "how-to" learning skills handouts that his students use. These handouts are based on the fastest and most efficient study skills that he has seen in the literature. The topics covered are goal-setting and attitudes about learning, reading textbooks, time organization, note organization, concentration environments, memory enhancers, test preparation, self-testing, test taking, and vocabulary mastery. He has also designed two learning skills diagnostics. One is entitled The Radial of Learning and the other is called a Learning Skills Diagnostic. Dennis is also a Supplemental Instruction trainer and has coordinated SI programs for 16 years. He has also done on-site consulting on SI and learning skills programs. If he can be of help in any of the above areas, he may be contacted at dcongos@mail.ucf.edu.

C H A P T E R   8

SUCCEED ON TESTS

I. CHAPTER OVERVIEW _____

Interviews with unsuccessful first-year students revealed that lack of appropriate test-taking strategies was a primary factor in their poor academic showing. Many of these students had never been in a lecture class where two or three exams comprised the entire term grade. If the student received a very low grade on the first exam, it was very difficult, if not impossible, to raise the term grade to a passing average. When that depressing fact became a reality, some simply gave up, stopped attending class, and accepted failure without finishing the term. During the same series of interviews, successful students related that both knowing how to prepare for an exam and knowing what strategies to use during the exam were important in achieving good grades. These students made deliberate plans to succeed on tests.

The place to start when helping students succeed on tests is to help them understand what tests are for. Students need to realize that tests provide motivation and feedback for their learning process and can result in a strong sense of accomplishment when they succeed. Regardless of whether any of that matters to them at this point, they need to recognize that tests are a part of college – one that they must learn to deal with successfully.

There is more to preparing for exams than studying. Taking care of oneself physically and getting in the right frame of mind is crucial, too. Students should prepare for exams over the long-term by taking charge of these necessities while honing in on important things in the short-term. It is also important to help students develop strategies for conquering test anxiety, such as positive self-talk, appropriate preparation, and learning relaxation techniques. You may even take some time in class to practice these techniques to help students get the feel for them.

Working to succeed on tests doesn't end when the studying is over. Once the exam has actually begun, there are numerous critical things students can do to help ensure success. Time management during each exam must be planned at the beginning as one determines the demands and amount of material. It is also important to realize that many exams contain clues that can help one remember otherwise forgotten information. Essay questions take a particular amount of preparation, even within the testing period. Students must be ready to plan, communicate precisely, and write legibly.

Once the results are in, there's more to do. Guide your students through the post-test process: reviewing their results to consolidate learning and plan for how they will approach the next exam, as well as recognizing the circumstances in which it is appropriate to challenge an instructor's judgment and determining when it is advisable not to. And last but not least, students should be made to recognize the impact of doing consistently poorly – so much so that they waste a semester with a very bad grade.

Academic integrity is a necessary topic that should be addressed in this course. Cheating offers a good in-class discussion topic; new research indicates that widespread cheating in college is a reflection of the significantly larger cultural problem. Use the student handbook to highlight the consequences of dishonorable behavior.

II. IMAGES OF COLLEGE SUCCESS

Your students may already know Albert Einstein's failure story from earlier educational experiences. Because his personal learning style was so different from what was expected at his school, he was not able to perform at an acceptable academic level. This Image of Success illustrates clearly that a match between an individual's preferred learning style and the expectations of the institution can make the difference between success and failure, and in rare instances, between failure and demonstration of genius. Einstein was poised to create a new way of thinking about a complex subject and resented the teaching style that stifled his thought patterns. The brief synopsis of his educational failure at the Luitpold Gymnasium stated that he purposefully failed exams so that he would be dismissed from the school.

Do students today deliberately fail exams? What reasons might be offered by a student who planned to fail? Homesickness? Parents who insist on a career path that is not what the student wants? Perhaps the student did not want to go to college at all. Why would failing exams even be considered as a way out in this case? Discussion of these questions can sensitize students to possible problem areas encountered by friends or roommates, if not themselves. Perhaps the student who deliberately fails an exam wants to go to another college. What happens when the college of choice has a place available but the student's grades are too low by that time to be accepted? The goal here is to help students realize that deliberate failure of an exam has potentially disastrous consequences.

Did Einstein have a learning disability? What role might a learning disability play in failing an exam today? What are some potential solutions to this problem?

III. CLASS ACTIVITIES

Break The Ice!

1. **Why Testing?**

Why is testing such a popular way of evaluating student progress? How does your institution evaluate? By testing? By term projects? By a combination of the two? Invite a faculty member or graduate student who received a degree from a tutorial college to speak to your students. Ask the speaker to talk specifically about evaluation in a tutorial system. Who decides whether or not the student passes? What kinds of grades are given? How does this grading system affect future employment? Although a few such colleges exist in the United States, this educational system is more likely to be found in England and in European colleges and universities. Ask the speaker to talk frankly about advantages and disadvantages of a tutorial system. Does it place more or less responsibility for learning on the student? What if a student believes that the evaluation has been unfair? What recourse does the student have? Is this system less competitive?

2.   **Types of Testers**

In general, students tend to fall into three categories of test-takers: those who test well, those who do not test well, and those who are competent test-takers because they have learned how to prepare for exams. In small groups, let individual students relate which of these three groups fits their personal test-taking profile in high school. Did their test-taking profile change depending on subject matter? Did some students achieve high scores on the ACT or SAT but not in classes? Pay particular attention to those students who had difficulty with testing in high school. Assist these students as they articulate their problems. Were they too nervous? Did they fail to prepare adequately before the test? Did they misunderstand test instructions? Did they not have enough time to finish? Were they slow readers?

Keep a list of their reasons for poor test performance in high school. Refer to this list as you discuss Chapter 8. As each reason surfaces in the chapter reading material and discussion, ask students to write a one-minute journal entry relating what they now know about how to overcome this test-taking problem. How can the suggestions given in this chapter make a difference in college testing situations? This can be an on-going assignment as chapter discussion continues.

Discussion and Reflection

1.   **Testing Across Disciplines**

Ask students to bring a copy of the syllabus for each of their courses. Compare testing and evaluation procedures among all the classes represented. Are there major differences in evaluation procedures among the various disciplines represented? What kind of testing occurs in humanities courses? In science courses? In math courses? Music or dramatic arts? Does each syllabus clearly state evaluation and grading procedures? What does one have to do to receive an "A"? Are some of the courses graded S/U or Pass/Fail? What percentage of the grade in each class is determined by testing alone? How many tests? Is there a final exam? If so, is it weighted more than other exams? Are any of the exams comprehensive? What difference does this make in preparing for and taking the test?

Words of Wisdom

1.   **Quotes for Discussion**

"Difficulties, opposition, criticism—these things are meant to be overcome, and there is a special joy in facing them and in coming out on top." Vijaya Lakshmi Pandit. This statement gives a clue as to the serious nature of college test-taking. When students submit their work through an exam, they often don't realize that they open an avenue for professorial criticism, and some are ill-prepared to accept and profit from critical analysis of their work. As students discuss this quote, ask them to be specific in relating the three key words—difficulties, opposition, and criticism—to the general topic of succeeding on tests.

"Character is destiny." Heraclitis. Talk in small groups about specific ways this quotation relates to the topic of academic integrity on your campus.

2.   **Quotes and You**

What are some hopeful quotations in this chapter? Do your students have favorite encouraging quotations to share with each other about test-taking? Students must balance hope for success with an appropriate amount of preparation and mix in just enough of an anxiety edge to heighten awareness. The focus of this chapter will be on achieving that balance and mix that will turn out to be just the right recipe for succeeding on tests.

Major Themes

1.   **Assessing Study Groups**

Poll your students to see how many of them are already working in study groups in other classes. Are the groups assigned by the instructor or teaching assistant? Are the groups formed independently by the students themselves? If study groups were assigned by the instructor, is a teaching assistant appointed to lead the group, or are the students themselves supposed to elect or rotate leadership? What advantages occur when students are totally responsible for leadership and management of the study group? Do your students study better in a group, or does the group tend to distract from test preparation? What are the advantages and disadvantages of studying alone? What are the advantages and disadvantages of studying with a group? Keep in mind that study groups that have worked together for several weeks may have an advantage over those that are formed immediately prior to an exam.

2.   **Test Files**

Does your campus have a test file system? If so, ask a small group to investigate the system and report their findings to the class. Are old tests provided by instructors? Are students allowed to contribute old tests to the files? Is there a fee for using the test files? Is it possible to photocopy old tests in the files? Are the tests annotated by student users?

3.   **Time Management and Tests**

This is an appropriate time to review again the time management techniques studied earlier. Look over students' study schedules. Is ample time allowed not only for reading material, but also for reviewing it? Are the study schedules realistic? Is there time for a thorough review immediately prior to the exam?

4.   **Healthy Test Preparation**

Ask teams of students to construct a "healthy test-prep" report to present to the class. Include suggestions for healthy eating, power snacks, adequate sleep time, physical exercises that wake up the mind, and other suggestions for feeling good before exam time. Give extra credit for teams that have unique and creative presentations.

5.   **Special Help for Test Taking**

For those students who have more than an occasional twinge of anxiety before or during exams, recommend a private session at the campus counseling center or attendance at a special test anxiety seminar. If a learning disability is involved in the test anxiety situation, assist the student in networking with the campus office that provides help for learning disabled students. The point is to empower students to do their best work on exams; if this means getting help in reducing test anxiety or finding alternate ways to complete an exam, then students may need a model of how to be assertive without being rude or negative.

6.   **A Representative from the Learning Center**

Invite a representative from a campus learning center to make a presentation on test-taking strategies for your students. Many first-year students profit most from this kind of presentation immediately before mid-term examinations. Ask the presenter to specifically address strategies for different kinds of exams: multiple choice, essay, short answer, matching, true-false, or fill-in-the-blank.

7.   **Dropping Courses**

Some colleges offer the opportunity to drop a course if the first test grade is below passing. If this is the case on your campus, ask a team to investigate the drop procedure and explain it to the class. Be mindful of any deadline dates that apply to this procedure. If students are allowed to drop a course because of failing grades, ask about the grade reporting policy. Will the dropped course appear on the student's permanent transcript? Will a "drop-failing" grade appear? What is the last date to drop or withdraw from a class without penalty? If a course is dropped, does this affect full-time student status? Ask the reporting team to address all these questions.

8.   **Test-Taking Integrity**

Do your students have ready access to copies of the student code of academic conduct? Where can this document be found? In the college catalog? In a student handbook? In a separately published brochure? Ask a student team to investigate these questions and secure student code copies for the class. A problem for many students concerns plagiarism. The definition may not be clear since some high schools are lax not only as to what constitutes plagiarism but how cases of plagiarism are handled. Students must be very careful about issues of academic integrity. Talk with the office on your campus that is responsible for dealing with incidents of academic dishonesty. Ask someone from this office to either talk with your class about campus policies or provide a set of case histories from their files for your students to use as discussion topics. Especially if you have access to recorded judgments or solutions to these case histories, these can be powerful tools for your students to role-play as judge and jury and then compare their findings to those actually recorded for the case.

Summary Projects

1.   If your campus has no published academic code of honor written in an abbreviated form so that it is clearly understandable to students, an interesting term project for a student team is that of creating such an honor code. Students may wish to consult such well-known documents as the University of South Carolina's *Carolinian Creed* or other similar codes. An Internet search may help in this research effort. This is a good project in which to blend academic honor code statements with traditions and customs of your institution. Upon completion of the project, help your students submit it

both to representatives of the student government and to the office of the Dean of Students with a recommendation for publication.

2.   Organize a test file center for your campus. First, lobby for assistance with such a center; visit with chief academic officers, the Dean of Students, and with directors of student academic support services. Investigate possible secure locations for such a center. Will the student government office lend support? Assist in locating secure physical space? Help with organizing volunteers to staff the center? Once these questions have been answered positively, write a proposal that can be presented to professors as they are asked to contribute old exams to the project. Ask upper-class students to contribute from their personal exam files, especially those students who are on the Dean's list! Check with officers who are responsible for student affairs and/or Legal Office to see if there are any prohibitions or restrictions on such a center. This is a very large undertaking and could be considered an appropriate project for several teams working together or even for the entire class as a service project for the campus.

IV. CAMPUS CONNECTIONS AND RESOURCES

Academic Support Services. If a student government representative is assigned to deal with student code violations regarding integrity in exam situations, ask that person to address your class on this topic. Some student government offices offer academic support services that will help students avoid problems in test-taking situations.

Disability Services. Test anxiety is a very real issue for many students. They know the information, excel in the homework, have studied and prepared for the exam; however, they tend to blank out and fail the tests. Have a disability counselor discuss test anxiety with the class. Discuss the symptoms of test anxiety and ways to manage the anxiety so students can succeed in courses. Discuss stress management and relaxation techniques. Provide students with resources and contact information for screening and testing for anxiety issues. Refer to Self-Assessment 1: "How Serious is My Test Anxiety?"

Code Speakers. Who wrote the code of academic conduct for students on your campus? Was this a student initiative? Was it handed down from a college governing board or administrative office? Who is responsible for any changes that might occur in the code? Do students have petition rights in attempting to make changes to the published code? If your campus has an office of legal counsel, send a student team to investigate this issue. Ask the team to either arrange for a speaker from the office to address the class or to bring back materials that would assist students in discovering the answers to the above questions in their small group discussions.

Transcripts. Have students bring in copies of their unofficial transcripts. Review how to read transcripts, specifically cumulative and semester GPAs. Teach the students how to calculate their GPAs. If they are in poor standing, discuss how repeating a course would change their GPA. Have them calculate their GPAs using new grades. Review academic standings and honors.

V. COLLABORATIVE LEARNING SUGGESTIONS _____

Is a Tutor Worth It?: Is it a good idea to find a tutor before an exam? Ask students to discuss this possibility in small groups. Why would a tutor be helpful? How long before the exam should a student see a tutor? Does your campus provide free tutoring? Is it effective? Are professional tutors available? What are the costs? How can students check on the credentials of professional tutors?   What kind of help should students expect from a tutor?

Exam Kit—Help!: Ask a small group team to fill an "exam prop kit" with materials useful to students during exams and then to show-and-tell their kit in a brief presentation to the class. Among the appropriate props are a blue book, various forms of Scantrons, several #2 pencils, a pocket pencil sharpener, a student ID (required for some exams on some campuses), a pocket pack of tissues, a calculator (if permitted), a black pen, paper clips, a pocket stapler, cough drops, and other imaginative (but legal!) exam props. Some instructors even permit small bottles of water during exams. Tell the team to find out what's permitted on your campus. Unpacking the exam kit in a dramatic demonstration fashion can provide humorous relief as students buckle down for an exam period.

Old Tests: Have students bring in copies of their old tests from different classes. In groups, have students review the tests, looking for examples of test-making strategies. Are the tests different based on discipline? What are some test-making styles of teachers? Are math tests graded differently than other disciplines? Why did the students get certain questions wrong?

Cheating: In groups, have students discuss why students cheat and what the consequences for cheating should be. Also include cyber cheating with online courses. What should students do if they think another student is cheating? What is the school's honor code? What action should they take if someone is trying to cheat off them?

Test Anxiety: In groups, have students list some common negative thoughts they encounter when taking tests. How do these thoughts or self-statements affect their test-taking behavior? Is their a strong link with attitude and behavior? What are some positive statements that can replace the negative? How will the positive statements affect test-taking behavior? Have each group share their thoughts with the remainder of the class for a deeper discussion on how self-talk can affect test-taking.

VI. ALTERNATIVE TEACHING STRATEGIES _____

Do students serve on academic disciplinary boards on your campus? If so, what are the criteria and procedures for serving on these boards? If students do not serve on these boards, who does? Exactly what are the procedures that the institution follows when a student is accused of cheating on an exam? What are the student's rights in such cases? What are the possible penalties if a student is found guilty of cheating on an exam?

The Duke University Center for Applied Ethics has released a videotape, "Academic Integrity: The Bridge to Professional Ethics". Student actors are featured in four brief vignettes that focus on academic integrity and ethical decision-making in college engineering courses. The Instructor's Manual accompanying the video contains a copy of the script, a summary of main ethical themes in each vignette, and several discussion questions. In addition, a section on Engineering Relevance and another on Comparable Engineering Scenarios are provided for each video segment. Although the topic is specific to engineering, each of the scenarios is general enough to apply to average college students in a variety of disciplines. First-year students who previewed this tape were impressed with the amount of discussion each scenario prompted and thought that the video was an excellent tool to introduce some difficult issues in the area of academic integrity. This video would also be appropriate for use in Chapter 4 of *Your Guide to College Success*.

Develop a practice test consisting of multiple-choice, true and false, matching, fill-in-the-blank, and essay questions. Some of the questions may refer to information learned in the previous chapters; others should be questions the students will have to make educated guesses on. Each test question should relate to a test-taking strategy (such as absolute terms in T/F questions are usually false). Assign different points to the different types of questions. Administer the test like it was a real one with a set time limit. Once the time is up, discuss effective test-taking strategies (such as allocating time based on point values, scanning the entire test before answering, paying close attention to the subjective questions while looking for clues when answering objective questions, etc.). Review the answers to the test and discuss the different test-wise skills demonstrated in the test. This is a great hands-on way to review test-taking strategies mentioned in the text book.

VII. LEARNING PORTFOLIO _____

1. Self-Assessments
Have students complete Self-Assessment 2, and then gather students into small groups to compare answers. What are some common areas marked "never"? Do students seem to have more trouble with any particular type of test? Discuss possible reasons for this and strategies for combating common problem areas.

2. Your Journal
Have small groups of students tackle the journal activity "Construct Your Own Exam" on page 239. Have them draft a 10-question quiz that tests material covered in this chapter. Allow them to select any type of test question they prefer and then compare test formats and question types. What did students find most challenging about this assignment? Consider drafting a sample quiz yourself and comparing your questions with those submitted by students. Was there any overlap? Small groups could also complete and critique each other's quizzes.

VIII. CHAPTER QUIZ SUGGESTIONS

1.   Use the Review Questions as a short-answer quiz. Points may be assigned equally at 25 points per question, or points may be divided unequally depending on the amount of class time and assignments devoted to various areas of the chapter.   In short-answer quizzes, complete sentences are not always necessary as long as the essential points of the answer are present.

IX. QUIZ

Multiple Choice. Choose the one best answer.

1. Most students say that tests in college
    A. are harder than tests in high school.
    B. require less preparation than they had anticipated.
    C. cover very little material, but in a very detailed manner.
    D. cover a great deal of material, but in a less detailed manner.
    E. All of the above.

2. Good strategies for test-taking success include all except:
    A. Getting a good night's sleep.
    B. Bringing required supplies.
    C. Cramming as much as possible the night before the exam.
    D. Bringing reference aids, if allowed.
    E. Organizing resources.

3. Role-playing is a good study technique for
    A. auditory learners.
    B. visual learners.
    C. tactile learners.
    D. humanities majors.
    E. science majors.

4. Terms such as *always, never,* and *usually* are particularly important to pay attention to in
    A. essay tests.
    B. procedural tests.
    C. multiple choice tests.
    D. true-false tests.
    E. All of the above.

5. Writing a lot more than asked to, or including information not asked for, on short answer tests
    A. is impressive to most instructors, as it shows your more complete knowledge of
       the subject matter.
    B. is usually a waste of time, as many teaching assistants are the ones who do the

grading, and they are told very simple answers; they don't have the ability or authority to grade further.
    C. suggests that you do not understand the concepts.
    D. suggests that you are pretending to know more than you do.
    E. All of the above.

6. Which of the following does not constitute cheating?
    A. Submitting essays you have purchased and paid for in full.
    B. Submitting a paper in a new class that you previously wrote and submitted for another class.
    C. Improper paraphrasing.
    D. Collaborating with another student on an assignment that is designated as an individual assignment.
    E. All of the above are examples of cheating.

True or False

7. _____You will experience more tests and quizzes in college than you did in high school.

8. _____It's a dangerous habit to try to predict what questions your instructor may ask on a test.

9. _____Most instructors devote at least a few minutes of the last class to narrow down the most critical material or give hints about what the exam will contain.

10. _____A little anxiety prior to an exam can be a good sign.

ANSWERS

1. **A**   2. **C**   3. **C**   4. **D**   5. **C**   6. **E**   7. **F**   8. **F**   9. **T**   10. **T**

X. TEST QUESTIONS _____

Multiple Choice. Choose the one best answer.

1. A test that asks you to solve math problems or find an unknown in chemistry is known as a(n)
    A. objective test.
    B. subjective test.
    C. procedural test.
    D. reflective test.

2. Multiple choice, matching, true-false, and fill-in-the-blank questions are all examples of
    A. objective tests.

116

B. subjective tests.
C. conceptual tests.
D. procedural tests.

3. Your most effective memorization strategy will effectively use your
A. short-term memory.
B. long-term memory.
K. C. mnemonics.
D. preferred sensory mode.

4. "Test-anxious" students may experience the following:
A. sabotaging their own grade.
B. increased pulse, heart rate, and perspiration.
C. interpreting neutral events as proof of their own inadequacy.
D. All of the above.

5. The Dean's list is
A. a roster of students recognized for academic excellence based on their grades.
B. a roster of students on academic probation due to poor grades who are in danger of having their admission terminated.
C. a roster of students who have applied to a university and are accepted with honors.
D. the list of all colleges and degree programs offered at a particular academic institution.

6. When instructors judge individual student scores in relation to the strongest score in the class, it is called
A. relative grading.
B. grading on a curve.
C. percentile scoring.
D. ranking.

7. A recent analysis comparing results across many years of surveys on cheating estimated that approximately _____ of both males and females cheated in college.
A. 25%
B. 40%
C. 60%
D. 75%

True or False

8. _____ If an instructor lets you have open access to your books and notes, you know the test will be easy!

9. _____ You should never read through an entire exam before you start. It can make you nervous and throw off your concentration.

117

10. _____It's possible to cheat and not realize that you're doing so.

Essay Questions

1. Discuss some different long-term versus short-term test-taking strategies. Why is it important to understand the differences between the two?

2. What are some things you can do to help control test anxiety?

3. Detail a good timetable for sensible study strategies.

ANSWERS

1. **C**   2. **A**   3. **D**   4. **D**   5. **A**   6. **B**   7. **C**   8. **F**   9. **F**   10. **T**

XI. MENTOR'S CORNER _____

Mary Pepe has been a Professor in the Student Success program since 1993 at Valencia Community College in Orlando, Florida. A majority of her students are self-proclaimed "hands-on" or kinesthetic learners who do not respond well to lectures. To keep these students engaged, Mary has developed several effective activities for the topics of note-taking, creative thinking, and test-taking.

E-mail Mary at mpepe@gwmail.valencia.cc.fl.us for a set of directions on how to conduct these hands-on lessons.

CHAPTER 9

EXPRESS YOURSELF

I. CHAPTER OVERVIEW _____

Being able to express yourself is a vital skill learned in college. Expressing yourself through writing is one of the best ways to get a message across. A pithy advertising slogan ("a diamond is forever"), a great book (*The Great Gatsby*), and a science report all involve writing. For those students who don't like writing, this your chance to win them over. The more they write, the better they will become. Writing is like cooking—you need to learn when to add spice and when to keep it straightforward.

Throughout *Your Guide to College Success*, your students have multiple opportunities to express themselves in writing. The Learning Portfolio at the end of each chapter provides students with good ideas upon which to think and then to respond in writing. Instructors who fail to require at least weekly writing assignments are not doing their students any favors. And, yes, it is necessary to read what students write and, if at all possible, to comment even briefly on their writing. Writing is, for most of us, learning by doing. We learn how to write by writing, and usually the more we write, the better we get.

Good writing begins with a well defined topic. Good writing exercises involve generating ideas and selecting, narrowing, and refining topics. Once a topic has been successfully chosen, it's on to the library. A good working knowledge of the library is essential in order for students to be able to accumulate the best evidence possible to support the positions that they take in their writing. In order to keep track of their progress and all of the materials that make up the writing process, it is necessary for students to develop an organization scheme, not only for materials at hand, but for obtaining additional sources of information.

Students will need to learn about the different kinds of writing they will be asked to do over the course of their college (and possibly professional) career. Knowing the purpose of their writing in each case, as well as whether it should take a formal or informal tone, is critical. The text presents several habits of good writers, which students should become familiar with and begin incorporating into their writing habits – particularly time management as it applies to developing and creating a paper!

Not only is communication via the written word highly important, but to be able to speak well to an audience is imperative as well. Students may not realize that even simple things like asking questions and participating in discussions in class helps give them experience with public speaking. They should capitalize on these opportunities to refine their oral presentation skills. Many of the same preparatory steps taken when writing an effective paper should be applied to putting together a great oral presentation. In addition, students need to work on the added elements of rehearsal and appearance for a polished presentation. You can help students become better public speakers by requiring them to present in front of the class. They can also incorporate multimedia elements into their presentations to practice working those factors into their delivery. By the end of the semester, students can become very familiar and comfortable with one another, offering a less threatening environment for practicing oral communication skills.

II. IMAGES OF COLLEGE SUCCESS

One of today's most well-known, loved, and respected authors is J.K. Rowling. Her series of Harry Potter books is tremendously successful because of its appeal to readers of all ages. The fact that teen-agers, college students, and older adults can enjoy and appreciate her writing as much (or more) than her original target audience of pre-teen children, is a testament to the powers of effective communication. While Rowling's story has been romanticized over the years, the fact remains that one of her majors in college was classic literature – certainly a useful foundation for becoming a successful author. However, just developing a good story doesn't automatically enable you to tell that story in an enthralling page turner. Have students think about their favorite books and authors. Are they familiar with their backgrounds? What training or education did they receive before writing their first big work? Have they ever thought that being able to write – or speak – effectively was simply a talent some people are born with and others aren't? Does J.K. Rowling or other authors demonstrate something in her writing that can't be learned? Prompt students to support their thoughts with specific examples from either the Harry Potter books or their favorites that they bring to class.

III. CLASS ACTIVITIES

Break The Ice!

1.   **Writing or Speaking?**
      Ask students to think about whether they would rather respond to a question in writing or in an oral presentation. Then take a vote in class. What are the results? How many students would prefer written exams? Are there any who prefer the prospect of oral exams? Why do many institutions still require both written and oral exams at the graduate level? Speculate as to why most college undergraduate exams are written. What happens to the undergraduate student whose strengths lie in speaking? What would happen if each of your students were required to take an oral exam in United States history, for example? Then ask students to create a list of reasons why both writing and speaking skills are essential for good communication.

Discussion and Reflection

1.   **Essay Exams and Stress**
      Why do some undergraduates fear essay exams? Have students recall the test-taking suggestions in Chapter 8. Your students may have experienced at least one essay exam at this point in the term. What were the results? If your students were not satisfied with their essay grades, what comments were supplied by the grader that would result in a better outcome on the next exam? Ask students to anonymously submit comments from

their essay exams. Which verbs in the comments give clues as to how students can improve their answers?

## 2.	Writing Lab Reports

What are the differences between scientific, lab-report writing and essay writing? Is it important to know how to do both kinds of writing? Why? Borrow a copy of an "A" lab report from a colleague in chemistry, biology, or zoology. Show parts of this report to your students and discuss why it is a good example of excellent work. Do the same for an essay exam in United States history, beginning political science, or first-year psychology classes. It may be possible to get these exam and report copies from the campus test files bank.

## 3.	Exploring the Writing Center

Does your campus have a Writing Center or tutorial lab? Arrange a brief field trip to the center and ask one of the professional staff members to speak with your students about the specific services offered there. Is the center available only to students or can faculty and staff use those services as well? What qualifications are necessary to work in the Writing Center? What services are excluded at this Center? What hours is the Center open? Are appointments necessary? What must students bring with them?

Words of Wisdom

## 1.	Quotes for Discussion

"A #2 pencil and a dream can take you anywhere."—Joyce A. Myers. Have your students discuss this quote. Have they ever felt they needed to put something down on paper—to clear their minds or focus their thoughts? By writing, a person can leave his or her hum-drum life behind or escape the chaos of a *too* exciting life. Writing is an "egalitarian" art form because of its simplicity—all that is required is pen and paper, unlike painting, which requires the purchase of paint and canvas, or film, which requires a great deal of capital. How has this quality of writing contributed to the great works in this country?

## 2.	Quotes and You

Outstanding athletes talk about getting "in the zone" when they are performing at top levels. How do you get "in the zone" for a writing project? If you have set aside a time every day to write, should you stop after the set time has elapsed? What if you are "in the zone" during a writing project? Will your writing get stale if you continue past the point you usually write effectively? Talk about individual preferences and experiences in light of set writing times versus extended "in the zone" times. How does individual learning style affect these decisions?

## 3.	The Library or Starbucks?

Present students with Anne Morrow Lindbergh's quote: "Good communication is as stimulating as black coffee, and just as hard to sleep after." Can they relate? Have them present examples of either a speech, conversation, or book that afterwards left them in a state similar to having had a cup of black coffee. What elements of the communicative experience made it so stimulating? Do they incorporate these same elements into their own speaking and writing? If they struggle with writing or public speaking, what do they think they need to learn or do in order to communicate more effectively in these ways? Have them look through the chapter in order to identify some of the most helpful sections that can help them communicate like those who stimulated them so greatly.

Major Themes

1.   A Career in Writing
Invite an alum who is an employee of a professional firm in your community to speak to your class about writing skills that are necessary in that profession. What writing skills are expected of an employee in an engineering firm? In a medical services office? In a manufacturing firm? In a public school teaching position? In a business services office? In a consulting firm? If several students in your class are considering majors and career fields in a particular area, ask your placement office to assist you in securing a speaker from a related professional firm who will talk with your students about necessary writing and speaking tools for employment and promotion in that field.

2.   A Daily Journal
Encourage your students to write daily in a personal journal. In addition to a personal history record, journals help students work through problems, find an outlet for personal expression, practice writing in a disciplined fashion, and explore creative ways of expression. If journaling is a part of your orientation course, it is essential that students understand that their journal entries are confidential information and may not be shared with anyone unless they have given written permission to the instructor to do so.

3.   Writing a Self-Portrait Poem
Assign a Bio-Poem as a form of expressive writing. A Bio-Poem is eleven lines long and is constructed according to the following model:

> Line 1 - your first name
> Line 2 - four traits that describe you
> Line 3 - who you are related to
> Line 4 - three things that you care deeply about
> Line 5 - three things you feel
> Line 6 - three things you need
> Line 7 - three things you give
> Line 8 - three things you fear
> Line 9 - three things you would like to see
> Line 10 - your city and street name
> Line 11 - your last name

Invite students to share their bio-poems within their small groups. See if the student's bio-poem matches what the other students in the group have learned about that student.

4.   Practice Speaking in Public

For students who are shy or fearful about speaking in public, provide opportunities to talk first in small groups. Remind small groups often that it is essential to hear from everyone in the group and to be good listeners while each person speaks. It is easy for aggressive, outspoken students to dominate a small group discussion. Be alert to this situation and intervene subtly if this occurs in your class.

As students become comfortable speaking within their small groups, encourage short presentations before the entire class. Define each of the presentations carefully so that students who may be uncomfortable in talking to the whole class have a clear idea of exactly what to say. For those who have unusual discomfort in public speaking, enlist the aid of a professional colleague from the communications department. Some colleges provide special assistance for students who must overcome speech disabilities, including excessive fear of public speaking.

5.   Group Discussion Reporters

Whenever you create small groups in class to discuss any topic then report their observations to the rest of the class, assign one student to be the reporter. Inform this student ahead of time that it will be his or her job to succinctly present the highlights of the group's discussion and conclusions to the rest of the class. They will need to listen well, take effective notes, then create a simple, yet substantial oral presentation that reflects the goal of the group discussion. Don't allow them to write something and read it, just emphasize the importance of synthesizing the material as the discussion progresses, then present it in a way that the rest of the class can understand and relate to. Select different students to serve as reporters each time you have these small group discussions so that all class members have at least one opportunity for this simple and relatively "safe" shot at public speaking.

6.   Introducing Class Members

Make a practice of assigning speaker introductions to individual class members each time you have a guest speaker or panel presentation in your class. Make sure that your students know this will be required of each of them at some point during the term and model the kind of introduction you expect so that they will have guidelines for appropriate introductions. Provide written feedback for each student's introduction of a guest speaker. As an alternative, you can assign students to introduce others from their small groups on a regular basis, until everyone has had a chance to speak and everyone has been introduced.

Summary Projects

1.   Require that your students submit an article or letter to the editor to the campus newspaper. Discuss this assignment with the staff advisor for the paper for suggestions and to prepare them for the incoming articles. See if he or she will agree to print the best ones. The goal of their article or letter should be persuasive in nature, as they will have the opportunity to communicate something to the entire campus. At the least the goal should be to draw their attention to an issue or an event on campus, in the most dramatic form, it could be to rally support for a particular issue or cause.

123

2.   Keep a portfolio of creative writing projects completed during the semester. Write a brief summary of your writing processes, successes and failures, and experiments over the term. Submit at least one of these projects for publication either to a campus outlet or a commercial one. What was the result?

3.   Volunteer as a speaker for a campus organization, club, or bureau in which you have particular interest or expertise. Audio-tape your presentation and write a review, contrasting and comparing the effectiveness of your speech and listing the ways in which you have improved over the length of the term. Ask a friend to accompany you to your presentation and to give specific feedback on your style and content. Include a summary of this peer feedback in your final review. Also include an outline draft of your speech, noting the occasion, date, and group to which you made your presentation

IV. CAMPUS CONNECTIONS AND RESOURCES _____

Campus Publications. Students usually have many opportunities to write for extra-curricular settings: the campus newspaper, yearbook, student literary journals, recruiting and retention publications, and pre-professional newsletters, among others. Encourage your students to seek out these opportunities to practice their writing skills. If a student in your class submits an article or letter for publication and it is accepted, congratulate that student in class so that peers will support and encourage each other to submit written work for publication as well.

Debate Teams. Debate teams are alive and well on many college campuses. If students have participated in debate at the public school level, encourage them to audition for the college debate team. Some residence hall advisors will assist students in establishing teams for local debate tournaments. Some debate events may offer college credit.

Speaker's Bureaus. Students have chances to practice public speaking skills through health-related peer education groups, social clubs, recruiting events, volunteer work with public schools in the area, and other student organizations. Students who serve as campus guides receive practice in informal speaking as they lead tour groups throughout campus buildings and grounds. It will be helpful to your students to take a friend with them as they make presentations so that they can have immediate, truthful, and yet sympathetic feedback on their public speaking skills. Students who serve as peer assistants in campus offices also have chances to improve public speaking skills in very informal and non-threatening situations.

Librarians. Invite a librarian to take the students on a tour of the library and learning resource centers. Provide the students with an orientation to all the resources available and step-by-step instructions on how to research topics in journals and periodicals. Many colleges and universities have information systems programs to research topics, which may intimidate new students. This orientation will reduce so much anxiety and provide the students with the information they need to succeed in all their writing courses.

<u>Faculty Speaker.</u> Many campuses offer a course in public speaking or oral communication. In addition, most curriculums require oral communication competency as part of the degree plan. Invite a faculty member from the Speech, Communications, or English department to discuss the importance of oral communication with students. Many students have anxiety about speaking in front of a group of people; discuss different strategies to help reduce their anxiety.

<u>Disability Counselor.</u> All colleges and universities have a counselor that specializes in learning disabilities. Invite the counselor to discuss the variety of disabilities that may affect the students' writing and speaking skills. Discuss strategies to deal with these disabilities and the resources available to assist them.

V. COLLABORATIVE LEARNING SUGGESTIONS _____

<u>Exercise 1:</u> Arrange for your students to attend a guest lecture either on campus or in the community. Many student organizations sponsor lectures each year that bring in nationally or regionally well-known speakers to address specific topics. Alcohol abuse is a topic that is often addressed by either one speaker or a series of speakers. Some institutions sponsor famous alums who return to speak to students about success in particular career fields. A particular division of your institution may sponsor a speaker series to which the entire campus is invited. Musicians, dancers, writers, or artists may be invited to lecture about their work.

Ask each small group to collaborate in writing a review and critique of the lecture. Since each member of the small group must contribute to the writing project, the group will have to meet outside the class hour to assign responsibilities within the project. Selecting a topic is the easy part: write a review and critique of the lecture or speech. Some suggested guidelines for the writing project include:

- State the name of the speaker, give the title of the lecture, provide the details of when and where the event took place, and list the names of the writers of the report along with their specific responsibilities in the writing project.
- Why was this particular speaker invited? What was the sponsoring organization?
- Briefly summarize the content of the speech.
- Was the presentation formal or informal?
- Were there accompanying slides, videos, charts, or handouts? If so, how did these relate to the presentation?
- Did the speaker seem to hold the attention of the audience? How?
- Was time provided for discussion or questions afterward? Did everyone have equal opportunity to ask a question or participate in the discussion?
- Was the speaker effective? Provide details in your answer.
- Would you recommend this speaker to a friend? Why or why not?
- Submit the printed report in an appropriate format and include evidence of working from at least one rough draft. Be sure to follow standard spelling, punctuation, and grammatical guidelines.

Exercise 2: Ask each small group to introduce one of the next chapters in the text by making a short introductory speech to the class that will preview the chapter. Each group member must participate not only in the presentation, but in designing and preparing for the presentation. Encourage the groups to use visual aids or other props to invigorate their presentations. The group may want to design a short exercise for the entire class to introduce the chapter, but group members should remember that the purpose of this exercise is to make a verbal presentation.

Exercise 3: In collaboration with the English and Speech faculty members, have students bring in a writing or speech assignment to class. In small groups, have students review and critique each other's work to assist one another in improving these skills. Students could even practice their speeches with one another.

VI. ALTERNATIVE TEACHING STRATEGIES _____

Connect the speaking part of this chapter to the academic advisor interview assignment in the Learning Portfolio section of Chapter 1. Upon completion of the advisor interview, each student must make a three-minute oral report to the class. In the oral report, include answers received to some of the questions during the interview and mention some of the things your advisor informed you about. Did you learn anything personal about your advisor, such as where they went to school, what they majored in, how they came to be an academic advisor, or why they wanted to work at your school? If so, be sure to include these interest elements into your speech.

If your campus newspaper prints letters to the editor, ask your students to write a letter to the editor expressing support for a particular campus office, club, or organization that offers services for entering students. State reasons why this group deserves recognition; what specific services provided by this group have been helpful to your students? Are there particular individuals within the group or office that have assisted your students above and beyond the call of duty? Mention their names in the letters. If the letters are published, bring copies to class for review.

As speakers make presentations to your class, assign one student or a small group to write a thank you note to the presenter. Mention some of the outstanding things about the presentation and express appreciation to the speaker for taking time to visit your class. Hand-deliver the notes, if possible. This is one way for your students to make connections with people on campus who can model how to navigate your institutional system. The more names and faces of campus staff and instructional personnel your students know, the better.

As they make brief oral reports to the class throughout the term, work with your students to avoid two particular phrases that have dominated contemporary American speech. "Like" and "you know" (or "ya know") don't always carry the meaning intended by the speaker. When these two examples permeate informal speech, it is often difficult to decipher content. Ask students to keep a tally of these two words in their own brief oral reports to the class and to keep a tally of these words as they occur in recorded sound bites of professional athletes and entertainers. Articulate speakers avoid over-use of common words. Will your students be more successful in interview situations and, subsequently, in their professional lives if these phrases and other similar ones are under control rather than over-used?

Most students will have at least one term paper due this semester. Have them bring in their course outlines from their different courses that require research papers. Make them set up a timetable, such as the one listed in the chapter, breaking down the research paper into smaller achievable tasks. This is a great way to practice their writing organizational skills, which will be a valuable tool for them both in school and at work.

VII. LEARNING PORTFOLIO

1.   Self-Assessments
Have students take the plagiarism quiz on page 269. Consider writing the statements on the board and asking for a show of hands regarding the acceptability of each one. How accurate are your students in their identification of plagiarism?

2.   Your Journal
If you use PowerPoint in any of your lectures, consider having students complete the activity "PowerPointers" on page 271. Produce some less-than-ideal slides and have your students prepare a critique.

VIII. CHAPTER QUIZ SUGGESTIONS

1.   Use the Review Questions as a short-answer quiz. Points may be assigned equally at 25 points per question, or points may be divided unequally depending on the amount of class time and assignments devoted to various areas of the chapter. In short-answer quizzes, complete sentences are not always necessary as long as the essential points of the answer are present.

2.   A useful, non-threatening quiz for the Writing and Speaking chapter is to ask each student to spend two minutes making a list of strengths and weaknesses in both of these areas. Then ask that they spend another two minutes defining a specific strategy that could be used to address <u>one</u> of their weaknesses. This pass/fail type quiz allows students who give honest answers to receive a "pass" grade for classwork; those who either don't answer or who give inappropriate answers are given the opportunity to rework the quiz outside of class time and resubmit their work for a possible "pass" grade.

IX. QUIZ

Multiple Choice. Choose the one best answer.

1. Basic reasons for writing include:
    A. Explaining an idea.
    B. Persuading or arguing a point.
    C. Describing an experiment or reporting lab results.

D. Reflecting on one's experiences.
E. All of the above.

2. _____ conveys your general position on a topic and should guide your research.
   A. The title
   B. The abstract
   C. The thesis statement
   D. The summary
   E. The overview

3. Writing without stopping for a set period of time is called
   A. journaling.
   B. extracurricular writing.
   C. expository writing.
   D. free writing.
   E. unplanned writing.

4. All of the following are important steps in delivering a successful speech except:
   A. Rehearsing.
   B. Polishing delivery.
   C. Reading carefully from your prepared speech.
   D. Effective use of media.
   E. Looking the part.

5. Presenting someone else's words or ideas as your own is called
   A. predication.
   B. copyright infringement.
   C. plagiarism.
   D. pragmatism.
   E. copying.

True or False

6. _____When doing research for a paper, you should try to find sources that argue *against* your assertions.

7. _____Any information you find on the Internet should be considered a valid source.

8. _____In writing a paper, each paragraph in the body should develop a separate idea.

9. _____Effective speakers should speak "above" their audience to demonstrate their preparedness and knowledge of the subject matter.

10. _____If you get particularly nervous when speaking in public, taking a tranquilizer will help you perform more smoothly and effectively.

ANSWERS

1. **E**   2. **C**   3. **D**   4. **C**   5. **C**   6. **T**   7. **F**   8. **T**   9. **F**   10. **F**

X. TEST QUESTIONS

Multiple Choice. Choose the one best answer.

1. Writing assignments that serve to explain an idea or provide information, such as research papers and essays, are called
> A. eloquent writing.
> B. exemplified writing.
> C. explanatory writing.
> D. expository writing.

2. The single most important part of the writing process is
> A. coming up with the right topic.
> B. researching effectively.
> C. organizing your arguments.
> D. revising your work.

3. _____ is/are unnecessary in a formal paper and slow down your writing.
> A. Using a lot of adjectives
> B. Using a lot of adverbs
> C. Using phrases such as "It is well known that" or "There are many things that"
> D. All of the above

4. The *conventions* of good writing refer to
> A. the various writing styles of individuals.
> B. the particular writing formats, such as reflective, expressive, descriptive, scientific, etc.
> C. the rules of writing.
> D. the manner of grading that applies to written assignments.

5. Which of the following is *not* true about proofreading?
> A. Because you know your work so well, it is very easy to spot errors.
> B. It's a good idea to take a significant break between finishing your paper and proofreading, even overnight.
> C. Experts often recommend reading your paper sentence by sentence from back to front to proofread.
> D. All the above statements are true.

6. According to the text, _____ is often the difference between a good speech and a great one.
> A. research of the topic
> B. humor in the presentation

C. the tone of the speaker

D. rehearsal time

7. If you are asked a question after a speech and are unsure of the answer, you should
    A. ask to have the question restated.
    B. admit that you don't know the answer.
    C. ask the questioner for his or her opinion.
    D. All of the above.

True or False

8. _____A large number of sources used for a project is admired by instructors, and will most likely assure you a good grade.

9. _____Instructors expect students to keep up with technological advances, thus most expect research done on the Internet.

10. _____If you are certain to cite the source, it is acceptable to import an author's words directly into your own work.

Essay Questions

1. What are some important ways to prepare *before* you actually begin to write a paper or draft a speech?

2. What is plagiarism? How can you commit plagiarism by accident? How might you get caught? Discuss ways to avoid falling into the plagiarism trap.

3. List at least three specific strategies for improving your public speaking skills.

ANSWERS

1. **D**   2. **D**   3. **D**   4. **C**   5. **A**   6. **D**   7. **D**   8. **F**   9. **F**   10. **F**

XI. MENTOR'S CORNER _____

Dr. Gina Claywell is Director of Freshman Composition and Associate Professor in the English and Philosophy Department of Murray State University. She coordinates the Freshman Composition program and has written a book—*The Allyn & Bacon Guide to Writing Portfolios*—about helping students in any class develop stronger portfolios. She uses portfolios in all of her classes, as they provide students with a model of revision while offering them the opportunity to improve their work the second time around. To contact Gina, e-mail her at gina.claywell@murraystate.edu.

C H A P T E R   1 0

TAKE CHARGE OF YOUR PHYSICAL AND MENTAL HEALTH

I. CHAPTER OVERVIEW _____

For many first-year college students who are in the traditional age category, this is the first time that they will be totally responsible for their own physical and mental health. We know from empirical evidence alone that some of these students will engage in very risky health behaviors during this first year on their own. Some of them will never have experienced a pre-college course that deals honestly and factually with health issues. The information provided in this chapter and the exercises that instructors select to accompany the text could, literally, make a life-or-death difference for these students.

Among the health problems that concern first-year students are those of extreme weight gain or loss. The "freshman fifteen" factor not only leads to physical health problems but can affect students' mental health as they see themselves as less attractive because of weight problems. Women especially may be prone to either bulimia or anorexia during this transition year of relative instability. Snack food and fast food diets with irregular meal times undoubtedly contribute to weight problems for many Americans, not just college students; however, first-year students are notorious for their poor eating habits.

Chapter 10 begins by discussing the importance of establishing and maintaining a healthy lifestyle. It offers students the opportunity to assess how they are functioning right now and provides tips for how to get on the right track regarding all aspects of healthy living.

One of college students' (particularly freshmen) worst problems is their lack of sleep and general sleep habits. The section on sleep will help students re-think the hours they keep and remind them of the negative impact lack of sleep has on their productivity. You can help them translate this point into end of the semester grades and their GPA.

Smoking among teens fluctuates every several years. Regardless of whether the statistics indicate that it is currently at a "low" or on the upswing, far too many college students smoke. Their newfound independence and sometimes purposeful decision to try things that have been forbidden often lead them to turn to cigarettes. Not as negatively stigmatized as illegal "drugs", and not illegal like alcohol, it may serve as an assertion of independence in a way that they don't see as being "that bad". Emphasize through the use of the text – and possibly a guest physician – how wrong that notion is. The addictive nature of nicotine should be highlighted along with the plethora of physical maladies and severe consequences that plague the smoker.

Alcohol is another "drug" that students often view as less harmful because they see it as something everybody does and almost a necessary ritual of the college experience. Of course, we know that drinking can lead to some very serious problems, the *least* of which may be poor school performance, with the most severe involving drunk driving and even death. You can never say too much or emphasize enough the dangers associated with drinking.

AIDS still seems like a foreign and improbable reality for most students. Whereas we can, for the most part, feel confident it isn't rampant on college campuses, there are numerous other problems that occur through poor sexual decisions. Students still have a lot of questions and seek a safe environment in which to discuss their concerns.

Prevalent, but not publicized, is the number of mental health related issues on college campuses. Because of the private nature of such circumstances, most students don't realize that many of their peers are going through or have gone through some difficult times during this transitional period. Everything from loneliness and homesickness to severe depression and thoughts of suicide plague college students. This course offers an important venue to address these issues and assure students that there are resources and a support system available to them on campus should they feel in need. They need to recognize that there is no stigma attached to having certain feelings – such as being overwhelmed, missing their friends and family, and not knowing how to cope – and it's both important and necessary that they take the steps necessary to address the problem as soon as possible.

II. IMAGES OF COLLEGE SUCCESS

Brooke Ellison's inspirational story should help your students appreciate their own health and serves as a launching pad for discussion of health issues as well as diversity. What do your students know about campus resources for students with mild, moderate, or severe health-related issues or limitations?

What other types of health issues might students need to overcome to attend or succeed in college? Do your students personally know any students with health issues that might range from anorexia to diabetes or physical disabilities? (Perhaps you also have students who experience health limitations themselves, and would be willing to discuss this with the class.)

Consider obtaining a copy of Brooke Ellison's autobiographical book or the video based on her life story and use brief snippets in class to further personalize this image of success.

III. CLASS ACTIVITIES

Break The Ice!

1.   **Exploring the Campus Health Center**
If you were unable to or did not take advantage of a visit to your campus health center as suggested in an earlier chapter, this is the time to enlist the assistance of the professional medical staff on your campus whose jobs are to assist students in becoming/remaining physically and mentally healthy. Ask students to read Chapter 10 before meeting at the health center and provide a copy of this chapter to the staff person

who will address your class so that both class and presenter are armed with the same information. Then ask the presenter to tell the class:

- Exactly what services are provided by the health center
- How students access these services
- What costs are involved and whether or not insurance coverage is available
- How (or if) private insurance carriers are accepted
- Who files insurance claim forms
- Whether or not prescription drugs are available through the health center and how the costs compare with commercial pharmacies
- What lab services are provided
- And whether or not mental health facilities are available to students at this center or elsewhere on campus

Most campus health centers or clinics will have a number of brochures or pamphlets that describe their services to students (and staff). Ask the presenter to have enough of these printed materials available so that each of your students will have a copy to take with them.

Perhaps the most important part of this presentation, however, will be how the presenter addresses your students in matters of physical health related to sexual practices. Again, it is quite possible that some of your students will not know correct terminology, preventative practices, nor where and how to access more information or assistance. Work with the presenter to ensure that the information is given in a non-threatening and purely factual manner. Make sure that students are given contact phone numbers if they wish more information; some of the phone numbers are national or regional "hotlines" that were developed solely for the purpose of providing current and correct information to the public. Your health center may have wallet-sized cards with free access phone numbers for STD, AIDS, and other crisis centers.

After this presentation, students should know how and where to get information and assistance with physical and mental health problems. It is important to stress that although an individual student may not need this information, many of them are in situations with roommates who may need assistance in accessing healthcare services.

2. Common Health Problems

Have students work in small groups and make a list of the most common health problems they believe are relevant to first-year students. Give the groups no more than five minutes to construct their lists, and then share them with the entire class. What are the items common to all/most lists? Did the "freshman fifteen" appear on any of the lists? Address each of the items on the small group lists by asking students to offer practical and effective solutions for each problem. Use these solutions as a springboard to open discussion of the chapter topics.

Discussion and Reflection

1.   Exploring Personal Strengths
Ask students to describe their own best attributes with the qualification that nothing can be mentioned about physical appearance. According to their perception of their own self-worth,

- What positive personality characteristics do you possess that are valuable not only to yourself, but to others as well?
- What are your own individual gifts and talents?

Each student should list four or five personal characteristics and then provide an annotation for each one. Tell each student to save his or her personal list and review it at the end of each month. If there are perceived changes, list them, but don't erase any of the original entries. This exercise may develop into an interesting and useful record of personal growth and discovery. The original entry may be completed in class, but don't allow more than five minutes.

2.   Relieving Stress
Invite a member of the physical education staff or one of the varsity coaches to demonstrate physical stress-relieving techniques for your class. Prepare for this visit by asking your class members to dress in exercise clothing. It is helpful if the class can meet in a large area, free of furniture, so that everyone has room to participate and experiment with the techniques demonstrated. If your campus has a student exercise facility, reserve one of the exercise rooms there for this demonstration.

Words of Wisdom

1.   Quotes for Discussion
This chapter emphasizes both physical and mental health. Group all of the quotations in this chapter as they relate to either physical or mental health categories. Discuss reasons for placing each quote in either the physical or mental health category. Can some of them apply to both? Why? Ask each student to select a favorite quotation from this chapter and then to defend the selection. Why is this quotation more appropriate or appealing than the others?

2.   Quotes and You
Abraham Lincoln said, "It is hard to make people miserable when they feel worthy of themselves." No doubt some of your students will immediately connect this statement to physical appearance. Weight gain, weight loss, or weight maintenance will be a primary concern for many first-year students as they adjust to new living environments, new eating places and schedules, and new personal and academic stresses that are often assuaged by overindulgence in snack food. At the same time, at some point during the first term, most students will have self-doubts about their academic capabilities and social prowess, no matter how well they were prepared for college-level

coursework and how many friends they had in high school. Keeping a positive total self-image will be an important goal for your students.

If you study this chapter toward the end of the term, your students should know their small group team members well enough to work on some self-esteem issues. Toward the end of the first term of college studies, many students begin to have self-doubts about their abilities to succeed in college-level work. Stresses about upcoming final exams, final papers, looming final grade reports, and personal issues begin to take their toll. Prepare for this exercise by describing it to students at the end of one class period; tell them you will do the exercise at the next class meeting and that you wanted them to think carefully about their responses. Then at the next meeting, ask small groups to work through a word-gift exercise.

The rules are simple: each student in turn is the recipient of short word-gifts from the peers in the small group. The recipient is not allowed to respond, but must listen to words of encouragement from peers in the small group. Peers take turns offering a one- or two-word gift to the recipient, mentioning special talents, positive personality traits, times of assistance to others in the class, and other gestures that have contributed to the well-being of the class or group. One student records the word-gifts to give to the recipient as a keepsake and reminder of their worth to the group. One caveat: for obvious reasons students should not give word-gifts related to physical appearance. Beware of attempting this exercise before students know each other well; generic compliments are not only useless, but they are sometimes insulting or hurtful.

Major Themes

1.   Your Personal Health Style
Ask each student to write a brief essay describing their personal health style. What health problems might be anticipated during the first term away from home? What resources are available to solve these problems? List three specific, personal goals for staying healthy during this transitional year.

2.   Getting Physical
What is each student's favorite form of physical activity? Write a brief plan of action regarding a personal exercise program for this term. Be precise about how this plan will be implemented and maintained. Is it practical? Effective? Enjoyable? Keep the plan for quick reference during the term. Write a weekly entry as to progress on the plan and adjust accordingly throughout the semester.

3.   About Sleep
Write a brief journal entry regarding your current sleep habits. Do you sleep enough? Is the sleeping area quiet and conducive to restful sleep? Do you ever have difficulty going to sleep? If so, is this connected to upcoming stressful events or activities such as mid-term or final exams? What are your favorite techniques for relaxing so that sleep comes easily? Are there sleep patterns that you need to change to have a healthier lifestyle?

4. **About Nutrition**

Brainstorm within your small group about healthy eating habits and places on or around campus where students can get healthy food. Then compare answers. How many students in your small group practice these healthy eating habits? Be honest! What changes can each student make to promote healthier eating practices? Do any of the students cook simple, healthy meals in their dorm (microwave and hotplate)? Share some of the most creative ideas and recipes with the entire class.

5. **About Smoking**

What services does your campus health center offer to students who want to quit smoking? Are there students in the class who have stopped smoking? Ask them to share their methods with the class. Review the reasons why students start smoking in high school. Speculate about why students might begin smoking in college. What steps could be taken to help students refrain from starting a smoking habit in college? Discuss current events in the national news regarding settlements by states with tobacco companies over smoking and health-related issues. Has any national legislation been passed that would ultimately affect your students? A quick search of the Internet should provide updates for discussion.

6. **About Drugs and Alcohol**

Ask students to share the information they received about drug use and prevention during their earlier school experiences. Did any of the students participate in programs like D.A.R.E.? Were these effective? Why or why not? What drug prevention programs or advertisements were appealing to your students while they were in elementary school? Middle school? High school? What advice would your students give to younger students at each of these levels about drug use or abuse?

7. **Using Music as a Relaxation Tool**

Ask students to share their favorite music for relaxation. Compare answers. What makes each selection appropriate for each student? Why does some music work as a relaxation device for some students and not for others? Are the selections related to earlier experiences of comfort and security? Are there students who do not use music as a relaxation device? If not, what do they substitute?

8. **Ways to Boost Confidence**

What are your favorite ways to boost your confidence and self-image? Do you give yourself pep talks? Do you reward yourself for jobs well done? Do you phone or visit with special friends who know you and who appreciate you? What can you do to enhance the self-confidence of others? Why do insincere compliments often backfire? Discuss these answers in small groups or in pairs with students who know each other well enough to be honest. Remind students that honest answers should remain confidential unless permission is granted to share with the class.

9. **Thinking about Depression**

How do the text authors suggest that students deal with depression? Give at least three answers that work well for college students. What are the primary causes of

136

depression in first-year college students? Brainstorm in small groups about practical, alternative ways to overcome depression. When should a depressed person seek professional help?

10.   Helping a Suicidal Friend
        Discuss ways in which a student can assist a friend who is considering suicide. What are the techniques that should be the most helpful? Are there things that should not be discussed with a suicidal student? If so, what are they? When should a student ask for help with a suicidal friend or roommate? Where can students on your campus receive assistance in dealing with someone who is considering suicide? Be specific. Is this help available at all hours? If not, what are the alternatives? How can your students recognize signs of trouble in potentially suicidal friends or acquaintances? Invite someone from the student counseling center to talk on the ways to deal with a depressed or suicidal friend/roommate, and the importance of getting help when you feel this way.

11.   Where to Go for Help
        Where do students on your campus go for assistance with mental health problems? Are there hotline numbers available? Will student health insurance cover the costs of mental health treatments? What printed materials regarding mental health care are available from your health center or counseling office? Ask a student team to collect a sample of these materials to share with the class.

Summary Projects

1.   For the creative student whose learning style incorporates a generous portion of humor, a project to gather a collection of cartoons related to college physical and mental health issues could be a significant addition to a teaching portfolio for the course. The assignment must define at the outset that the cartoons must be sensitive enough to be pertinent, but in no way offensive or in questionable taste. Such a collection could be added to the teaching tools of the orientation instructor and used to open discussions or to relieve stress after a class session that focused on difficult or painful health issues. The collection could include published cartoons, some that were created for this assignment by the student, or both.

2.   What are the major health risks on your campus? Using research collected from news media reports, library resources, public health open records, and personal interviews with local health professionals, write a summary paper that would identify principal health risk categories among students on your campus over the past five years. In addition, sort the research findings so that suggestions for education, treatment, and prevention can be identified.

IV. CAMPUS CONNECTIONS AND RESOURCES _____

Campus Health Center: After reviewing available campus health facilities, give a three-minute quiz and ask students to give specific directions regarding how to locate the campus health center. Be sure that students not only know the address/location of the health facility, but also the phone number and any emergency numbers that are pertinent to health concerns. If you have provided students with wallet-sized emergency phone cards, give extra points for those who can produce the cards in class.

If your class does not visit the campus health center as a group and if your health center gives student tours, ask each student to take the tour and provide confirmation that they have done so. Most health centers will provide special stamps for students who produce a class assignment request for a tour.

Counseling Offices: Ask student teams to research all the counseling offices available on your campus for mental health counseling. These offices may be located in the student health center, or they may be housed in other units. If there is more than one counseling unit, be sure that each class member knows the location of each counseling office. Are the services provided by different units similar or different?

Student Health Groups: Are there any student organizations or clubs that are devoted to health concerns? Some colleges have chapters of H.E.A.T. (Health Education Awareness Team), a peer education organization. Ask teams of students to research the campus official club directory and to locate information about student groups whose purpose is to address health issues. Bring information to share with the class about each of these groups:

- What is the stated purpose of the group?
- Who are the officers?
- When are the meetings?
- What are the qualifications for membership?
- What is the contact address or phone number?

Student Recreational/Exercise Facilities: Is there a student recreational facility on your campus? If so, what services are offered? Is there a separate fee for each time students use the facilities, or does payment of tuition and fees for the term allow access for all students? Are there special fees for part-time students? Do faculty and staff also have access to these facilities? Are the facilities often over-crowded? If there is someone designated as coordinator for this facility, ask that person to either speak to your class about the facility and services, or better yet, host your class at the facility and demonstrate some of the activities available to students. If you elect the latter, be sure to warn your class to dress appropriately!

Health Professionals: Many universities and community colleges have health science programs such as Nursing, Dental Hygiene, Nutrition, and Exercise Science. Ask a health science faculty member to come in and speak to your class about healthy living practices.

Disabilities Counselor: All campuses should have disabilities services that provide testing and accommodations for all types of physical, emotional, and mental health disabilities. Ask the disabilities counselor to speak to your class about emotional and mental health issues that relate to college students. He or she could also discuss how to

138

deal with stress, anxiety, and depression. Many students have specific anxieties relating to test-taking, math, public speaking, or social situations that may be discussed at this time. The counselor could provide individual counseling for these students in addition to providing them with resources and references to reduce their anxiety.

Library: What kind of books and journals does the library have relating to health topics? Do they have books about relaxation techniques, healthy eating, safe sex, relationships, meditation, exercise, and stress management? Have students turn in a list of books that interest them relating to these topics.

Health Insurance and Services: Most universities have health centers and provide students with health insurance; however, most community colleges do not have these services. Have students research what services are provided for students on campus and what health services are available off-campus. Have them research their health insurance policies either through their parents, work, school, or the company itself. It is important to know about co-payments, deductibles, prescription rates, dental plans, and mental health services.

V. COLLABORATIVE LEARNING SUGGESTIONS _____

Exercise 1: Assign student teams to research health information that is available at city, county, or state health facilities in the area. What printed information is provided by any or all of these government units? Is there a local hospital that has a health education program? If so, are students eligible to attend? Is there a cost? What other community health groups are open to student access or participation? For instance, is there a local alcohol abuse prevention program? Are there Alcoholics Anonymous meetings close to campus? Al-Anon meetings? Drug abuse prevention support groups? Smoking cessation support groups? Ask the student teams to coordinate and collate their research findings, to arrange the findings in brochure or pamphlet format, and to offer the results to an appropriate department on campus for possible publication.

Exercise 2: Ask student teams to conduct an Internet search on various health topics. Assign a different topic to each team: drug abuse prevention, alcohol abuse prevention, smoking cessation assistance, stress relief, relaxation techniques, and exercise programs. Each team must write a summary paper on their topic, listing pertinent Internet sites, printed material, and local resources, including speakers who would be available for classroom presentations.

Exercise 3: Divide students into two groups, traditional (single, recent high school graduate) and non-traditional (returning adult with a family and employment). Have each group discuss their top five sources of stress and the negative and positive ways they have coped with their stress. Have them discuss how the stressors affect their behavior and attitude. Have them come up with positive healthy ways to deal with stress. Once the two groups complete their discussions, have a couple of students from each group present the following to the class: top five stressors, how stress affects their behavior and attitude, and five positive ways to deal with their stressors. The class could then discuss similarities and differences between the two lifestyles.

Exercise 4: Learning how to properly breathe and relax is vital to healthy living. Most of us take short breaths throughout the day and forget to really breathe. This exercise will teach students how to take deep, cleansing breaths that revitalize the body. Have the entire class practice deep breathing. First, turn the lights off in the classroom. Second, have the students close their eyes and place one of their hands on their stomach. Tell them to focus specifically on their breathing and nothing else. Have them inhale slowly through their nose while focusing on their lungs filling up with air like a balloon. They should feel their stomach expanding with each breath. Then, have them exhale though the mouth allowing all the air to escape from the lungs and stomach. Have them repeat this exercise several times taking deeper and longer breaths with each turn. This exercise teaches the students how to breathe correctly and deeply. If time permits, have the class practice deep relaxation techniques such as the one listed in the text book on page 290.

VI. ALTERNATIVE TEACHING STRATEGIES _____

If your institution is participating in the interactive CD program, *Alcohol 101,* assign student teams to participate in and complete this experimental program and to write a comprehensive critique. Compare the critiques and address any conflicting opinions. Why do the students believe this program to be effective or ineffective? If your institution is not a participant, ask students to write for information and a sample kit. The address is: The Century Council, 550 South Hope St., Suite 1950, Los Angeles, CA 90071-2604. Students should follow up by reviewing the sample and speaking with the unit or department on your campus that might be interested in sponsoring the program.

A second alternative is to join an existing campus program that focuses on preventative health measures. Some campuses sponsor a week-long effort to educate students on alcohol abuse issues; many of the activities are organized and implemented by students themselves with sponsorship from various departments on campus. Does your campus sponsor a health fair during the term? Is it possible for your students to volunteer as assistants for this project? It may be possible for your student teams to write a critique of the activities and publish their work in the campus newspaper.

Divide your class into three groups to research and present on healthy living (eating, sleeping, and exercise), safe sex (sexually transmitted diseases and safe sex practices), and stress management (sources of stress and positive ways to manage stress).

Have all students try one new healthy habit for a week. They can choose from trying out a new type of exercise, relaxation technique, change in eating habits, change in sleeping habits, change in smoking and drinking habits, or any of the suggestions listed in the book. At the end of the week, have students discuss their experience with the class. Was it difficult to practice the new habit, what were the challenges, what were the positive outcomes, did they feel different, and will they continue with the new healthy habit?

VII. LEARNING PORTFOLIO _____

1.   Self-Assessments
Have students complete the lifestyle questionnaire on page 296. Were they surprised with their overall scores? What are some common lifestyle weaknesses and strategies for addressing these issues?

2.   Your Journal
Have students complete the sleep journal outlined on page 300. What did they discover about their sleep habits? What percentage of your class gets less sleep in an average night than they originally thought, or than is considered healthy? How might this impact their daily performance?

VIII. CHAPTER QUIZ SUGGESTIONS_____

1.   Use the Review Questions as a short-answer quiz. Points may be assigned equally at 25 points per question, or points may be divided unequally depending on the amount of class time and assignments devoted to various areas of the chapter. In short-answer quizzes, complete sentences are not always necessary as long as the essential points of the answer are present.

IX. QUIZ _____

Multiple Choice. Choose the one best answer.

1. Of the 10 leading causes of death, _____of them can be reduced by lifestyle changes.
   A. 3
   B. 5
   C. 7
   D. 9
   E. 10

2. Exercise has been linked with
   A. generation of new brain cells.
   B. higher self-esteem.
   C. improved mood.
   D. greater life expectancy.
   E. All of the above.

3. *STD* stands for
   A. Suicide Then Death.
   B. Socially Themed Depression.
   C. Sexually Transmitted Disease.
   D. Sexually Targeted Date.

4. A man's lifetime risk of having depression is _____, while a woman's lifetime risk is _____.
    A. 5%, 10%
    B. 10%, 5%
    C. 10%, 25%
    D. 25%, 10%
    E. 50%, 50%

5. The basic food groups include all except the following:
    A. milk group.
    B. fruit and vegetable group.
    C. grain group.
    D. vitamin group.
    E. meat group.

True or False

6. _____In a national survey of first-year college students, heavy TV viewing was found to be related to poor health.

7. _____Exercise can actually generate new brain cells.

8. _____Smoking accounts for more than one-fifth of *all* deaths in the United States.

9. _____Insomnia can be impacted by lifestyle choices such as use of alcohol and nicotine.

10. _____A study found pessimists had twice as many infections and doctor's visits as optimists.

ANSWERS

1. **C**   2. **E**   3. **C**   4. **C**   5. **D**   6. **T**   7. **T**   8. **T**   9. **T**   10. **T**

X. TEST QUESTIONS_____

Multiple Choice. Choose the one best answer.

1. Which of the following exercises is *not* aerobic?
    A. Sprinting.
    B. Walking.
    C. Cycling.
    D. All of the above are aerobic.

2. Traditional-age college students should get 10 hours of sleep a night to function at optimal levels; however, researchers have found that college students average about
   A. 14 hours of sleep per night.
   B. 8-9 hours of sleep per night.
   C. 6 ½ hours of sleep per night.
   D. 5 hours of sleep per night.

3. The highest healthy body fat content is _____ for women, and the average woman has _____ body fat.
   A. 35%, 38%
   B. 40%, 48%
   C. 17%, 26%
   D. 22%, 32%

4. The term for the amount of weight typically gained during the first year of college is
   A. the freshman 5.
   B. the freshman 15.
   C. the freshman 50.
   D. None of the above; college students typically *lose* weight their first year.

5. Which of the following statements is *not* true?
   A. Bulimia can cause gastric and chemical imbalances in the body.
   B. Bulimia can cause long-term dental damage.
   C. Bulimics can control their eating.
   D. All of the above are true.

6. Each year, approximately _____ people are killed by drunk drivers.
   A. 8,000
   B. 14,000
   C. 20,000
   D. 25,000

7. Sexually transmitted diseases affect approximately
   A. 1 of every 23 adults.
   B. 1 of every 18 adults.
   C. 1 of every 10 adults.
   D. 1 of every 6 adults.

8. Mental health professionals don't classify a person as depressed until sad feelings linger for
   A. a week or longer.
   B. a month or longer.
   C. 3 months or longer.
   D. 9 months to a year.

True or False

9. _____Male college students engage in riskier health habits than female college students.

10. _____Passive smoke causes as many as 8,000 lung cancer deaths a year in the U.S.

11. _____*Anyone* who is sexually active or uses intravenous drugs is at risk for getting AIDS.

Essay Questions

1. Discuss the differences between depressants, stimulants, and hallucinogens. Why might students be tempted to use each type and what are some related risks?

2. Discuss sleep and the college student. Do students typically get enough sleep? How much is enough? What can you do to get enough? How can it affect you if you don't?

3. Discuss depression. What are the characteristics? How prevalent is it? What is its connection to suicide? Can it be cured? If so, how?

ANSWERS

1. **A** 2. **C** 3. **D** 4. **B** 5. **C** 6. **D** 7. **D** 8. **B** 9. **T** 10. **T** 11. **T**

XI. MENTOR'S CORNER _____

Alice Lanning is a past author of this Instructor's Manual and has taught her college's First Year Experience course fourteen times, each time with some different "twists" depending on the needs of the students. Her teaching evaluations indicate that students especially enjoyed her health units, multicultural diversity units, and campus resources units. She believes her ideas would be most appropriate for large, state institutions (18,000+ undergrad student body), but would be happy to share thoughts and successful exercises with any FYE instructor.

Her health unit includes in-class work with a "drunk-driver" kit from her health education office (goggles that distort vision while students "walk a highway line", or attempt to do so), student-led discussions of how to handle difficult situations that arise from underage and/or binge drinking, Alcohol 101 CD-ROM assignments, and in-class presentations by students who have been convicted of DUI.

Multicultural diversity issues are addressed by presentation/discussion sessions with minority campus leaders, assignments that require students to investigate other cultures through campus events, assignments that require students to interview students from another country/culture/ethnic group to investigate commonalities as well as differences, participation in a cultural event on campus other than one of their own

144

culture, class attendance at a Native American pow-wow (unique to her particular state culture), and other mind- and culture-stretching activities. Campus resources assignments and projects have always been evaluated very highly by students.

You can contact Alice Lanning at: alanning@ou.edu.

CHAPTER 11

BE A GREAT MONEY MANAGER

I. CHAPTER OVERVIEW _____

Along with their newfound independence as young adults, college students are often faced with financial responsibilities for the first time. Many freshmen are used to dealing with money in terms of an allowance from parents and income from a part-time job to make car payments. However, college often results in an entirely new set of money issues, including having to pay for tuition, living expenses, and learning how to balance work and school.

It is important that freshmen become aware of numerous issues regarding money management. In particular, they need to understand the basics of where to keep their money and how to budget. Different kinds of bank accounts are presented, along with how to create a budget and use a check register or a debit card. Establishing some savings is also addressed, since the text helps students draw the connection between being a good money manager now and how they will handle their finances after graduation.

One of the major stressors students face during college is having enough money to afford their education and living expenses. Record numbers of students are now working and going to school, something that can result in poor school performance, constant course withdrawal, and even quitting school altogether. Students are encouraged to pursue jobs that don't have constant work demands, enabling them to balance reading and study time. They are also introduced to the notion of seeking out a work-study program that will enable them to earn money by working part-time on campus – the most beneficial work situation to have. If work is not an option, or not their first choice, students are given explicit information about various types of financial aid. Students are encouraged to make an appointment with a financial aid advisor on their campus to learn what options may be available to them. Scholarships, grants, and loans are discussed in detail, including how students can pursue obtaining such financial assistance.

As a target group for credit card companies, freshmen must understand how credit cards function and learn both the benefits of having one and the dangers of using one. The concept of using a credit card "in case of emergency" is illustrated by demonstrating the need for students to clearly define what constitutes an "emergency", and discuss with their parents, as appropriate, the circumstances in which they will be financially responsible.

At some point during their college experience, students may find themselves in debt. This chapter provides several steps students can take if their financial situation takes a downward turn. The entire chapter is pulled together through a meaningful conclusion that discusses the incredible value of a college education. Despite the challenges inherent in paying for school and covering living expenses while a student, if college success is mastered and the goal of graduation is achieved in a timely fashion, the payoff is invaluable.

II. IMAGES OF COLLEGE SUCCESS _____

Irresponsibility resulted in the creation of the hugely popular video service *Netflix*. Because Reed Hastings was annoyed by late fees at the video rental store, he decided to solve his problem. He also solved thousands of other people's problems as well, with the initiative stemming from his own financial frustration. Hastings story is that of a positive response to money issues, but few college students have the experience or common sense to deal with many new financial responsibilities that may arise as they begin life as independent adults. Given your students are likely to have been on their own for most of the semester at this point, ask them what they have discovered so far about being financially independent. What are their frustrations? How do they solve their problems with money? Are these wise solutions or potentially problematic moves. Assess your class's money savvy prior to delving into the chapter. You can then select the activities and topics to place the most emphasis on in order to help them make wise fiscal decisions.

III. CLASS ACTIVITIES _____

Break The Ice!

1.   The Cost of a Break
Provide a calculator for each group. The assignment is to count the cost of missing one class. Students who attend public institutions that receive tax support will need to know what percentage of their educational costs is provided by public support. Other steps may be added to the following formula to account for local necessities, but the essentials are as follows:

- List the cost of basic tuition per term.
- Add to this cost any student fees commonly assessed per term. Health fees? Health insurance? activity fees? facility fees?
    - Add the cost of books and supplies per term.
- Add the cost of room and board per term. If you are a commuter living with parents, spouse, or relatives, estimate your share of room and board costs.
- Add any transportation costs: personal vehicle (payments, insurance, fuel, upkeep, parking fees, etc.), shared commuter costs, public transportation costs (for commuters), campus transit system costs.
- Add entertainment costs: movies, video rentals, sports/concert tickets, meals, membership dues for student organizations.
- Personal items: laundry, health supplies, clothing, medications.
- Total the cost per term of all these items.

- Multiply the number of hours you are in class each week by the number of weeks in the term.
- Divide the total cost by the number of hours you are in class per term. This is the average cost per class hour. Can you afford to miss class?

2.   Exploring Financial Resources

What are some of the financial resources available for college students? Students bring an extensive knowledge base with them to your class. Ask each small group to prepare a list of financial resources that are accessible to students to support their college costs. Share the lists with the entire class. Among the answers will likely be:

- savings from self and/or parents and relatives
- monthly support from parents and/or relatives
- scholarships and grants
- loans
- work-study jobs on campus
- off-campus jobs

Encourage elaboration within each of the categories listed. Probe into answers that involve loans. What are the interest rates? Your campus financial aid office can provide examples of loan payment schedules so that students can see what will be due when they graduate. What percentage of an average college graduate's monthly salary may need to go toward student loan payments?

Discussion and Reflection

1.   Personal Financial Plans

Have students create personal financial "plans". Have them itemize and prioritize both short-term and long-term financial goals. These may include both *items* that they desire (new CD player for their car, their own home), *experiences* they would like to have (going on a road trip for Spring Break, traveling through Europe), and *life circumstances* they hope to attain (not having to work while going to school, being able to get married and have themselves or their spouse stay home with children). Students can share their goals and dreams that require financial success, then work together to brainstorm ways in which they can actively pursue those goals now. Students can also assess themselves relative to their classmates in terms of how ambitious their financial goals are, the degree of importance they place on things requiring money, and their current financial functioning and the extent to which it will enable them to achieve their dreams.

2.   Credit Card Use and Abuse

Invite a speaker from the Consumer Credit Counseling Service or similar non-profit organization to talk with your class about the advantages and dangers of credit cards. Ask the speaker to cite case studies of students who demonstrated both responsible and irresponsible credit card use. As an assignment following this presentation, ask student teams or groups to investigate the ease of obtaining commercial credit cards on your campus. Are credit checks necessary? What are the limitations on first-time card holders? What are typical interest rates?

Have students discuss what they know about credit cards. Do they have one? Do they use it? If so, what for? Do they pay off the balance each month, or just make the minimum payment? How does this fit in with their budget? Are they noticing that they spend more than they expect? If they don't have any personal experience, do they know anyone who does – a roommate or friend? What have they noticed with regard to their ability to be financially responsible with credit cards? Have students discuss ways to use credit cards responsibly (and stick to it!) as well as defining what constitutes an "emergency" for those who have a card solely for that purpose. How widely do definitions vary?

Words of Wisdom

1. **Quotes and You**
Ask students to consider the following quote: "I finally know what distinguishes man from beast: Money worries." How much do your students worry about finances? Credit card debt can be a real source of stress for college students. Some students have felt so overwhelmed by debt that they have committed suicide. How much do your students care about money? What sort of life-style do they imagine having—lavish or middle class? What sorts of luxuries do they imagine? Do any students get sucked in by Hollywood glamour? Ask them how commercials can play into our desires and our debt!

2. Present your students with the quote: "If you can eat, wear it, or drink it, it is not an emergency." Ask them to identify what they believe truly constitutes an emergency requiring them to spend money, or use a credit card, etc. Have them respond to each others' "emergencies" by developing a solution that doesn't involve spending a lot of money. Might they add anything to the list presented in the quote above (such as "listen to it", "watch it")? See how small you can get your class' list of true spending emergencies.

Major Themes

1. **Guest Speakers**
Invite a service representative from a local financial institution to address your class about how to prepare a budget and stick to it. Ask the speaker to mention ways that college students can save money even while they are undergraduates. Some financial institutions offer students the opportunity to belong to investment groups for a very small monthly fee. Student investment clubs often have professional assistance available from commercial financial institutions.

2. **Delayed Gratification**
Ask small groups to create delayed gratification statements for students who tend to overspend their budgets. What are some of the carrots that students can hold in front of themselves as rewards for delaying unnecessary expenditures?

3.   Your Big Night Out!

For residential campus students, assign the following small group activity. You have $20 to provide entertainment for you and a friend for next Friday night. You must begin and end the evening at your residence hall location. Make a detailed budget of how you will spend the $20. Don't forget to include costs for food and transportation. Be resourceful, but don't exceed the $20 limit. Award a pizza to the group voted by the class as the most creative within the guidelines. Then hold a drawing for $20 and ask the winner to actually try out the winning idea and report the results to the class.

4.   A Different Type of Job

Have students look in the classified ads from both the campus newspaper and local community papers. They should search for positions that might enable them to work in a situation where periods of study might be possible. See if students can identify other types of jobs that would provide both the opportunity to earn money and accomplish some school-related activities.

5.   Scholarship Search

The Internet has numerous websites linking students to scholarship opportunities. Have students either visit the campus Financial Aid office for scholarship websites, or use a search engine to identify sites. Each should create a list of scholarships they may qualify for and collect application information. Have an application prep session, in which you guide students through the process of filling out the application forms, planning out and writing required essays, suggestions for whom to ask for letters of recommendation, etc. Review "Show Scholarship Savvy" on page 315 of your text for pointers.

6.   What's It Worth To You?

Have students either make a list or write in essay form the reasons it is important to pursue their education *now*. Encourage them to delineate the factors that make it imperative to wholeheartedly give themselves to succeeding in school, despite the sacrifices it may take. Have them include the benefits to their life both now and in the future, as well as reasons for them not to wait, or go through school sporadically – possibly taking off semesters occasionally to work more or save more money. Why is it important that they explore financial aid options so that they don't have to work full-time or even part-time while in school? What difference might it make to them to stay on track and keep up their momentum to finish within 4 or 5 years, as opposed to plugging away for 6, 7, or 8 years, thinking they'll "eventually get there"?

Have them share lists and ideas – anonymously if necessary. Follow the presentation with a class discussion on the incredible value of school and the benefits of managing money in such a way as to be able to take advantage of it now.

Summary Projects

1.   An in-depth report on commercial credit card use among freshmen on your campus is a most appropriate topic for a final research paper. With written permission, creative students might videotape interviews with professional credit card advertisers and

then follow up with interview videos of students representing both pro and con sides of the credit card debate. A written summary could complete the project.

2.   With the plethora of scholarships available to students, every student should be able to locate at least one or two to pursue. Have students research scholarships either through the Financial Aid office or the Internet and put together an application to submit. Prior to sending off their applications, have them submit them to you for review. Grades can be given for extensiveness of searches – yielding appropriate scholarship opportunities – the neatness and completeness of the application for submission, as well as the effort and presentation of any additional application requirements such as essays or letters of recommendation. Encouraging students to pursue and take the time to apply for scholarships will give them first-hand knowledge of all that may be available to them and experience with what it takes to apply. The results may be quite rewarding!

IV. CAMPUS CONNECTIONS AND RESOURCES _____

Invite a representative from the financial aid office to make a brief presentation to your students. Request that the speaker bring copies of printed resources that are available in most financial aid offices. If emergency loans are obtainable, ask the presenter to give specific instructions about accessing this resource. Also ask that the speaker tell students about the availability of and application process for scholarships that are based on first-term GPA.

If your campus has a separate placement or employment office (or financial aid officer who is responsible for on-campus employment), secure a speaker from that office to inform your students about how to apply for jobs both on campus and in the community. Ask the speaker to bring application forms to the class and review specific instructions necessary for completion of the forms. What additional documents are necessary to apply for a job? Are interviews required? Are the interviews with a job placement counselor or with the specific job supervisor or both? What tips will help a student have a successful interview? How many hours should a student expect to work and still make acceptable grades? Is there a difference in pay scale for campus and off-campus jobs? Will this extra employment affect scholarships or other financial aid? Most speakers will appreciate a brief list of topics that the instructor would like addressed during the presentation as well as a time limit for presentations.

Most colleges and universities offer business courses. Invite one of the faculty members to talk to your students about financial planning and management. Discuss the advantages and disadvantages of student loans, cost of living, and other money matters. Review how to keep records of spending, how to balance checking accounts, and how to develop a budget plan.

Have students visit the financial aid office and the college catalog to review scholarships available based on major or department, financial need, GPA, community service, veteran relations, nationality, and any other factors. Students will realize that there are many scholarships available for everyone. Require students to complete the FAFSA online and to apply for at least one scholarship. If the students are in community college, have them research the scholarships and grants available at the transfer institution. Have them review the requirements and deadlines for the scholarship applications.

V. COLLABORATIVE LEARNING SUGGESTIONS _____

1.   After reading the *Expand Your Resources* section, "Beyond Coupons", assign each small group to add at least five other suggestions to the list that are specific to their campus. For instance, what are the common money-saving coupons that appear in your campus or local newspaper? Are there discounts for students at late-night movies? Combine the suggestions and publish a class newsletter on your campus Internet server as a public service project. Invite other students to add to the list and then offer the complete list to the campus newspaper as background material for a feature story.

2.   Have students form teams of financial aid experts. Group students and assign them a particular type of financial aid to research and become knowledgeable about. Include work-study, scholarships, grants, and the various kinds of loans. After each group has done its research, have them put together a detailed presentation, including handouts, web addresses, etc. and share the information with the class. Groups should be prepared to discuss how their particular form of financial aid can assist students in their current financial situation, as well as the implications it can have for the future. They should provide explicit materials for students to see, and information as to how students can go about obtaining the particular forms of aid.

3   Have each student anonymously write down his or her top five concerns and worries about money on a piece of paper. Some of these concerns may be listed in Self-Assessments 2 and 3. List the different concerns and worries on the board. Group students into 5 teams and assign them one of the issues. Have them discuss strategies for dealing with the money concerns and then present them to the remainder of the class for discussion. Discuss some alternatives for compulsive spending. It helps students to know their concerns are a commonality among college students. This exercise will provide them with ideas and support to help them with financial issues.

VI. ALTERNATIVE TEACHING STRATEGIES _____

Use the Internet site under the Financial Aid heading of the Resources page to investigate other Internet and online financial aid services. Students can share information gleaned from these sites as well as other sites they may discover from using the browser connected to their server. It will be helpful for students to evaluate the information they discover, especially in terms of current information provided, ease of access to the information, and cost of the service, if any.

      Work with students on debt management. Based on the tips presented in the text, have them brainstorm ways to solve debt issues. If they aren't currently having difficulty, have them identify ways in which they might be at risk for problems. Imagining that those problems should arise, guide them through the process they might go through in order to get back on track financially. Make sure they consider the most realistic scenarios.

Provide students with a budget planning program and require them to use it for a month before reviewing the chapter. Require them to keep track of their income and expenses. At the end of the month, have them review where their money goes. Are they spending more than they make? Where can they reduce expenses? How can they increase their income? Discuss these options with the class.

VII. LEARNING PORTFOLIO

1.   Self-Assessments
Have students complete Self-Assessment 3 on page 328. Were students concerned about their financial scores? Why or why not? Discuss some strategies students can implement now for greater financial health and independence.

2.   Your Journal
Have students complete the activity "Simplifying my Life" on page 329 and then brainstorm in small groups about ways to streamline their lives. What common strategies were reached? What were some of the most creative ideas?

VIII. CHAPTER QUIZ SUGGESTIONS

1.   Use the text review questions or quiz questions *prior* to beginning the chapter. Test students to see how prepared they are to manage their money successfully. Often students believe they will have no difficulties managing their finances, or that there's nothing to having a credit card. Once they are faced with answering specific questions regarding the important issues addressed in the chapter, it will open their eyes to all that they have to learn from this unit.

2.   Have students create their own quiz questions, demonstrating what they feel are the most important facts to take away from this chapter. Compare and contrast student quizzes to assess where your class stands as a whole. Are they thinking along the same lines, or are there very disparate views as to the issues of significance?

IX. QUIZ

Multiple Choice. Choose the one best answer.

1. The term for a record of how much money is being spent versus how much is being earned is
    A. bank statement
    B. check register
    C. debit

D. budget

E. financial analysis

2. Looking back at what you earned and what you spent over a period of time prior to making financial decisions is _____ budgeting.

    A. time frame

    B. reflective

    C. proactive

    D. reactive

    E. superficial

3. A strategy for helping to finance your college education includes:

    A. college loans.

    B scholarships.

    C. work-study jobs.

    D. internships.

    E. All of the above.

4. When you use a debit card,

    A. money is charged to your account and you will be billed monthly.

    B. money is immediately taken out of your checking account.

    C. money is immediately taken out of your savings account.

    D. the bank loans you the amount until you replenish your funds.

    E. you are expected to make immediate payment in cash.

5. Establishing good credit includes all of the following except

    A. maintaining a high GPA.

    B. managing a checking or savings account appropriately.

    C. paying bills on time.

    D. having a stable employment history.

    E. timely payment of all loans.

6. The federal loan for students is called

    A. work study.

    B. the Pell Grant.

    C. the Stafford Loan.

    D. the FAFSA.

    E. a scholarship.

True or False

7. _____All scholarships are based on financial need.

8. _____It is silly to stress over credit card debt in college, as you will be able to pay it off easily once you get your first full-time job.

Fill in the Blanks

9. The two primary types of bank accounts are _____ and _____.

10. Three considerations for approaching budgeting are _____, _____, and _____.

ANSWERS

1. **D**　2. **D**　3. **E**　4. **B**　5. **A**　6. **C**　7. **F**　8. **F**　9. checking, savings

10. time frame, proactive, reactive

X. TEST QUESTIONS _____

Multiple Choice. Choose the one best answer.

1. The place to start when managing money is
   A. to create a budget.
   B. to consult a financial advisor.
   C. to acquire a credit card and use it.
   D. to invest some money.

2. Anticipating your upcoming expenses and making sure they do not exceed your projected income is _____ budgeting.
   A. time frame
   B. anticipatory
   C. proactive
   D. reactive

3. According to your text, saving money is all about making
   A. money.
   B. a budget.
   C. choices.
   D. deposits.

4. Which of the following might a bank charge you a fee for?
   A. Having checks.
   B. Processing each check you write.
   C. Monthly account maintenance.
   D. All of the above.

5. A check card is also known as a(n)
   A. debit card.
   B. charge card.
   C. ATM card.

155

D. credit card.

6. Government programs that employ students in either community service positions or on campus are called
    A. work study.
    B. Pell Grants.
    C. the Perkins' programs.
    D. federal internships.

True or False

7. _____When working out your budget, you should only include your *regular* monthly income and not money from special occasions, or textbook buy-back money, etc.

8. _____"Financial success" is defined differently depending on who is defining it.

9. _____It is a good idea to keep a balance on your credit card to establish good credit.

10. _____Neither prospective nor current employers have the right to look at your credit report.

Essay Questions

1. What are some advantages of establishing a monthly budget early in your college career?

2. For students who have to work, discuss the kinds of jobs they might pursue in order to better their chances of college success.

3. Discuss the importance of defining "emergency" in relation to good money management.

ANSWERS
1. **A** 2. **C** 3. **C** 4. **D** 5. **A** 6. **A** 7. **F** 8. **T** 9. **F** 10. **F**

CHAPTER 12

EXPLORE CAREERS

I. CHAPTER OVERVIEW _____

This chapter, presented last in the text, not only discusses issues associated with exploring careers, but also connects many of the ideas presented in prior chapters that contribute to the theme of this book. The first semester of college may seem like an unlikely time for freshmen to look carefully into a future career. Right now, they are only completing the first of numerous core courses – some will not be taking a single course that is directly related to their major. Some students don't even have a major, so a chapter titled "Explore Careers" is probably seen as not only unnecessary at this point in time, but nearly impossible as well. However, when presented in the context of all that has come before, the material in this chapter can be viewed as highly beneficial.

It begins by going back to the basic building block of success – knowing your values. Students often believe that "values" refer only to morality – the choices they make to be "good" or "bad". *Your Guide to College Success* repeatedly acknowledges that it is our values – what is important to us in life – that are at the core of deciding where we want to go and what we want to do when we get there. Identifying one's values will provide the direction and the motivation to take us in that direction. In the college student's case, one direction that needs to be identified is in terms of a career. It is amazing how clear this can become when it is approached from the simple perspective of what we value.

Once values have been acknowledged and career ideas begin to flow, students must assess their skills. This will enable them to identify what areas they need to work on to help them achieve their career goals. Evidence is building that clearly links personality traits to success in particular careers. Many of those connections are presented in the text and students can go back and refer to them, now taking a closer look at how they can use that information to help guide them towards a career.

Finding good potential careers goes beyond knowing yourself. It is highly beneficial for students – even as freshmen, or *especially* as freshmen – to explore the *Occupational Outlook Handbook* in order to gather detailed information about career trends, projected salaries, and the job market outlook. While our values should set the foundation for our goals, an element of practicality is necessary for making the best decisions. As students are exploring careers from both the personal and realistic perspectives, it is important to encourage them to investigate several choices. This is where their status as freshmen serves as a good argument for the assignment. They have a multitude of opportunities and experiences ahead of them, and they should remain open to a variety of possibilities and take their time to narrow their direction.

Career counselors and the campus career center are vital resources available to students. They may initially write off this service as something they won't need for a couple of years; however, introducing them to what they have to offer now will be appreciated. Encourage or assign students to visit their career center to discover all the ways in which it can help get them a head start on defining their career paths.

It is also never too early to begin networking and making contacts with people who might help in the future job process. Students should begin brainstorming a list of contacts – even people they have not yet met, but simply have heard of through others – that might be able to get their foot in the door for an internship or co-op. The Internet offers a tremendous storehouse of resources and the sooner students can learn their way around finding job-related information, the more power they'll have towards making sound decisions.

It's also good to give students a "heads up" now about what skills employers look for the most in potential employees, as well as the importance of researching jobs and companies prior to considering applying. They should begin learning the basics of how to write an appropriate resume as well as the techniques important for succeeding in a job interview. All of these lessons may be necessary earlier than they think, as summer jobs, internships and co-ops are becoming the norm for students who expect to have an edge in the job market.

II. IMAGES OF COLLEGE SUCCESS

There are many important and inspiring lessons students can learn from Giselle Fernandez' story. Her career accomplishments are notable, particularly for someone who is young and a minority in her field. What she has done in her career demonstrates how far people can go when they follow their passion.

Just as interesting and significant is the fact that journalism was not Giselle's first pursuit. She strongly believed that she wanted to go into politics. So certain was she of this, she moved across the country from her home in order to live and study in an area more apt to help her reach her goal. Students can take some time to think about the choices they make now, and how they believe they will impact their future career. It is also a good opener to discuss sacrifice, and some of the more challenging decisions that students might be faced with making in order to follow their dreams.

Giselle's experience working in a senator's office is something most people probably think would solidify her decision and direction in politics; however, just the opposite happened. Her realization that politics was not what she wanted to do took some very deep insight and courage to acknowledge. This is a wonderful example of the learning process in action, and it provides an opportunity to point out that not everything students imagine will happen exactly as planned and they can always make choices to alter their course toward a more desirable goal.

III. CLASS ACTIVITIES

Break The Ice!

1.   Academic Motivation

Many institutions provide excellent speakers on the topic of academic motivation. Who are these people on your campus? Perhaps there are speakers available from the Office of the Dean of Students, the counseling department, or particular academic departments whose faculty members are recognized as being inspirational motivators for their students. Ask officers from the student honor societies to recommend speakers who can provide a motivational presentation to your class. Often a professional advisor who has teaching experience can provide this service.

2. Writing Cover Letters

Have students write a cover letter for their future resume. Tell them to imagine themselves upon graduation, introducing themselves to a potential employer. The letter should present a good picture of who they are, a summary of some of their accomplishments, and their ideas as to how they can contribute as an employee. Of course, none of the information should be job specific. Students should just use this as an exercise to plan out what they would like to be able to say about themselves when they are ready to begin their career. Encourage students to keep the paper and refer to it in the future. It can serve as a great motivator to get through the challenges of school, as well as a nice reminder of what they value in themselves and how they believe others will value those characteristics in them.

Discussion and Reflection

1. Exploring Career Testing

If your campus provides a center with resources for career testing, ask if it is possible for your students to be given one or more tests that can help them discover an appropriate career field and a degree area that leads to employment in this field. Among the measures that can be helpful are the Myers-Briggs Type Inventory, the Strong Interest Inventory, Holland's *Self-Directed Search*, the *Discover* test, and others that assist students in matching interests and abilities with career fields. If students know how and where to find help when they want career information, this may be more valuable on an individual need-to-know basis rather than requiring the entire class to complete one of the career assessment measures before each of them is ready. Students will also need to know whether or not career testing is free or whether additional fees are involved. In most cases, individual interpretation of the career measure is necessary to achieve maximum benefit.

Words of Wisdom

1. Quotes for Discussion

"Whatever you can do, or dream you can, begin it. Boldness has a genius, power, and magic."—Goethe. Have your students discuss this quote.

2. Quotes and You

Many students will already have identified a favorite motivational quotation during their high school years. It may have been one suggested by an athletic coach, a music instructor, a close relative, or a favorite classroom teacher. Ask your students to write their favorite motivational quote on a transparency using colored pens or other devices that will highlight the meaning of the quotation. Then discuss the quotations in class. Which ones might continue to serve students through this first year in college?

Students who are creative may wish to write their own motivational statement to share with the class. Some students may recall a high school class motto from a graduation announcement that was particularly meaningful to them.

Are there quotes from athletic superstars that are pertinent to the content of this chapter? How do professional athletes motivate themselves to succeed? What advice have your students heard from successful public figures about going to college, completing a degree, and then becoming successful professionals? Quotations may be inspiring as heroes "talk the talk", but sooner or later students have to "walk the walk" and do the work necessary to be academically successful. Discuss the problems between hearing the rhetoric and then following through with appropriate action.

Major Themes

1. Who are You and What Do You Want to Do?

Lots of research has matched personality characteristics with ideal jobs. Have students take the MBTI (either in class or through the campus career or counseling center) and assess their personality using the Big Five categories. Once they have delineated their personality characteristics along these lines, have them look over the list of jobs suited to the different personality types. Have them make a complete list of what job types match their characteristics. What specific jobs can they think of that fit the match? They should try to make a complete list regardless of whether or not they initially like the job descriptions that match their characteristics. Have students share their ideas as to specific jobs relating to each category. Have some students thought of jobs others did not? Do those ideas prompt other considerations? Might they be able to create a unique position within their field that encompasses the ideal characteristics listed in the text? Encourage students to think about careers and job possibilities in ways they have not yet considered.

2. Interviews: Role-Playing

The ideal job candidate has rehearsed for interviews. Your students will have an opportunity to rehearse their interview strategy if they complete the academic advisor interview suggested in Chapter 4. It is extremely helpful if you can help prepare your students for this and other interviews by role-playing exercises in small groups. It is also important that students understand why they practice interview techniques.

If you require a advisor interview, not only will students benefit from talking in this manner with a university staff member, they will also gain practice in interviewing for future jobs. Some of your students may have qualified for federal work-study jobs on campus, most of which require a personal interview. Ask your students who are in the process of interviewing for campus jobs to compile a list of interview questions that might be appropriate to any job. Then share these lists with the class and discuss how students can answer truthfully while emphasizing their skills and previous work experience.

3. Informal Ways to Consider a Major

Does your college offer brief, non-credit seminars or workshops that allow students to explore various majors? Ask students to contact the career services office on your campus to see if this option is available. If so, when and where are the exploratory sessions held? If this is a service feature of an office at your institution, ask a team of students to pick up publicity information from the exploring majors seminars and share the information with others in the class. Suggest that students attend the seminars with a partner from the class who is interested in the same field. Make a brief oral report to the class about the seminar. Was it helpful? How does one follow up on the information? Will there be other similar seminars this term?

4.   It's Never Too Early to Network

They may only be freshmen, but students can get a head start on their career path and pre-graduation experiences through networking. Have students make a list of people whom they could potentially network with. Remind them that it begins with simply inquiring as to opportunities that might be available to them – regarding part time work, an internship, co-op, research assistantship, or summer job. They should consider their parents' friends, their friends' parents and their friends and business acquaintances. Faculty and staff are very important contacts, so students should consider whom they might try getting to know better. Older students and teaching assistants can be sources of useful information and can be contacts as well. Once students have generated their lists, they should make a plan to meet with at least a couple of people on the list, simply to "feel them out" regarding opportunities for the future.

5.   An Employer's Ideal

There is a general consensus as to what employers value in an employee. Go over the list of top skills desired by employers then have students identify where they stand with regards to each. Which ones are they already strong in? Which ones need the most work? They should be able to provide examples illustrating the former, and then delineate what they need to do in order to strengthen the latter. Help them to identify current opportunities in college to develop these essential skills.

6.   Write to Impress (and Get Hired!)

During the job search process, students will need to write to potential employers in a variety of ways. Resume writing is often the primary focus; however, it is essential to be able to write an effective cover letter, as well as employment inquiry letters, and thank you letters. Have students produce an example of each type of correspondence. Although the content may be scant, have students practice each form of resume. Also, they should practice writing a letter inquiring about a particular position in a company, as well as a follow-up thank you letter. Remind students that in most cases, what they write will be the first impression they present to potential employers, and their written communication skills are vital.

Summary Projects

1.   One orientation instructor assigns a career-selection final project for her class. Each student is required to select a field of special interest and thoroughly research that field through the resources provided not only in the main campus library, but also through the departmental library most closely connected to the proposed career field and

the campus career services center. Students are encouraged to interview a professor who teaches in that career field as well as at least two persons who are currently employed in that area of specialization. Part of the final paper includes a section in which students describe their own personal characteristics, abilities, or interests that relate directly to the proposed major field. Each student includes a degree plan that outlines what courses should be completed in what sequence and lists various options for fulfilling course electives.

IV. CAMPUS CONNECTIONS AND RESOURCES _____

Campus Career Placement Office: If your campus has a Career Services or Career Planning and Placement department, ask a representative of that office to speak to your class about the services provided to all students, not only graduating seniors. Most career planning offices encourage students to register long before the senior year for assistance in resume construction, reference letter collection and storage, and assistance with applications for summer internships and apprentice positions available even to students who have completed only limited college work. Be sure to acknowledge if additional fees are required to register with the office; this will have an impact on whether or not students register early. Some career planning departments urge students to do minimal research on possible career fields before registering, but many will assist undeclared students with career options and ways to research possible fields of interest.

Departmental Career Advisors: Are there special career advisors within academic departments who are available to talk with students, either in groups or individually, about career fields related to specific majors? If so, arrange visits with these advisors for any of your students who are interested. This may occur as an extra credit assignment for those students who are still searching for an appropriate major and/or career field or as a follow-up assignment for students who have already selected a major and want to know alternative career paths that might be connected with a particular major.

Departmental Careers Courses: Ask students to look through the college catalog and identify credit classes within particular departments that are career-investigation courses. Often this kind of course is offered for entry-level or second-year students who are still searching for a major. Some institutions offer special credit elective courses in career and life planning for students who are undeclared majors. Are these courses available on your campus? If so, ask junior and senior students who have taken the courses to talk with your students about the relative usefulness of the courses. Encourage your students to investigate career fields through this course design even if, after completing the course, it means that they will no longer be interested in that particular field. Sometimes learning what a student *doesn't* want in a career field is as helpful as knowing what a student *does* want. Eliminating a career field through a special class at this point may save a considerable amount of time and money invested in a field that will ultimately not suit the student's interests or abilities.

Career Resource Center: Assign students to visit the career resource center on campus to research their three top career choices. Many career centers have a variety of books and references in addition to websites providing career information. Ask students to review the educational and training requirements, salary, advancement, nature of work, job outlook and demand, and working conditions of their top career choices.

Career and Transfer Counselors: Ask students to meet with a career or transfer counselor to develop a career and academic plan. Counselors can provide students with information regarding the universities and colleges that offer programs relating to their career choices. Counselors can assist students in developing a plan including prerequisites for acceptance into educational programs. For example, a student interested in medical school needs to develop an academic plan relating to the prerequisites and academic requirements to be accepted into certain medical programs.

Library: The library on campus holds many resources and much information relating to careers, such as up-to-date labor market information and journals.

Student Employment Services: Many employment offices on campus assist students in developing functional or chronological resumes. Mock interviews may also be set up so students may practice their job interviewing skills.

V. COLLABORATIVE LEARNING SUGGESTIONS _____

1.   As mentioned earlier, work-study jobs provide opportunities for positive work experiences during college. Many students hold part-time jobs while attending classes full-time. Research suggests that most of these students benefit not only from extra money earned to supplement college expenses, but also from the responsibilities gained from regular work experience and learning the time management techniques necessary to juggle classes, study time, work schedules, and personal time. Another advantage is the opportunity to investigate a particular career field to discover whether or not it matches the student's abilities and interests. A part-time job in an accounting office may convince the student that a business degree is definitely not a good match, while a part-time job in a dentist's office may well lead to a career in a health field.

Conversely, some of the dangers involved in working while attending classes include:

- Neglecting class attendance and/or study time for work responsibilities
  - Earning promotions at work that are financially enticing, thereby encouraging a student to stop out or drop out without completing a degree
  - Trying to work too many hours while trying to keep a healthy grade-point average, usually resulting in a drastic drop in GPA.

Ask your students to work in teams to create comparison lists of advantages and disadvantages for students who hold part-time jobs while attending college classes. Put the lists on transparencies and then compare lists from each of the teams. What items

163

appear on most or all of the lists? Are these realistic for students on your campus? Ask one of the teams to contact someone from your office of institutional research to find statistics that relate to the success rates of students who work part-time while attending classes. Is there an average "point of no return", a specific number of class credit hours plus a specific number of job hours worked per week that add up to a success/failure prediction? What does this suggest to individual students in your class who are working part-time jobs while attending classes?

2.   Create groups of students according to major and/or area of career interest. Have each group learn what they can regarding their future career field in the *Occupational Outlook Handbook* and other informational guides. Once groups have completed their research, have them make a presentation to the class in order to inform their classmates about the various outlooks and implications of pursuing each area of study.

3.   In collaboration with English faculty, students may be assigned a research paper relating to careers. Students will learn how to research information using the Internet, library, and journal articles in addition to learning about their career options.

4.   In collaboration with Speech faculty, students may be assigned to present on a career of their choice. The presentation should include the nature of the work performed, employment outlook, educational and training requirements, working conditions, likes and dislikes, salary, and career-related personality traits. Students could interview a person in their career of choice for a real point of view. They could also use many different media resources as part of their research.

5.   Faculty members are a great resource for career information. Many are involved in current research in the field and many have had experience working in their field. Students could set up meetings with different faculty members to discuss options in their chosen field or faculty members could be guest speakers for the class.

VI. ALTERNATIVE TEACHING STRATEGIES _____

1.   Some institutions are presently experimenting with service learning concepts. Ask students to research which, if any, departments on your campus offer this option. If service learning opportunities are not a part of the education experience at your institution, search for peer colleges that offer these kinds of programs. Collect descriptions of service learning projects and compare what each of these provides to students who are involved. If possible, interview students who have completed these kinds of projects. What were the advantages? Concerns? Disadvantages?

2.   Have students conduct an Internet job search. Provide them with a list of items to discover, such as jobs requiring a certain major, salary, years of experience preferred, graduate degrees required, etc. Collect their information and resources used to pass on to future students and use for future projects.

3.   After completing the *Self Directed Search* or *Discover* career inventories, divide students into six groups relating to Holland's Job Families: Realistic, Investigative, Artistic, Social, Enterprising, and Conventional. Have each group research different careers and characteristics for the job family and present it to the class.

4.   Have students bring in their resume to class. Break them into groups of three and have them review and critique one another's resumes.

5.   Have students practice their interviewing skills with each other through the use of mock interviewing. First, students would prepare their answers to the most common interview questions. Second, they would take turns interviewing one another. Last, they would critique each other on the quality and delivery of the answers.

VII. LEARNING PORTFOLIO

1.   Self-Assessments
After completing Self-Assessment 1 on page 348, collect a general list of those values students consider important in a career. Which values seem most popular? Discuss strategies students can begin implementing now to help utilize these values in a later career.

2.   Your Journal
Have students rate their communication skills by completing the journal activity on page 351. Discuss some general strengths and weaknesses that are common across small groups.

VIII. CHAPTER QUIZ SUGGESTIONS

1.   Use the Review Questions as a short-answer quiz. Points may be assigned equally at 25 points per question, or points may be divided unequally depending on the amount of class time and assignments devoted to various areas of the chapter. In short-answer quizzes, complete sentences are not always necessary as long as the essential points of the answer are present.

IX. QUIZ

Multiple Choice. Choose the one best answer.

1. Holland's personality type that would be ideally suited for a job in teaching or counseling is
    A. realistic.
    B. social.
    C. artistic.

D. enterprising.

E. scientific.

2. According to the 2006 – 2007 *Occupational Outlook Handbook*, the
_____industries will provide the most new job in the near future.

    A. computer

    B. service-producing

    C. heath care

    D. education-based

    E. A and C

    F. B and D

3. Making contact and exchanging information with other people regarding career information is

    A. socializing.

    B. multitasking.

    C. networking.

    D. mentoring.

    E. capitalizing.

4. Which of the following is a common type of resume?

    A. Chronological.

    B. Reference.

    C. Structural.

    D. Presentational.

    E. Topical.

5. A good strategy for a job interview involves

    A. being prepared.

    B. knowing your resume.

    C. anticipating questions.

    D. following up promptly.

    E. All of the above.

True or False

6. _____An important first step in choosing career options is to know your *values*.

7. _____Signs are showing a stronger interest in societal welfare among college students.

8. _____Ideally you will have, or soon develop, a singular career focus in your first year of college.

9. _____Writing a "thank-you" note after an interview will be looked at as "kissing up" and is advised against.

10. _____If you are struggling to decide on a career path, a *career counselor* at your school will tell you what to do.

ANSWERS

1. **B**   2. **E**   3. **C**   4. **A**   5. **E**   6. **T**   7. **T**   8. **F**   9. **F**   10. **F**

X. TEST QUESTIONS_____

Multiple Choice. Choose the one best answer.

1. John Holland developed one of the most commonly used systems for examining the link between _____ and _____.
   A. college major, first job
   B. college major, personality style
   C. college major, future income
   D. personality style, career choice

2. The resource that tells rates of job growth, job availability, and ranks pay among jobs requiring college degrees and those that don't is called
   A. Petersen's Big Book of Jobs.
   B. The Employment Outlook Manual.
   C. The Occupational Outlook Handbook.
   D. The Occupational and Employment Guide.

3. Employers in a national survey ranked these as the three most important skills of a prospective job candidate:
   A. intelligence, computer knowledge, writing.
   B. academic functioning, computer knowledge, leadership.
   C. oral communication, interpersonal relations, teamwork.
   D. leadership, intelligence, teamwork.

4. Employers recommend that students get work-related experience beginning
   A. their first year in college.
   B. the summer after their freshman year.
   C. their junior year.
   D. their senior year.

5. In a recent national survey of employers, _____said that their entry-level college hires had co-op or internship experience.
   A. 25%
   B. 40%
   C. 55%
   D. 60%

6. Service learning involves
    A. working for a company in a field related to your major.
    B. engaging in activities that promote social responsibility and service to the community.
    C. upperclassmen volunteering to tutor freshmen on strategies for choosing a major and, ultimately, a career path.
    D. special college courses designed for members of the armed services.

7. Researchers have found that when students participate in service learning
    A. their grades improve.
    B. they are more likely to choose a humanities-based major.
    C. they choose a career path faster.
    D. they usually quit their job, or greatly reduce their work hours.

True or False

8. _____It is important to have only one career to focus on once you begin college.

9. _____In a national survey, employers recommended that first-year students get work-related experience, good grades, and experience in extra-curricular activities.

10. _____Co-ops pay a salary, and many offer academic credit, too.

- **Essay Questions**

1. Describe at least three strategies to "knock 'em dead" in a job interview.

2. What are the basic skills that will benefit individuals as they enter the work force? Provide examples of experiences that would be particularly beneficial to a wide range of career options.

3. Describe Holland's six basic personality types and some ideal jobs for each. Does any one type represent your personality? Why or why not?

ANSWERS

1. **D**   2. **C**   3. **C**   4. **A**   5. **D**   6. **B**   7. **A**   8. **F**   9. **T**   10. **T**

XI. MENTOR'S CORNER _____

Wendy Hope teaches her college success class with an unusual twist—as an "Intro to Business Culture" class. She teaches the course from the viewpoint of an employer and asks her students to find out how college success skills will benefit them in the workplace. For more information about this unique approach, e-mail Wendy at: wclairek@hotmail.com.